A CONCISE ECONOMIC HISTORY OF MODERN CHINA

(1840–1961)

Frank H. H. King

PRAEGER • PALL MALL

Published in the United States of America in 1969 by Frederick A. Praeger,
   Inc., Publishers, 111 Fourth Avenue, New York, N. Y. 10003

Published in Great Britain in 1969 by Pall Mall Press
5, Cromwell Place, London, S.W. 7, England

Library of Congress Catalog Card Number: 70-76549

S. B. N. 269.67181. · 1

Printed by

Mgr. T. A. Pereira,
Examiner Press,
Dalal Street,
Bombay-1.

PRINTED IN INDIA

PREFACE

An economic history of modern China is particularly difficult to write in our present state of knowledge. Whereas, after expenditure of considerable resources on vast research projects, a generally accepted synthesis is beginning to emerge for the period of the People's Republic and there is a growing literature on the war-time inflation, work on the period before 1937 is disconnected and tentative. With statistics either inadequate or meaningless and with few quantitative reference points, it is doubtful if a satisfactory economic history will be written for many years.

The present work presents a synthesis of the results of recent research on the Chinese economy in as coherent a sequence as possible. The varying emphases as the story moves from one period to another in part reflect the state of research, in part the different economic questions which appear of major interest. There is apparently no unifying analytical framework for the entire period 1840-1961; each few years presents different problems of interest to the economist.

Since this is based on both my own and others' research, I must acknowledge my debt to those sources on which I have most frequently depended. They are referred to in the text and stated more fully in the list of readings. In a sense, this present book may be considered a guide to the issues which are discussed more fully in the monographs and studies cited.

Throughout I have assumed that the reader will have access to a standard history of modern China, preferably that of John K. Fairbank, Edwin O. Reischauer, and Albert M. Craig. I do not assume that the reader will necessarily have any knowledge of the Chinese language or will wish to use, at least for the present, Chinese-language sources, and I have minimized use of any Chinese terms and phrases.

Professor Thomas R. Tregear, my colleague of Hong Kong days, has been kind enough to contribute the maps, for which I am most grateful.

I wish specifically to acknowledge the kind permission of Harvard University Press to include material and some direct quotations from my *Money and Monetary Policy in China, 1845-1895*, which they published in 1965, Cambridge, Massachusetts. This material is mainly to be found in chapters I and II.

I wish also to acknowledge the considerable financing of my own research for this work by the University of Kansas, where I am presently a Professor of Economics, and to express gratitude for the hospitality of St. Anthony's College and Merton College, Oxford, during the current academic year.

                                                     Frank H. H. King

University of Kansas,
April 1967.

CONTENTS

TABLES

TABLES

Chapter 1

SOME PROBLEMS OF CHINESE ECONOMIC HISTORY

PERIODIZATION

Since even the most elementary conclusions concerning the economic history of China are still highly controversial, it is pleasant to be able to begin an introduction with at least one generally accepted statement: modern Chinese history begins in the year 1840.

Post-1840. Historical periodization, essential for the Marxist, has for others a degree of descriptive usefulness, providing objective analysis remains unhampered and providing too much time is not wasted in establishing the relevant dates. But 1840 seems to have a surprising consensus behind it. "Surprising" because 1840 is a date most obvious for its relevance in the history of China's foreign relations and seems hardly appropriate either for the Marxist or for the patriot. Nevertheless, the Chinese can see in this date of foreign success, the beginning of that struggle, culminating in the May Fourth Movement of 1919, which produced the revolutionary drive of the 20's and 30's and the eventual success of that revolution, led by the Chinese Communist Party in 1949. Indeed, as Albert Feuerwerker has reported, Chinese historiographers give the dates 1840-1919 as the period of China's modern history, 1919-1949 as contemporary history, and post-1949 as the Epoch of the People's Republic of China.*

* References are found in the lists of suggested readings at the end of this volume.

1

This is not quite satisfactory for the purposes of the economic historian. Indeed, several alternatives might be suggested, all of them useful for their specific purposes. The first period might comprise 1840-1895, as being one of increasing foreign contact and pressure but retaining the essential decision-making initiative to a Chinese government traditionally conceived. We might then cut across the 1911 revolution to 1930. In this period the Chinese are forced to take steps which radically alter the nature of the state and, therefore, its ability to plan and enforce economic policy. For 1930 to 1949 a nominally unified China tries but fails to solve the manifold economic problems which warlordism, the Japanese invasion, and the civil war impose. From 1949 indeed begins a new epoch which should be described separately. Alternatively, one can argue that these "long waves" are not as helpful as the shorter periods which contain more coherent policy periods—1851-1862, the reign of the Hsien-feng Emperor was characterized, for example, by monetary experiments forced on the government by the events of the Taiping rebellion. The following reign period, T'ung-chih (1862-1875), marked a determined effort, known in the language of the dynastic theory of Chinese history as "restoration," to reassert the fortunes of the Ch'ing, e.g. attempts were made to restore the coinage. The period of 100 days reform in 1898, the abortive attempts to redesign the imperial government along nation-state lines, the economic activities and theories of Sun Yat-sen, the growing impact of the "dual economy" of treaty-port and hinterland, the height of nationalistic success in the early and mid-thirties—all these had their prologues and epilogues and could form the basis for the delineation of short-term historical periods. The Communist period with its reconstructions, plans, leaps, and reactions lends itself even better to such schema.

The reader will probably have noticed that many of these suggested "periods", whether long or short, appear to depend upon political events or on changes in economic policy or organization. Does this suggest that the vast economy of China was dominated or directed centrally so that changes in government must be the key to an understanding of China's economic history? If we exclude the two years 1956-1957 when central planning is supposed to have had a significant impact, the answer must be "No!" The basic agricultural economy was largely unaffected by such centrally directed changes until the revolutionary reorganization of agriculture in the 1950's. For reasons we shall wish to examine, government were unable to formulate or to execute plans designed to radically change the nature of the Chinese economy. We must not, of course, conclude from this that the Chinese economy was somehow "unchanging", for this would be to ignore the devastation of the Taipings, the changing commercial cropping patterns, efforts at flood control and irrigation, settlement of Manchuria and, in the modern sector, the whole subject of development of industry.

The tendency to periodize in terms of Government or policy changes stems from the type of question that we may profitably put as economists studying the Chinese economy. Without anticipating later comments in this introductory chapter, we can suggest that the problem of government reaction to foreign economic stimulus and the subsequent efforts to respond at various levels of understanding to the need for development—in the sense of "modernization"— tends to give such a focus to the study of an economy which might otherwise warrant a different approach.

Having accepted 1840 as the beginning of modern China—and its economic history—we reject the further Communist periodization on the grounds that it does not serve our analytical needs. A more pragmatic approach seems appropriate. This rejection includes also the pre-1840 structure.

Pre-1840. If now we turn briefly to that problem of periodization before 1840, we find further dispute and even less satisfactory results. If, following the Marxists, China's slave economy became feudal with the end of Shang or with the Chou dynasties, how is the next 2-3,000 years to be characterized or delineated? Such an analysis perpetuates the myth of unchanging China and Communist historiographers present a picture not unlike the popular European misconception of

China as "stagnant", backward, and traditionalist. Nevertheless, such an interpretation, which has had the support of Chinese Communist Party Chairman Mao Tse-tung, is followed by the suggestion that foreign imperialism stifled a latent capitalism, transformed China into a semi-feudal, semi-colonial economy, and effectively strangled those spontaneous native revolutions which would have shaken China free from feudalism and led her to modernization. Thus only after the Communist victory in 1949 and the subsequent land reform was, according to this interpretation, China's feudal period ended. To the Marxist the history of modern China is, then, precisely this imperialist opposition to both her political independence and her development of capitalism.

These sweeping indictments take the argument out of the realm of Marxist polemics and stage-building by posing questions capable of factual study and professional analysis. Unfortunately, our knowledge of China's recent economy is not such as to make the answers to these questions so dramatically posed at all easy to discover—the tentative answers which are now available certainly do *not* support in full the anti-imperialist charges, and should lead us to seriously question their validity. And thus, perhaps for the purpose of setting the historical record straight—facts and analysis against nationalist or Communist myth—we find another focus for the study of the economic history of modern China. We have not only to ask concerning China's reaction to the Western economic confrontation and to development, but also as to whether Western actions in China hindered or assisted this development, and whether, in either case, the actions were premeditated or calculated.

With another problem, that of pre-1840 industrialization in China, we need not concern ourselves. During the mid-1950's China's historians were concerned as to whether or not a "proto-capitalist" society had developed by the end of the Ming dynasty. If so, a Marxist might interpret the risings which effectively brought about the downfall of that dynasty as representing a combination of hand-factory workers and peasants. This rising was to be stifled by the Manchus who established the "feudal" Ch'ing dynasty. The repression was confirmed and strengthened by the Imperialists. The degree to which such economic developments did indeed take place before 1840 are, of course, worthy of research for their own sake. The official Communist interpretation is that only by the mid-nineteenth century was the latent capitalism sufficiently strong to overthrow the feudal order and by that time Imperialism had been established—hence the importance of the 1840 date. For our purposes we can agree that the Chinese saw modernization as distinctly Western and reacted to it on this basis. Those attempting to make economic change more palatable naturally sought purely Chinese precedents and found them in the most unusual and disconnected places. But to the Chinese confronted with foreign pressure and traditional values, these attempted reinterpretations did not in fact have much impact.

CHINESE STATISTICS

In the study of economic history the economist must be primarily concerned with the selection and arrangement of data appropriate to the answering of questions which yield to his analytical tools, that is, which give relevance to the body of economic theory. Thus, whatever social or political predelictions the economist may have, he will attempt to begin with the collection and analysis of quantitative data. It is just here that a basic problem in the understanding of China's economic history arises. The statistical base is grossly inadequate, and to prevent misunderstandings something of the pre-1949 problem should be stated here. There is a natural tendency of the practical scholar when not finding the ideal to substitute the available. The development economist knowing the gross inadequacy of some country's national income statistics may nevertheless use them with the plea that you have to start somewhere. It is difficult to follow the logic of this argument.

Defects of Ch'ing statistics. For China we do not have, nor can we expect to see compiled Empire-wide statistical series of, for example, prices, wages, silver-copper exchange rates, nor can we expect to have even trade or balance of payments figures with the normal degree of accuracy. Statistics involving money or which are expressed in some unit of account are complicated by the nature of China's monetary system, and they will often hide the consequences of unrealistic exchange rates or the addition of various weights of the monetary metals under the assumption that units with the same name are similar. Tax revenues suffer from this defect, and in addition, through faulty coverage do not state with any assurance of accuracy the cost of the state to the economy.

These defects result from many separate and independent factors. First, the Chinese economy was not a unified "nation-state" economy, and there are still few national markets in which a single price prevails. Therefore, national indices for the pre-1949 would not be very helpful, and series derived from a lucky "find"—some shopkeeper's records, an enterprising foreigner's observations etc.—will not necessarily be valid outside the town for which they provide a record. Secondly, the Ch'ing government had no statistical service and had no reason to know the economic situation unless some crisis or disturbance required reporting and permission for correction. Thus, we may know of famines but not of annual crop production; and we may know of famines only to the extent that foreigners reported on them, officials considered it necessary to "memorialize" the Emperor, travellers' reports, or the general literature describes them. But these are not quantitative sources.

Interpretation. Even such basic material as government revenue and expenditure and trade are fraught with problems of interpretation. Here we must distinguish between quotas and actualities. The mints were, for example, assigned annual output quotas, but this does not mean that such quotas were realized, even approximately realized. Nor does this necessarily suggest a breakdown of government control, simply the force of local economic or other circumstances which required almost constant deviation from the authorized. Such deviations might or might not be reported. For taxation we are again confronted with the quota problem: but revenue consisted of more than sums sent to or made available to the capital. Indeed, the maze of imperial and local taxes, revenues from such monopolies as salt, payments made by the people for specific services (sometimes regarded erroneously by foreigners as illegal or "squeeze"), "voluntary" contributions by merchants and officials, and labour services in various guises, makes the total tax burden apparently impossible to assess.

Foreign trade statistics may seem at first to avoid many of these difficulties.   There was an Imperial Maritime Customs Service, national in scope and staffed and directed by foreigners in the employ of the Chinese government.   Their statistical services, backed by consular trade reports, would seem unexceptional.   Yet they suffer from the poor reporting of bullion trade and from the handling of Hong Kong, an important element in China's trade picture.   For a time, these figures exclude trade in "native" junks and do not include internal trade.

Alternatives.   What then can be our information on the Chinese economy ?   We must first of all make what use of the figures we can by correcting for obvious omissions, correctly understanding the scope, evaluating their accuracy on the basis of what we know about the purpose of the collection and the method of its compilation.   And this work can then be supplemented by descriptive reports of the same phenomena, when these are available.

From the Chinese we must read and interpret the memorials of leading officials who are reporting on economic events within their jurisdictions.   But this involves recalling that the facts transmitted to the Emperor are likely to be selective and designed to support the policy recommendation which follows. We can also read the diaries and non-official literature, but we will find that economic problems, although undoubtedly of concern to officials, were infrequently the subject of their off-duty writings.   The writings of Chinese who had opportunity to observe foreign economies are not strong in their analysis of their applicability to the Chinese scene.

From the foreigner we have the consular reports and the reports of the Imperial Maritime Customs as a basis.   These are to be supplemented by digesting the copious company records which survive.   This task remains to be done, although some very fruitful work has been begun in this direction.

   Post-Ch'ing material.   As we leave the Ch'ing, we find that visiting economists, investigating committees, reports for evidence at international conferences, the discussions of war-time financial problems, and the copious accounts of the subsequent inflation and the breakdown of the economy in the post-war period have their statistical bases.   The year-books of various publishers and the newspapers provide statistical information. We have a background for analysis, but the statistics remain unofficial, inaccurate, and sectoral in coverage.

   Moving then into the Communist period, we have the growth for the first time of a statistical service designed to provide the basis for national planning on the Soviet model. By 1955 this service is in effective operation, but the Great Leap Forward of 1958-59 rendered the service inoperative and it has not recovered. Nevertheless, the interest in events in mainland China since 1949 is so great that this absence of statistical services has been compensated for, at least in part, by the intensive study of the data which do become available.   Put together by competent economists and statisticians, some quantitative picture of developments in contemporary China can be pieced together.

CHINA'S FAILURE TO MODERNIZE

   Validity of economic theory.   Although we have said that the purpose of the economist in dealing with China's economic history is to apply the relevant economic theories to the material available, to some this would seem to beg the question.   Surely, China is in some way different.   Chinese values, Chinese traditions—these are so different as to bring into question the relevancy of theory generalizing observations of Western circumstances.

   There is some validity to any complaint against an economist who did not take account of the varying inputs in his models, but this is not an invalidation of the models.   The feeling that the Chinese must be different in some relevant way and that Chinese institutions are responsible for the lack of development is often the consequence of failing to identify the economic factors involved—factors which often go far to explain the observed phenomena—and a misunderstanding of the assumptions and practices of economists and Western business.

False contrasts. Thus one historian suggested a shortage of capital in China on the evidence that the subscribed capital of newly-formed manufacturing enterprises was not immediately paid up! Another felt that the Western custom of primogeniture was responsible for some difference, neglecting the fact that the English mercantile community of the eighteenth century did not practise primogeniture.

This uncritical attitude is also reflected in the tendency of foreigners to assume that the failure of the Chinese to utilize machinery in any given instance is an example of their conservatism or of the corruption or worse of their government. Thus the withdrawal of machinery in a Newchwang bean press, which was primarily the consequence of the high cost of the operation and the unsuitability of the machinery to the process, may also have been accompanied by interference from the local guild and officials, or mandarins, but by the time the story is retold ten years later, only the non-economic factors—the interference of guild and officialdom—is recorded.

China's lack of information. Indeed, one may wonder that China developed to the extent she did in the early years of foreign contact. The impression is sometimes gained that China "rejected" modernization, as if she had been offered it. Fairer to the Chinese would be the comment that China failed to go out and seek modernization. As for the advice and counsel of businessmen, missionaries, and foreign diplomatic officials, it would have been a rash society indeed which accepted it. The early foreign merchants knew little of manufacturing enterprises and many of their initial schemes failed financially, including the long-lamented Shanghai-Woosung railway, a classic example of bad costing, poor engineering,

and unwise siting. Secondly, foreigners were more enthusiastic than they were practical and the supplementary sources
of information available to the Chinese, including a few
technical training bases and technical periodicals in Chinese,
were relatively unimportant. Offers of direct technical
assistance or of training abroad were unavoidably entwined
with political implications, which were real and unavoidable.
This would apply as well to railroad and mining enterprises
which involved the extra-territorialized foreigner in unlimited
contacts with the suspicious Chinese of the interior. We
must conclude that China had little basis for judging the
merits of the random proposals foreigners presented, excepting,
perhaps, in the military field. Here, moreover, China responded.

  The institutional explanation—China is "Oriental". That
historical events take place within an institutional framework
is a commonplace generally accepted. If we find that these
institutions are ill designed for modernization and are, in fact,
preventing it, we cannot accept this as a causal factor—at
least until we have asked why the institutions themselves do
not change. Certainly there were peculiar circumstances in
China which made these institutions more difficult of change
than those of the West, but there is no *a priori* reason why
this should be so. We may find that the weakness of the
economic stimuli to development and growth, in the sense of
modernization, was equally important.

  Again it may be objected that there was something
peculiarly "Oriental" in the Chinese approach. There was
no economic man, in the sense of a conscious maximizer in
China ; the rising merchant aspired to be an official, the clever
young man a Confucian scholar. In the Confucian ethic
there was no room for the maximizing manufacturer in
the perfectly competitive model ; in an oriental society there
is more than economics. Unfortunately, this approach
does not lead anywhere interesting. There is little in the
Christian doctrine as understood in late Mediaeval times to
support the maximizer. Nor is there anything incompatible
about developing manufacturing industry and seeking official
status—businessmen have been knighted and raised to the

peerage. Chinese families were large—there was room among the sons for scholarship, official status, *and* business. Indeed, this is not an unknown pattern among the Hong Kong and overseas Chinese. On the other hand, recent studies suggest that the Western "maximizer" is best described as a "satisfier", as a role player. That some Chinese played the role of manufacturer and played it well is generally accepted. This was not a barrier to nor apparently was it sufficient for modernization.

When the Empire fell and the Republic failed to establish sufficient authority to develop a comprehensive development—or indeed any economic—policy, the institutional argument may have been more relevant, although in a less interesting way. The fact that civil war or the impact of warlordism, the destruction of the Japanese and the subsequent dislocation of the economy in the final struggle of the government with the Communists should prevent effective development of the economy is so obvious that it goes little way to give a peculiarly Chinese answer to the events.

One can argue, on the contrary, that the Chinese institutions were too well developed for the West to be able to have the necessary impact. The newly developing trade at Canton, for example, could be fit, verbally at least, into the context of the traditional Chinese tributary system. China's response to military defeat was limited precisely because she saw the defeat within the context of frontier disturbances. To the extent that she did respond, as in the so-called "self-strengthening" movement, it was purposely limited to meet specific military needs, interpreted in technical terms. And yet, such a reaction could have formed the basis for the construction of those "overheads" which make development by the private sector more likely, so that, even here, we find the actual response not incompatible with modernization.

The European example. Perhaps we are being unreasonable to suppose that a vast Empire should develop in an entirety. If we took the parallel of the British Empire rather than Great Britain, we would not find any such universal trend. Nor is the parallel so far fetched, since British control

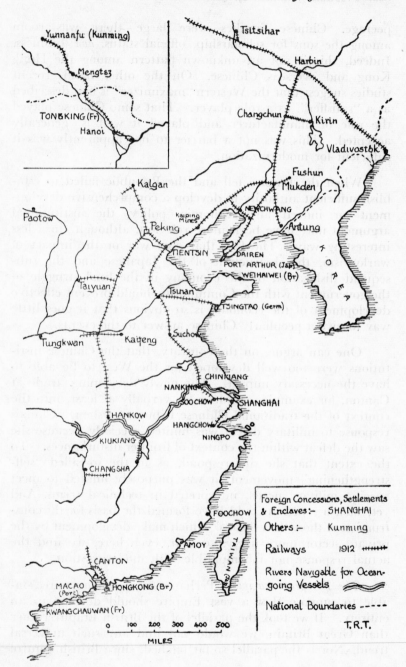

Foreign Concessions, Settlements
& Enclaves :-   SHANGHAI

Others :-   Kunming

Railways   1912 ┼┼┼┼┼┼┼

Rivers Navigable for Ocean-
going Vessels   ∿∿∿∿∿

National Boundaries -----

T.R.T.

of the separate political identities which compose her Empire had key resemblances to the Chinese model. The Colonial Regulations against which governors might petition for exceptions as local conditions required, bore, as we shall see, a resemblance to the statutes of the Ch'ing as administered by the Six Boards in Peking and modified *ad hoc* to meet the memorialized requests of provincial authorities. Or we can take the example of Europe, which in only certain areas can be called modernized, certainly by World War I. If then the bulk of China's development was in those areas controlled to varying degrees by foreigners, i.e. the treaty settlements and the ceded enclaves (see map on p. 12), we can account for this in economic terms, perhaps with a modified dual-economy model, in which the institutional favourability of certain specified areas is openly admitted. But this favourability is relative and explains why, given its existence, development naturally concentrated in those settlements and enclaves. It does not provide an institutional explanation of "China's" failure to modernize. That, we might conclude, is neither surprising nor requiring of a non-economic explanation.

The entrepreneurial explanation. The idea that the Chinese were different effects the entrepreneurial theory of development, the economists' dubious counterpart of the great man interpretation. . . if Arkwright had been there . . .but he was there . . . But where will we find a Chinese Arkwright arising out of China's family system, its schools of classical education, and its system of values weighted against the individualist and profit-seeker? Thus runs the argument. Studies of the merchants show, quite naturally, that their training moved them in trading and financial dealings more readily than in manufacturing. There are, however, studies of successful manufacturers whose stories read surprisingly like a narrative of the American dream! Cheong Chi Pio, for example, was born in Macao in 1853 and apprenticed at the age of sixteen to a furniture manufacturer and general contractor. This suggests "humble" origins. A foreigner gave him $300 to start business on his own as a ship's painter. He subsequently became a decorator and contractor, expanding his business through advertising. He was still later instrumental in founding the Hongkew Iron Foundry in 1881, an ambitious undertaking in which he lost heavily. This is not spectacular, perhaps. But there were others like him ; it was not impossible for society to produce such men, and we cannot explain China's failure to modernize or her failure to foster the type of man who in early industrial England contributed so much.

The problem is, of course, that each national development task comes at a different time in history and requires different organization to meet new problems and industrial structures. Perhaps more relevant to our problem would be the question as to why more men of the calibre of Sheng Hsuan-huai did not arise, or whether there was, given the economic situation, room for more such men. We may consider, in any case, whether it is relevant to China's specific development problems to lament the absence of a Protestant ethic or whatever other cultural touchstone appears responsible for British economic development and consider instead that, in the world of large industries and oligopolistic markets, *satisfying* rather than *maximizing* seems to be consistent with industrial progress ; competition, in the sense intended by the earlier economists or imagined by them in the classical writings, probably never was an essential requirement for Chinese economic development.

Role of corruption. Much, too, has been made of corruption as stultifying the chances of growth in the Chinese economy. There is, however, no *a priori* reason to suppose that corruption as such would necessarily work for or against growth and modernization. If the right to build some manufacturing enterprise will apparently bring great profits to the entrepreneur, he may be willing to bribe officials for the appropriate licence, thus sharing with them the anticipated quasi-rent! But, admittedly, this does not do justice to the proposition.

For although corruption as such need not prevent growth absolutely, it may be symptomatic of broader evils which make development in our sense at least unlikely or more hazardous. This is not to suggest that it is the cost at the margin which decides the entrepreneur against the investment, for this is to suggest a nicety of calculation which is unlikely and begs the question to the extent that it supposes corruption will be prohibitive in degree. No, rather we must suppose that there is a basic problem with the governmental-legal system in which a system of corruption on the Chinese scale is possible. That it was part of such a system is manifest from an understanding of this corruption not as something outside the system but as a shading growing out of the system and being rather an unacceptable growth of what was otherwise permissible than something distinct and objectively ascertainable. For, whereas there was corruption in the common sense, the term is more widely used to describe any excessive payment in a system where the normal or proper payment was not precisely delineated. This must, of course, be further distinguished from the outright seizure of private property in times of warlordism and civil disturbance, a possibility we have allowed for in our previous suggestion that such times are in general not suitable for modernization and growth and that there is no need to seek more subtle factors.

Reluctance to make basic reforms. That the Chinese system of government *per se* was a factor making economic growth difficult is a suggestion also to be found in the writings of Chinese nineteenth-century officials and observers in Europe who were questioning, on the basis of their overseas experiences, the very basis of the self-strengthening movement in China, i.e. the policy which advocated technical change without basic reform of apparently unrelated but actually significant spheres of policy. We shall be better able to judge the validity of these charges in the following chapter, but suffice it to admit here that it was precisely this apparent necessity to make basic changes which armed the opposition to modernization. The question remains, therefore, how necessary was basic change?

The self-strengthening movement could have provided the economic overheads for Chinese modernization. Had it done so, the private sector would have found it more profitable to make industrial investment and the pressure on the conservative forces might have been more effective. That there was opposition from the scholars, from certain officials, and from perhaps a majority of the so-called "gentry" or land-owning and degree-holding classes who ever considered the problem is unquestionable. But this opposition would not be unique to China or single China out for special consideration. Opposition to change is normal ; opposition to industrialization has been a feature of every industrializing nation. Even foreigners in China objected to certain specific projects which seemed to threaten established positions. Progress is not always obvious, even to a nineteenth-century Englishman.

Thus we are thrown back to the proposition that what is different in China must be the lack of sufficiently great economic stimulus. Studies of specific projects would appear to bear this out. We have seen, as one example, in the case of Cheong Chi Pio that his investment in the Hongkew Iron Foundry involved him in considerable losses. Other cases might easily be cited. Unfortunately, we are not sufficiently advanced in our study of China's economic history to state with certainty which industries would have proved profitable at which times and under what circumstances. Certainly, the proper course for the would-be industrialist was not as obvious as either contemporary foreign observers thought or recent historians have supposed.

In the chapters which follow we shall approach the subject as a problem in economic analysis operating in an unusual institutional context which, whether it is decisive or not, must be considered as effecting the working of the model. In this task we shall be severely restricted by the lack of an integrated statistical system and by the damaging qualifications which must be made for those sectoral and local statistics which are available. Thus the final product will be more descriptive and speculative than economic historians are currently willing to tolerate. If this stimulates further study of the modern Chinese economy, the task will have been worthwhile.

Chapter II

THE TRADITIONAL ECONOMY AND THE
WESTERN IMPACT, 1840-1895

To some historians the Chinese state has appeared as a parasitic appendage exploiting but providing scant, if any, services. To others, the state reflects the essence of "Oriental" civilization, arising from the necessity of providing public works for rice cultivation, and so, in a sense, essentially economic in origin. We may take a less judgemental position, insisting that the Chinese government provided essential economic services and encouraged others, while admitting that the cost of these services was at times excessive. With a view of China as a rural, self-sufficient, traditional economy, changing little, requiring little, the idea that the government was a costly luxury imposed from without might appear plausible, but this view is an over-simplification. In this section, therefore, we should first examine the traditional economy and note the role of the state therein. Secondly, we should describe in more detail the state's economic organization and functions with a view to examining its role in the reaction to foreign economic stimuli in the last years of the Chinese empire.

THE TRADITIONAL ECONOMY : A SURVEY

Population. On the eve of Taiping rebellion in 1850, the population of China was probably close to 430 million. Today it may stand at 720 million. Considerable efforts have been made to reconstruct the growth of the Chinese population, but the cataclysmic impact of the rebellion, in which some 20 million lost their lives, has made projections from the eigh-

17

teenth-century base unreliable and estimates during the Republic, which ranged from 420 million to 480 million, are not reliable.

Traditional agriculture. China was indeed an agricultural economy with peasant cultivation of rice and other cereals as the basis. But even this does not describe a simple economy. Rice culture assumes a store of capital in the form of local irrigation systems protected by dykes, river works and including transport facilities and storage. And this peasant agriculture had, in 1840, just concluded a dynamic expansion into new areas and with new crops, maize, sweet potato, vegetables —and opium. Commercial primary production, centering on tea, silk, cotton, opium, fish, and minerals, gave to the rural economy a monetary dimension which could have proved of great significance as the basis for expansion on the eve of modernization. That it did not do so can be at least partially explained.

Despite the relative dynamism of the previous century, China had not been able to solve her agricultural problems. A rapidly expanding population with new crops in new areas provided a challenge which the Ch'ing was not able to meet and the facade of prosperity which characterised the reign of the Ch'ien-lung Emperor (1736-1795) had crumbled seriously by 1840. With the disturbances following the shift of foreign trade north from Canton, open rebellion swept south China and the Taipings were born, taking Nanking as their capital in 1863.

For behind the skills of age-old techniques lay hidden the fact that Chinese agriculture was backward, especially in seed selection. The small size of the farms, the social customs which limited the optimum use of the land available, the destruction of forest cover, and the untamable rivers—especially the Yellow River—left little margin for the peasant farmer should anything arise to disturb the delicate balance. But drought and flood statistics indicate that during the Ch'ing dynasty (1644-1911, but the figures exclude 1847-1861 and the period after 1900) there were, on an average, 27 droughts and 44 floods per century in the home province of Chihli alone. In the great drought of 1876-1879, affecting 300,000 square miles, some 9 to 13 million people may have perished. The Yellow River, which lay with its bed above the level of the surrounding countryside, changed its course in 1852 and flowed north of the Shantung peninsula with resulting calamitous floods ; in 1887-1889 it made a further disastrous change, with protective dykes impeding the drainage of the flood waters to the sea.

War and rebellion. Coupled with these natural disasters were rebellion and foreign wars, although the impact of the latter was local and of greater long-term significance. The Taiping rebellion of 1850-1864 was followed by a Muslim uprising in Yunnan in 1856 and the Nien rebellion. The Taipings destroyed China's richest provinces and the vast financial problems surrounding the conflicts diverted government attention from all other economic problems. The Grand Canal became useless and other public works were neglected, but one may assume that the task of controlling the Yellow River would have taxed the resources of any Chinese regime, as it continues to do today. After the end of rebellion in the west and northwest by 1873 and the conquest of Sinkiang in 1877, China found herself with costly foreign involvements which lost her considerable territory and economic rights. The disaster of the Sino-Japanese War in 1895 and the Boxer Uprising in 1900 forced China to reorganize her government along more modern lines. But the foreign wars involved foreign debts which totalled some 45.3 million *taels* by 1890 and became a serious economic problem with the fall in the value of silver and the rise in the total after the Boxer Protocol in which China agreed to pay a total indemnity of 450 million *Haikwan taels* (or £65.7 million Sterling equivalent).

Thus foreign contacts grew as China's internal crises mounted. This is not to be described as the decay of the dynasty, but rather as a period of mounting problems the solution to which the Imperial government tried vainly to find, and, having failed, disappeared.

Table 1. THE SHANGHAI STERLING EXCHANGES,a 1867-1895

December 31b	Pounds Sterling per Shanghai Tael	Index 1895=100
1867	0·2947	201
1868	0·2917	199
1869	0·2947	201
1872	0·3021	206
1873	0·2854	194
1874	0·2869	195
1878	0·2358	161
1879	0·2604	177
1882	0·2490	170
1883	0·2594	177
1889	0·2008	137
1890	0·2343	160
1894	0·1348	92
1895	0·1468	100

a. TT rate Shanghai on London. See also Table 7 below.
b. Years of change in direction.

Source :   North-China Herald.

Here then is an agricultural economy with a significant commercial sector and with considerable skills and physical capital accumulated, but subjected to a series of natural and man-made disasters which it could not surmount. And beyond the agricultural base, with its supporting crafts of village and market town, there was a superstructure of some sophistication, yet still strictly limited. Mining was limited both by primitive techniques and by the unwillingness of the government to permit unlimited and unfettered exploitation by private lessees. Yet these mining enterprises and the salt, tea, and silk trades suggest the existence of a commercial organization of some scope. Guilds in the larger towns regulated trade. The use of money was widespread and banking institutions provided many of the services—remittances, deposit and loan facilities—required of the mercantile community. But the impact was still local and limited. True, goods must be transported, but the routes were traditionally defined ; taxes must be collected and tribute rice sent to the court in a non-rice growing part of China, but the impact was restricted. Not all taxes were remitted to Peking, and the Grand Canal, while it remained open, was unique in China. Economic overheads were limited to transport, but in most parts of China there were no roads suitable even for wheel-barrows and pack animals ; men carried the goods. Provided with a vast river network, China still had problems, since river works could not be maintained and traditional craft travelled but slowly.

This was the state of the "traditional" economy in the period after 1840. Upon it were superimposed the state and the foreigner, attempting to create the conditions for growth —to support either self-strengthening or modernization. We shall first explore the nature and role of the state in the Ch'ing economy.

CH'ING GOVERNMENT AND ECONOMIC POLICY

The role of the centre. The impotence of the autocrat is a somewhat complex phenomenon, but it must be understood if the role of the nineteenth-century Ch'ing state is to be put into perspective. An Emperor may appoint and dismiss, reward and punish at his discretion, but he may become sin-gularly powerless in the initiation of policy. He may be trapped by the structure of the government of which he is the head. Providing established policies are adequate, this para-dox of absolute but ineffective power is disguised, but if signi-ficant change is required, the power structure can remain only if it is thoroughly and dramatically reorganized. Had the dynasty been Chinese—it was Manchu—this might have happened.

The Emperor stood at the apex of the governmental hie-rarchy in Peking, but what did this imply ? William F. Mayers wrote :

The central government of China, so far as a system of this nature is recognized in the existing institutions, is

arranged with the object rather of registering and checking
the action of various provincial administrations, than with
that of assuming a direct initiative in the conduct of affairs
...Regulations... are on record for the guidance of every
conceivable act of administration; and the principal
function of the central government consists in watching
over the execution of this system of rules.

Stated thus the situation appears fantastic ; no wonder foreigners in their confusion beat vainly at the doors of the capital only to be frustrated by the refusal of the Peking authorities to adopt this or that reform. Those who understood
China, Sir Robert Hart the Commissioner-General of the
Imperial Maritime Customs, for example, warned that Peking
was the last place to take the initiative. Reforms had to be
urged on provincial officials and were there subjected to perhaps a similar fate, but for significantly different reasons.
This we shall discuss below. But the role of the centre must
be understood first.

Confucian political theory. Consider the Confucian nature
of the Chinese state and the conflict between the Confucian
ideal and the Legalist practice. Confucius condemned government by statute or by the imposition of pains and penalties;
instead he urged government according to the principles of
virtue, that is, the reduction of the common people to order
thorough observance of the Rules of Propriety. The government of China was, therefore, a Legalist bulwark against the
decline in Confucian virtue ; its function was to act only when
inaction had been unsuccessful. Officials from the Emperor
downwards were supposed to effect their rule by the example
of their virtuous conduct. Should this prove inadequate,
disturbances would follow—evidence of failure—and the
power of the state called in to correct the problem, which was,
from a metaphysical point of view at least, a consequence of
the failure of the officials' virtue. But matters beyond the
routine had to be memorialized to higher authorities and
eventually approval sought from the Emperor. At best,
therefore, the Emperor's policies were reactions to disturbances

and were based on recommendations received in the same communication which reported the problem itself.

The central government as referee. Thus the central government is seen in more practical administrative terms as the referee seeking to enforce uniformity based on precedents established in the early years of the dynasty. But certainly in the economic sphere, there is no reason to suppose that uniformity would be possible in an Empire so diverse, with markets so separate, and with tax regulations themselves on several bases. With the further economic disruption caused by the growth of foreign trade and other economic contact, a key issue had to be decided : since change was inevitable, where would it be initiated ? At the local, provincial, or imperial level ? The answer would be significant not only to the survival of the dynasty but also to the survival of the central government which was threatened not so much with losing its power as with losing its purpose, not so much with being the victim of a successful civil war but with simply disappearing. Of course, what we have called a "key issue" was never considered by the Emperor as such, and the decision, which was to permit the necessary economic reaction to occur below the imperial level, was perhaps not consciously made in this context.

Indeed, in permitting the economic business of the state to continue much as before, the central authorities probably viewed the changes forced on those areas of China most affected by the foreign contacts as undesirable but unavoidable deviations from the norm. Such deviations had not been unknown in the past ; there were precedents. But their magnitude and frequency, combined with the political events which were concurrent with them, produced an entirely new situation and prepared the way for the vacuum of power which followed the 1911 revolution.

But what other course could the central authorities have pursued ? Economic policy was but a part of total imperial policy, and that aspect which dealt with foreign economic contacts was particularly subject to political considerations. John K. Fairbank has suggested that China's basic problem in her "barbarian" affairs was not her unpreparedness for such foreign contacts, but rather the opposite. China had long established a system for dealing with territories beyond China proper, a system which varied in detail from area to area and dynasty to dynasty but which was essentially based on two concepts; first, that the relationship was a tributary one ; secondly, that basic negotiations and continuous contact— to the extent necessary at all—were matters for the authorities at the point of contact, i.e. on the frontiers. Indeed these two principles were not entirely independent and were based on the not unreasonable assumption that China would not have to change to accommodate "her guests"—as one official put the matter in rejecting a British reform proposal. Thus China, faced with a new type of foreign contact, met the problem in the traditional way, missing the chance to reorient its political approach and making it less and less likely that the centre would be able to respond with well-thought out policy alternatives to the new economic problems. The new foreign department, the Tsungli Yamen, was forced on the Chinese government by the terms of the treaties of Tientsin at the conclusion of the second round of Sino-foreign conflicts, but the real conduct of foreign affairs remained with the frontier officials, even though one, Li Hung-chang, as Superintendent of Trade for the Northern Ports, became for all practical purposes close to a *de-facto* minister of foreign affairs. He did not become so, however.

The possibility of reorganization. While this course of events was not surprising, it need not be considered as "inevitable". The central authorities were functionally organized into six boards of which two, the Board of Revenue and the Board of Works, had primarily economic assignments. These were responsible for economic administration within the capital area in addition to the Empire-wide supervisory roles we have alluded to. There was, therefore, a nucleus around which a national economic ministry might have been constructed. Similarly, the civil service of China was, in its senior, recognized positions, an Empire-wide service, recruited on the basis of an examination system—with notable and growing exceptions in the nineteenth century—which, coupled with the censorial tradition, could have been counted capable of affecting a national economic policy. Indeed, it may be argued that this is just what happened when the failure of the Boxer Uprising forced the Chinese to reorganize their government under foreign pressure.

The question of the centres's failure to reorganize has thus been pushed back a stage. It must be admitted that there was potential for a reformed role for the centre ; why did it not take it ? The answer may be that the centre thought it was doing just that. The centre considered its actions in the face of foreign intervention sufficiently decisive, sufficiently authoritative, to achieve its purpose—the preservation of the political concept of the Chinese empire and the execution of those policies, including economic policies, necessary for the people's livelihood. The existence of an adequate machinery for policy consideration, approval, and execution blinded the regime to the fact that more was required. Thus the Hsien-feng Emperor pursued a vigorous monetary policy in the late 1850's ; the T'ung-chih administration was singularly active in directing the "restoration" of the dynasty's power—and of the war-devastated areas of central China ; there was never any question but that important policy questions were referred from the provincial authorities to the centre throughout the nineteenth century. The Emperor and his advisers might well have asked in astonishment : What more could be done?

Policy control. At least in one sense, however, the policy referrals from province to centre must be considered perfunctory. Peking had the power to reverse recommendations, and sometimes did so. But on what basis could such decisions really be made ? The memorial which urged a policy also presented the situation which called for them. Naturally, the two parts of the memorial were intended to be mutually supporting. The relevant Board might be referred to by the Emperor and might urge maintenance of the traditional regulations, but if economic conditions made this impossible, what course could the Emperor take ? And since the initiative came, as it was supposed to do, from provincial officials, the problem was presented to the Emperor as a purely local one.

It did not provoke consideration of a national policy change, at least, not one to be undertaken by a national executive. Thus, a proposal for a silver coin might be approved for one province and subsequently approved for another and so on, but this need not have resulted in a national coinage proposal with mints run from Peking. That officials in the capital were not without initiative or economic ideas may be seen from the proposals which they memorialized and executed—but, and this is important, for the capital, that is, in their capacity as local officials.

Underlying this failure to reorganize in the face of foreign pressure were several factors of a complexity which would take us too far afield if we were to consider them in detail. First, the experience of the 100 days' reform in 1898, which was stopped by a *coup d'etat* staged by the "reactionary" Empress Dowager, Tz'u-hsi (1835-1908), suggested that the authority of the centre was subjected to practical limitations not so much of power as of capability. Reform from on top has already been successful. The question of whether the officials believe in or want the reforms is certainly not an irrelevant question, but it may not be the operative factor in the failure of the reform. Secondly, opposition was expressed to the policy of meeting foreign pressures with accommodation rather than political manoeuvring or force. This opposition cannot, however, be regarded as a weakening of central relative to provincial power, because the opposition came from without the formal government structure and its impact was on all levels of government. Certainly some officials were sympathetic to it, others were not. But the important point is that the "gentry" were for the most part opposed to the sort of change which the reformed central authority would be needed to affect, and, therefore, their influence was opposed to the necessity of change. That the government was influenced by this pressure from gentry as it was from the fear of unemployment of the masses were machinery to be introduced, indicates the power limitations of a traditional autocracy. The Ch'ing may have realized that they were powerless to cope with the disturbances change would have brought and thus change or reform were ruled out as political possibilities.

Ch'ing economic policy. We must, therefore, examine Ch'ing economic policy and institutions within a context of central static administration and provincial response to economic stimuli and limited central permissiveness. This examination can perhaps be better undertaken in two stages. Here we shall consider those activities traditionally conceived as within the scope of Ch'ing administrative concern. Secondly, we shall consider the specific response to the possibility of industrialization—but only after the economic impact of the foreign sector has been stated. Government economic policy involves both its role as referee in the market, that is, the establishing and supervising of rules under which the private sector is to operate, and also its budget making, that activity in which the government allocates to itself certain activities and resources, redistributes income, and undertakes the task of stabilization.

In discussing the Ch'ing's role as referee, one should remember that the government was not the only "authority" in the Empire. That it was the ultimate, legal authority—and we are not here concerned with areas in open rebellion where government rule was admittedly temporarily in suspense—is not being questioned, but certainly there were powers interposed between the individual and the official in normal intercourse. We refer, of course, to the family, the clan, the guild, and, on a different level, the secret society. Thus at least some of the functions of government were undertaken by these institutions, a fact consistent with the Confucian concept of government as a residual power where other influences fail. That officials exercised their "virtue" through these institutions and supported them is true, but they were not government creatures and must be considered part of the private sector.

The traditional Chinese official economic role may be summarized by the saying : "To encourage agriculture and the mulberry tree". Thus both agriculture and manufacturing, considered obviously as cottage industry, had an important place in official thought. We find in Chinese literature and official documents numerous examples of officials who promoted the people's livelihood by experimentation, by taking with them the fruits of their experience in a previous position, by adjustment of tax burdens. But there were severe limitations as to the effectiveness and scope of these individual measures. First, there would be little "follow through"—foreigners, for example, were startled to find Chang Chih-tung's Canton mint experiment continued by his successor! Secondly, the official might have been more eager than qualified, and for a modern example, contrast the painstaking work of the Joint Commission for Rural Reconstruction on Taiwan with the more sporadic, even overenthusiasm of development-minded Thai district officers. Thirdly, the official had many responsibilities and his industry-promotion could not always have priority. Connected with this would be the official's probable interest in literary pursuits, his disinclination to stir up the countryside, especially the gentry, co-operation with whom would be the basis of successful, *i.e.* peaceful, administration. Finally, the official must undertake his experimentation strictly within his own area of jurisdiction. He could take neither a broad view, seeking the co-operation of neighbouring areas, nor could he take a long-term view—the immediate spectre of unemployment and banditry and the ever-likely transfer severely restricted the horizon of his consideration.

The Confucian official as economic administrator. The mention of literary pursuits should remind us that the Chinese official was the product of a classical education and that this had the same limiting effects as it had in India and is having today in Britain. But this classical education did not prevent the Chinese official, as it does not prevent the Indian or British official, from being interested in or having some competence in economic affairs. More than this, the Chinese official had, within his official *yamen* or administration, local minor officials who might be fully qualified in business affairs and able to give some economic advice, or he might himself come from a merchant family. Young officials serving with seniors concerned with such problems had time to learn what there was to be learned. In the latter half of the nineteenth century, officials might call on foreign advisers—or might have them without the request—but these were usually effective only for the design and supervision of projects already considered and approved by officials, usually under the umbrella of the "self-strengthening" movement. As we have seen, the range and competence of such foreign advice was limited by the background of the foreigners available to the official.

Since, however, power was shared with non-governmental institutions and with unpaid, local gentry advisers, we must not restrict the policy impact of the government solely to officials. Certainly local gentry were active in organizing public works, even in financing them, and in exceptional circumstances it was on their initiative that modern-style factories were built. Their main function came, however, in the minor administrative tasks which are part of keeping an agricultural economy with significant commercial aspects in operation. In this maze of activities they were in fact supreme ; the Imperial authority stopped at the district magistrate and extended from there only in the form of devices for assuring loyalty, including taxpaying, and, at the discretion of the official, encouragement in public services. Indeed, so thinly spread were the Chinese bureaucracy that this distribution alone provided a limitation to policy. Little local work could be done without the active co-operation of the gentry. While it is obvious that the Imperial authorities could focus on high priority public works, the Grand Canal for example, they could neither initiate nor supervise the myriad of small public works throughout the countryside. Similarly, officials could not themselves supervise markets, judge on the matter of weights and measures, insure a full-bodied coinage in local circulation. They could, as their inclinations directed, show relatively more concern with this or that problem ; they would have to intervene if trouble threatened, that is, if the extra-governmental agencies failed to solve the problems assigned them. Under such circumstances, it was enough to keep the economy running and to respond to particular problems as they arose. Long-run planning was out of the question.

The Confucian ethic did not, therefore, prevent literary-trained officials from concerning themselves with economic policy, within the limited scope described. The charge has been made, however, that Confucian training biased officials in favour of agriculture to the neglect of commerce and industry. While there is something of interest in this criticism, we must be cautious. China was and is an agricultural economy. People's livelihood then—as now—depends upon the agricultural sector. Especially after the devastation of the Taipings or of some great famine, the task of the official would naturally be focussed on agriculture. One might argue further that *pari passu* commerce and industry would benefit most from improvement in agricultural techniques. Indeed, one might cite the failure to standardize quality of the silk and tea crops in proof of this. Yet it is also true that the official attitude was actively biased against the merchant. The reasons for this as stated by Chinese writers were manifold and conflicting and are not unsimilar to those found in any agricultural society. But the consequences may have been especially significant. Official attitudes combined with the imperial system prevented the merchant from having, as a class, political power or, perhaps, even influence. The merchant remained identified solely by his economic function. If he had political influence, it came from his purchase of political rank or his relationship to officials, and in this he joined the existing power structure ; he did not create a rival focus of power. Certainly this meant that any inclination he might have to encourage modernization of industry would be subject to the tolerance of that official concerned with maintaining local and short-term order. The merchant could not then replace such stultifying authority with his own. Yet assessment is difficult because we cannot assume the merchant would be the harbinger of progress ; this comes as much from individuals as such—and these may as likely, or more likely, be in handicrafts as in commerce.

THE CH'ING CURRENCY SYSTEM :
A STUDY IN TRADITIONAL POLICY

If officials shared responsibilities in their role as referee of the economy, they had the sole responsibility in the field of currency policy. Banks supplemented the currency supply with issues of notes which had local acceptance and with current accounts sufficiently transferable to classify as money. Nevertheless, monetary policy and the basically significant task of insuring an adequate supply of legal-tender coinage were responsibilities of the Ch'ing official bureaucracy and as such considered a traditional function of the state covered by the regulations or statutes of the dynasty, co-ordinated by the Board of Revenue in Peking, and applied by governors, provincial treasurers, and local officials. The monetary system, therefore, provides a singularly useful example of the nature and limitations of economic policy in the traditional imperial state.

The Ch'ing currency system was bi-metallic, viz. copper and silver, the relationship between the two, as implied ideally by the terminology, required an exchange rate of 100:1 by weight but in fact varied according to the market and the state of the coinage. Since both the copper and silver sectors present problems unique to Chinese money, each will be considered separately. We shall then consider the general characteristics of the system and the nature of Chinese monetary policy with examination of certain specific policy measures.

The copper sector. Copper played its role in the Chinese monetary system only in coined form, indeed the round copper-alloy "cash" with its characteristic square centre hole was the only coin traditionally cast or considered the responsibility of authorities. Weighing ideally 0.1 liang it should thus have taken 1000 to exchange for one liang (or *tael*) of silver. The crude manner of casting and the low value of the cash coin gave rise both to wide variation in weight of officially minted coins and to counterfeiting. This combined with the low value for weight itself gave rise to a rather complex but quite logical payments system, the basic characteristics of which it is important to understand.

Cash coins were paid out separately for small payments, but in general transactions were paid in "strings of cash". These were literally cash strung together in ten groups or sub-strings, each worth 100 units of account (*ch'ien*), totalling 1000 *ch'ien*. Naturally, there would be less than 100 coins in each sub-string ; less than 1000 in each string, since the cost of stringing—involving not only placing coins on a string but also selecting the acceptable combination of full-weight, counterfeit, etc., coins and tapering them by size on the string—had to be made by the purchaser of the string. Thus 98 strung coins might settle a debt of 100 *ch'ien*, while 10 coins, unstrung, would settle a debt of 10 *ch'ien*. We assume in this that the variety of coins in the string or casual small offer is appropriate to the time and place ; the figure 98 for 100 itself making just such an assumption, since some markets might expect a sub-string of, say, 97 coins ; the government would require 100 coins, i.e. the taxpayer would have to bear the cost of stringing. Those familiar with metallic coinage systems may wish to consider the discrepancy between say 98 and 100 as being the premium tendered for, in effect, the guarantee of acceptability in the stated market.

This payments system was complicated by the fact that two major variations existed in northern China. In the Peking-Tientsin area a string of cash consisted of 500 coins (less premium), and thus one coin would appear to have been worth two *chung-ch'ien*, as the unit of account was specified to distinguish it from the previous or (*chang-*) *ch'ien*. Farther north in Manchuria the *hsiao-ch'ien* system prevailed where a debt of 1000 *ch'ien* could be satisfied with 160 coins. But these complications can all be fit into the model, and those involved in such calculations should refer elsewhere for a fuller account.

The silver sector : taels. Traditionally, there was no silver coin in China. But this usually accepted statement requires immediate qualification. Silver was shaped for monetary uses into a standard form, usually referred to as a "shoe of sycee". This shoe resembled a coin in that its weight and fineness were certified on it, its production had to be paid for, and it was susceptible of value fluctuation independent of the silver metal. It differed in that the "coinage" was informal, with shoes differing in weight and fineness from the generally accepted standard, and private in that the government's interest in such "coinage" was no more than in any other economic activity of the private sector. But despite these qualifications, we may conclude that the shoes of silver treated much as silver bullion and that China was, for international purposes, on a silver bullion standard.

If we take the silver sector's basic unit of account as the *tael* and assume it can be satisfied by payment of a lump of silver in acceptable shape weighing one liang and 1.000 fine, then one tael could also be satisfied by copper coins weighing 100 liang, i.e. 1000 cash. But the actual tender would be, say, 980 *strung* cash, of course. Thus, the units of account were related : 1 *tael* = 1000 *ch'ien* ; the metals were related according to the actual payments system. Silver bullion, slightly debased to allow for charges involved in shaping, weighing and assaying, but apparently weighing the equivalent of say 50 liang, 1000 fine, would exchange for 50 strings of normally sized cash coins, each string consisting in turn of 980 cash.

The metallic currency was supplemented, as we have mentioned, by the notes or current accounts of "native" banks—a term used by foreigners to distinguish between the traditional-style banking partnerships and the foreign and Sino-foreign joint-stock enterprises. Exchange operations between market centres were arranged by the so-called Shansi banks, although too frequently transfers involved the actual physical movement of the coins or bullion.

Monetary policy—goals. Ch'ing monetary policy was first of all involved in maintaining this traditional system. It was further required to meet the impact of foreign coins, the silver dollars of Spain and Mexico, and those foreign practices and concepts given some practical weight by their implementation in the treaty-ports by the foreign exchange banks. Examining traditional policy first, we find that it was involved with maintaining the standard of the cash coinage, preventing counterfeiting, maintaining some stability of exchange between the silver and copper exchanges, and refereeing the role of the native banks. While we must conclude that in all this the government was singularly unsuccessful, monetary policy was soundly conceived and executed within the range of economic feasibility. For at least some of the policies were conflicting—thus the ideal model could not be maintained with an exchange rate of 1:100 weight for weight, as implied by the definitions, if, given copper and silver supply conditions, the weight of the coin were not to be changed.

The key element in Ch'ing policy was the regulation of the government mints by the Board of Revenue under the statutes of the dynasty. But here again it must be made clear that the Board of Revenue in Peking, while responsible for general supervision of the currency regulations, actually had control of and was directly responsible only for the output of its own mints in Peking. Even in the capital area there were other mints, supervised directly by the Board of Works. And the bulk of the imperial regulations refer in detail to the management of the Board's Peking mints, while only the specifications of size, weight, alloy and supply sources are relevant for mints outside the capital. Thus, on the one hand, the Board of Revenue was responsible for inspecting dies sent from provincial mints, for commenting on memorials concerning the coinage sent to the Emperor and referred to it ; on the other hand, it was bound by detailed instructions, including the number of workmen and overseers in its local mints.

As its responsibilities were traditionally defined this meant that the Board of Revenue could not be the source of a coherent monetary policy. It had no power to inspect the quality of provincial coins actually minted. It could comment on provincial memorials only if they were referred to the Board by the Emperor, and then the Emperor might or might not accept their advice. Thus, if a provincial governor on the advice of his treasurer memorialized for permission to mint cash of a different weight from the national standard, giving reasons why local conditions required this, what could the Board of Revenue contribute other than an appeal to uniformity? And if the Emperor then rejected the recommendation of the provincial authority, what followed? If the governor had correctly assessed the situation, coinage must cease, a crisis might follow, and the governor would have to forward another request. This time he might state that coinage at the new weight had already begun and merely ask permission to continue! The centre had shown lack of purpose, not lack of power.

There is evidence that for the first 150 years of the dynasty, changes in the coinage were made with Empire-wide effect. Thus, we note several edicts ordering changes in the number of coins minted, their composition, and their weight.

This is firm evidence that the centre was responding to stimuli of universal application and that the changes were made to keep the coins from the melting pots, to keep supplies coming from the mines to the mints, and to maintain orderly silver-copper exchange rates.　From the less universal changes approved in the nineteenth century we may conclude that the basic motives of policy were the same, but that local conditions varied so widely in response to natural disaster, civil disturbances, and foreign impact, that currency uniformity was no longer possible.

If the formal purpose of these currency measures was approximate maintenance of the "ideal" relationship expressed in the 100 : 1 exchange rate between cash and silver, what further considerations motivated Ch'ing monetary policy? First, the Ch'ing was fulfilling its referee role, i.e. taking steps to permit the economy to function and the people's livelihood to be satisfied.　Secondly, orderly management of government finance would require some foreknowledge on the part of the government and the taxpayers as to the amount of tax due. Taxes assessed in *taels*, implying payment in silver, but actually collected in cash, provided an opportunity for exchange manipulators to profit unnecessarily.　That the rates did fluctuate seasonally is natural and sound, but the officials made some attempt to maintain stability.

Monetary policy—specific example. Some methods the Ch'ing used to affect monetary policy have already been alluded to.　But, from time to time, exceptional situations arose which required specific remedies.　Governors might attempt to prevent the export of cash from their provinces, local treasurers might attempt to "equalize" the exchange rates by supplying the needed metal from the local treasury, an edict or local regulation might decree the more extended use of either cash or silver, e.g. payment of troops in cash where silver had been used before, regulations might be promulgated to prevent the melting down of coin to make utensils, and, unfortunately, police methods might be authorized to enforce economic measures which ran contrary to market forces.　This complex of direct measures was supplemented by mining policy, by policies with regard to the import or export of copper bullion and coin, and by the extraordinary device of the so-called "big-cash".

The Hsien-feng inflation. The use of big-cash was an innovation of the Hsien-feng period (1851-1862) and was part of a series of measures designed to overcome the disruption caused by the Taipings. In cutting off the copper supply from the Peking mints, the Taipings threatened the currency, and the Board of Revenue was instructed to mint cash coins worth 10 *ch'ien* or more but at less than proportionate weights. In 1853 the casting of iron cash began and in the same year the government undertook, for the first time since the early years of the dynasty, to issue government paper notes. These measures were not, it is important to understand, initiated by the Board of Revenue after having the whole monetary problem placed before them. Rather the proposals had come individually from various provincial sources and had been imposed on the Board of Revenue at least to some degree against its will. Nor were the measures uniformly applied throughout the Empire ; indeed, the list as shown above applied only to Peking.

The temptation to over-issue a token currency and paper money was too great to be overcome, and the consequence of the new monetary policy was a serious inflation in the Ch'ing capital. That this was foreseen by some officials, including some members of the Board of Revenue, is quite clear. A particularly interesting memorial demonstrates the ability of a Confucian official to think in parallel with, say, Adam Smith :

> If the state decides a cash coin has a denomination of 100, then it is 100 ; 1000, then it is 1000. Who would dare to disobey ? The measure is successful. Yet although the official is able to determine the price of cash, he is not able to limit the price of commodities. As for the 1000-cash, people would not dare to use it as a 100-cash. But as for goods valued at 100 *ch'ien* the people would have no difficulty in considering them worth 1000 *ch'ien*.

Thus wrote junior vice-president of the Board of Revenue, Wang Mao-yin, an official perhaps more widely known today as the only Chinese mentioned in Marx's *Capital* ! Compare the above with the following from Adam Smith's *Wealth of Nations* :

> A positive law may render a shilling a legal tender for a guinea ; because it may direct the courts of justice to discharge the debtor who has made that tender. But no positive law can oblige a person who sells goods, and who is at liberty to sell or not to sell, as he pleases, to accept of a shilling as equivalent to a guinea in the price of them.

Although the outcome of this make-shift monetary policy was inflation, we cannot conclude that the imperial officials and Manchu official advisers were unaware of the implications of their policies. Faced with a desperate need for funds and without the administrative capacity for devising and enforcing immediate tax increases, officials saw currency debasement as the only possible solution. The real policy question was rather, how much debasement, how many government notes before the economy is adversely affected ? They realized, furthermore. that their policy would be more successful if accompanied by other measures—what we should call in England today a "package deal". These included limitation of the manufacture of copper utensils, fixing the proportion of notes and big-cash relative to standard cash to be paid to troops and officials, and control of exchange shops to insure their acceptance at face value of the token coins and notes. As counterfeits became more common, officials began harassing peasants bringing goods into the city, ostensibly to search for counterfeits, actually to exact bribes ; this, too, the metropolitan officials were aware of and attempted to stop.

Monetary policy—foreign advice. We might conclude from a survey of monetary policy that Confucian bureaucracy failed not so much in devising intelligent and sophisticated economic policies but rather in executing them. The Ch'ing was weak administratively, and this set a severe limit to the

effectiveness of economic policy decisions and also, since officials were often realists, to the formation of the policies themselves.   Thus foreign advice designed to tax the capacity of
the officials as administrators would have to be rejected on practical rather than philosophical grounds.   Although this tends
to anticipate the later discussion on the foreign impact on
China's economy, some consideration of foreign monetary
advice might nevertheless be relevant here, at least by way of
illustration.

Foreigners viewed China's monetary system from three
distinct vantage points : first, as wholesalers, that is, merchants concerned with the financing of the China trade ;
secondly, as residents, that is, with the day-to-day monetary
transactions ; thirdly, as reformers *per se*.

As merchants, the foreigners had two approaches, the
first being to assure the stability of an acceptable and adequate means of payment, the second being to allow the Chinese
compradore and merchant to handle the details of currency
matters and to take the risk involved.   The general attitude
was expressed in the thought, "We did not come to China
to reform the currency."   Merchants sought through the
several treaties to insure that customs dues would be uniformly expressed, that the several coins and bullions in circulation would be accepted at their silver par, and that the
officials would manage their local currency problems to prevent banking crises with the possible losses to foreigners.
These merchants distrusted the idea of a Chinese national
currency as they distrusted officials and governments—Chinese
and British!   Only when the cash-silver exchanges became
chaotic and threatened the supply of the tea or silk crop, or
when particular silver dollars reached an unrealistic value
did the merchant seek to intervene in the monetary problems
of China.   His outlook was pragmatic.   And, in any case,
he was shielded from the more annoying inconveniences
by his relegation of such matters to his Chinese agent or compradore.   This in itself might be deplored as giving too much
economic power to the Chinese merchant, but there were
other reasons why power existed, and monetary reform would
not have broken it.   The foreign merchant, without know-

ledge of the language and barred from the interior, faced Chinese determined to keep the internal trade in their own hands. The foreigner left them too with their monetary problems.

The merchant was also a resident, and as such he was concerned with day-to-day payments. But here, too, he was shielded by the fact that his servants would do the household purchasing and his own retail activities could be financed by signing "chits" on his compradore. He need rarely handle cash.

The reformer *per se*, be he merchant, missionary, consular official, or newspaper editor, had specific objections to the monetary system—and specific remedies. Some reformers, indeed, professed to see in the monetary system with the frequent negotiations, changing exchange rates, and quibbles over the quality of coins, a small-scale model of the ills of the Chinese state itself. Furthermore, he professed to suppose the monetary system was holding up China's modernization —how could you have railways in a country in which arguments over the currency of a coin were so protracted that the train would leave without you ? Their remedies were, however, economically unsound and politically impractical. In our discussion it is important to remember this first point, so often neglected, that both objections and remedies were often ill-founded.

A key objection found even in official British correspondence was that the Chinese monetary system was "barbaric" because it was, in the important silver sector at least, basically a bullion system. Receiving such a letter from China, a British Treasury official minuted, "Why barbaric ?" and noted that David Ricardo had proposed a similar system for Britain which had, unfortunately, been modified. The reformer also lamented the state of those coins actually circulating in China. He urged, in the copper sector a modern minted coin, in the silver sector a national dollar. With some reason the more cynical foreigner felt that counterfeiting was the key problem—counterfeiting and tampering with the coinage—chopping, sweating, clipping. While in England critics of the Bank of England in the 1820's had complained that its notes were too easily counterfeited and had urged a full-bodied coinage as a solution, in China people turned from a faulty coinage to banknotes!

In making these proposals for a national coinage, the foreign adviser never felt the need to show the superiority of a coinage over the bullion system nor its economic feasibility in a nation of separate market areas.   The Hong Kong mint experience of 1865-1868, although its success would have depended in part on Chinese cooperation, actually failed because the exchange rates made it unprofitable to bring bullion to the mint for coinage.   Certainly, the position subsequently changed, but the foreigners' coinage proposals did not take these more complex matters into consideration ; they wanted reform and were not concerned with details. The Chinese, however, were sufficiently aware of economic affairs to be just so concerned.

China's first modern mint—implications for development. By 1889 China had a modern mint. Here is a case study of modernization which may assist our understanding of Chinese reactions in the industrial sector. The successful founding of the Canton mint through the initiative of Chang Chih-tung, then governor-general of the Liang-Kuang, indicates that modernization was easiest and success most likely in areas where the traditional responsibility of the Ch'ing economic administration could be more efficiently undertaken without undue impact on other sectors—that is, ironically, without those linkage effects which economists rightly consider so important in the promotion of development. A parallel case would be the founding of the China Merchants' Steam Navigation Company to effect in part the traditional task of transporting grain from the Yangtze to the capital *after* almost irreparable damage had been done to the Grand Canal. In the case of the Canton mint, the scheme derived from an imperial edict of 1877 which ordered the establishment of mints using foreign machinery for the minting of cash coinage, i.e., an attempt to improve the traditional coins for which the Ch'ing had always accepted responsibility. The edict itself may be considered part of the currency re-form measures initiated in the Tung-chih restoration period

(1862-1875), again part of the traditional conception. Actually, as Li Hung-chang discovered in his temporarily unsuccessful Tientsin mint, modern machinery was apparently not adapted to the striking of a coin with a centre hole, since it broke them in the process. It was Chang Chih-tung's suggestion that a modern mint also be permitted to mint silver coins, a dollar and subsidiary coinage, that made his experiment successful.

Here we find several themes combined. First, the reform or modernization—and, typically, we tend to confuse the two—came within the traditional policy scope of the dynasty, at least initially. Secondly, the suggestions of foreigners relative to the scheme were ill-advised. The Canton mint did not prove the feasibility of the national coinage for which the foreigners had so long been pleading ; it was the subsidiary coinage which financed the first years of the mint's operation. Thirdly, the uncritical or direct application of foreign methods in China often presented technical as well as economic problems ; modernization was not simply knocking at the door and waiting for a conservative officialdom to open, rather it had to be carefully adapted despite the misconceptions of foreign reformers themselves.

The acceptance of the dollar coin. The advent of the dollar itself and its role in the Chinese monetary system may also provide an insight into the workings of the Ch'ing administration when faced with something "foreign". Since the silver sector was traditionally based on bullion as a means of payment, the introduction of dollars *per se* would not provide an innovation providing they were accepted for their silver content, i.e. as bullion. And this indeed is how the East India Company and the Co-hong merchants with whom they dealt must have regarded it. This is the basis of the first treaty agreements—although later there are ambiguities and qualifications—and of the official assays, during which Chinese and foreign consular officials agreed as to the silver content of a new coin and, therefore, the rate at which it was to be accepted in payment of duties. Nevertheless, coins have a convenience and gain a reputation which in turn can give them a

value independent of their silver content, a premium for relia-
bility, convenience, and acceptability. As dollars flowed into
China, they became a common means of payment and it was
natural that in the private sector prices should eventually be
quoted in a *dollar* unit of account. When this happened it
was possible that the exchanges should attach to this unit and
vary independently of the silver exchanges, a fact students
must consider in following the rates of dollar-using ports. Of
all this the imperial authorities took no account, except to
insist that *de jure* the dollar must be considered as bullion only.

In fact, however, local officials could not ignore the dollars. To the extent that they treated them as a form of
bullion, they were or appeared to be, as stated above, merely
following the traditional policy. But once coins cease being
solely accepted by weight and for wholesale transactions prior
to being melted into featureless bullion, their specific characteristics and problems have to be faced. And officials did
consider their impact on tax payments, their rate of exchange
and the problem of "equalizing" that rate, and, eventually,
the problem of an adequate supply. For once in use, the
dollars became a necessity, and mint policy changes in Mexico
or silver purchase policies in the United States could have an
unwarranted effect on the Chinese monetary system—not
only in Ch'ing but as long as China remained on silver. Thus,
it was a natural extension of the traditional coinage task of
the dynasty to undertake the minting of a Chinese silver
dollar. That first minting came typically as the result of a
memorial from a provincial official and was granted on the
basis of the needs of his area—not on the basis of a needed
national policy change. Thus China's "national" dollar was,
in origin, a provincial dollar whose circulation, when once
accepted, became practically Empire-wide, though still issued
from provincial mints.

Limitations of reform. Chinese officials were willing to
consider recommendations of limited impact and to implement them to the extent that they fell within the traditional
scope of Ch'ing administration. A modern mint in Canton
could succeed ; a 100 days of reform, a series of reform edicts

without precedence or relevance from above could fail. We may conclude tentatively that the imperial regime in this field of monetary policy had shown itself capable of adaptation providing it was permitted to proceed with caution and providing the impact could be measured. As the scope of certain key provincial officials became enlarged both as to responsibility and as to areas, so the outlook of the reforming or modernizing official might become wider. By the Sino-Japanese war, "provincial" no longer meant "confined within one or two provinces", a fact illustrated by the concerns of Li Hung-chang whose interests involved industry, naval affairs, actual contacts with foreigners, civil defence, inter-provincial financial arrangements, and other functions within the area of Shanghai and the north. In all this he remained, however, a provincial official, his policies only with difficulty being fit in part into an imperial concept. The centre failed to incorporate his administrative concepts into the traditional fabric ; when Li Hung-chang fell from power in 1896, the task had to be redone, already too late, under the direction of the successful foreigners. In fact, as we have noted, the task of giving new purpose to the centre was never achieved. Officials might innovate and modernize as the stimuli dictated, but their actions never became part of a centrally administered system.

Whether this may be described as a failure depends too much on what might have been. We began describing the monetary system and Ch'ing monetary policy as part of the traditional role of imperial administration as referee of the private sector and its economic transactions. The outline of policy in the last few pages suggests that the Ch'ing reached a high stage of sophistication in this role and that the private sector, given time, found the officials adapting their regulations and their preconceptions to meet some of the more pressing needs. Given time and sufficient economic impetus, economic development in the sense of growth of national product and modernization might most probably have forced further changes, with the referee willing to respond. But time was a crucial factor ; the forces of the New Imperialism and of Japanese expansion threatened the break-up of China.

After the Boxer Uprising and until the early 1930's, foreign influence had a direct and immediate impact on the Chinese economy. China had lost the chance to develop while remaining master and thus the question of the Confucian official's final willingness to thorough reform was never put to the absolute test. Yet it was probably not the official philosophy or political concepts which limited the Chinese government's response. The bureaucracy was victim of inadequate administrative techniques, and the government—both imperial and local—lacked the power to permit, not to mention foster, change. This criticism is nowhere more clearly seen than in the tax structure, a subject to which we must now turn.

CH'ING FISCAL ADMINISTRATION AND POLICY

A government may act, we have said, as a referee in the market ; it may also take more direct action in allocating resources to itself and in redistributing income. We have now to examine these activities and note immediately that here we shall be especially hindered by the lack of statistics. As we noted in chapter one, statistics are available, but aggregates are particularly unreliable and absolute figures which have no reference mark, e.g. tax receipts without any concept of national income magnitudes, have little economic significance. Estimates have been made and they are referred to in the concluding lists of suggested readings.

Statistics of the government sector. The Ch'ing court, indeed the entire bureaucracy, has been referred to by social historians as "parasitic", feeding on the production of the people, returning little or nothing. Since official salaries were unrealistically low, we might conclude that they were paid for their contribution to the national income ; we might conclude further that the extra payments they received, "squeeze", constituted a transfer payment affecting the ultimate distribution of income but not its size. This, of course, is to moralize about national income statistics and to attempt to distinguish between official salaries and other emoluments and forced payments as if we were dealing with a government operating with advanced accounting methods. The fact is that the Ch'ing administration was inefficient by modern standards, and thus the Chinese taxpayer paid more for the services rendered than we would tolerate in a more modern society. But all this is quite irrelevant. There was a government, there was a "civil list", and services were rendered ; no particularly Chinese problem is created.

When, however, we come to consider the size of government payments and receipts, we do come across an insurmountable difficulty. Statements of expenditures and receipts are only partial records of transactions with the government sector ; a percentage—what percentage must remain unknown—is unrecorded. And in the recorded section, the figures are difficult of interpretation because we can never be sure whether we are reading figures for what ought to have been paid or expended but which was not, what ought but may have been, or what ought not but actually was. The structure of Ch'ing finance, which looks so simple and straightforward in the nineteenth-century translations and abstractions from official documents was an administrative maze, a makeshift which defied analysis and which shrewd contemporary observers, like Sir Robert Hart, saw as the key to the economic problems of the Chinese Empire.

Expenditures. The central government was in one sense but a local administration for the metropolitan area of the capital ; it also had certain other direct responsibilities for public works, especially the Grand Canal. Similarly, provincial authorities took direct responsibility for some works, but a vast percentage of such public investment was undertaken at the local level, financed by contributions in kind or by unrecorded payments. There is no total figure for the empire. As for salaries, these were but part of a complex of payments, some in kind, some in money, some for actual services performed, some in "squeeze" or through manipulation of the exchange rates—their total escapes the possibility of precise summation. Were one to attempt to distinguish between payments made at the different levels of government, the problem would be more complex, for we cannot hope to unravel the transfers of receipts among officials, the levies of the court, and the more recognized and open inter-provincial transfers.

Receipts. If we turn now to government receipts, it seems at first as if the system were more clearly defined. Since China was an agricultural nation, quite obviously the tax structure must rest on some form of land tax—considering a tax on income as administratively out of the question. And indeed we do find the traditional breakdown of land tax providing the bulk of revenue, supplemented by taxes on goods in transit, on the customs and receipts from licences and from government monopolies, especially salt. This last is, of course, equivalent to an excise tax.

At each turn, however, there are problems. First, tax farming, normal in pre-modern administrations, makes it difficult to assess the tax burden. Secondly, there were many taxes on land, including the so-called grain tribute, at times commuted and at other paid in kind, which had to be transported at considerable cost to a rice-eating court in a non-rice-growing area of China. Then too the land tax was in one sense "fixed", that is, the normal size of the quotas or bullion quantities accountable to Peking were fixed, but not the actual tax burden on the peasant nor the actual amount remitted to Peking. Thirdly, taxes on goods in transit, referred to as *likin*, an innovation of the Taiping period, were so miscellaneous and variable that they provide particular problems. Fourthly, the extent of special "contributions", forced levies, payments in kind and labour services cannot be estimated.

If the payment of customs duties would appear a clear spot in this picture because of the role of the foreign-staffed Imperial Maritime Customs, we would be mistaken. The Maritime Customs first of all did not concern itself with the "native" junk trade, and secondly, did not until after the 1911 revolution become responsible for the actual collecting of the monies received. The customs reported only the amounts to be collected, leaving the officially commissioned customs banks to actually collect the revenue. Indeed, foreign merchants who had fought so hard for a clear statement of customs duties and a simple method of payment, having won the former, gave up the latter by permitting their Chinese compradores or other Chinese merchants to handle duty payments. Then, too, the *Haikwan tael*, the unit of account in which duties were valued, could be paid by different weights of bullion in the different ports. Not even here was there a national system.

Evaluation of the fiscal system as a base for modernization. Since we cannot study the problem in terms of specific quantities, we must rely on indicators, on indirect evidence. Perhaps this is in any case more satisfactory, for we are concerned with the economic significance of the public sector and not, since we can never have national product statistics, with absolute sums. On the expenditure side we can ask whether there is evidence that state activities were curtailed because of lack of funds ; on the revenue side we can ask what flexibility existed. Was the public financing system adequate for a state attempting modernization ? If the answer is "No", we may have here a factor limiting the Ch'ing's economic potential for change.

Consistent with the general structure of the Chinese state, the public sector was, with few exceptions, based upon locally executed decisions with central government supervision. Central government activities themselves, including the court, national public works, the Manchu military organization, and the metropolitan local government, were financed from four sources : the quotas of provincially levied taxes, principally the land tax ; local taxes in the metropolitan area ; revenues collected on a supra-provincial basis, e.g. salt excise and customs duties ; and special levies, sale of rank, "gifts". If to modernize, the central government had to redefine its functions, we must consider whether it could have financed such new functions. How flexible was the central government's revenue structure ?

The first impression is that with fixed provincial quotas, a tariff set by treaty, and a practical limit on salt taxes, flexibility came only from the special levies. Growing court expenses and the cost of even the traditional functions of the centre suggest a sufficient reason for permitting provincial authorities to undertake experiments which might well have been national projects.   The centre had, after all, no tradition of direct tax administration, all collections were directed by provincial officials.   Indeed, Sir Robert Hart and other foreign observers saw rightly that without fiscal reform, modernization directed from the centre would be impossible.

There was, nevertheless, some flexibility.   Provincial quotas could be enlarged, especially when the demand for additional funds was joined with an exposition of new expenditure requirements and, sometimes, as with indemnities, foreign pressure.   But this was not the traditional way, and, although the centre had the power to force such payments, it was easier to follow precedent and permit the province to undertake both project and financing.

Not that the province had a limitless source of funds.   Too often local administrations found themselves unable through famine or civil disturbance, to collect the traditionally approved taxes.   In the chaos of the Taiping rebellion, the transit tax (*likin*) was introduced, although it was planned that the incidence should fall on artisans and merchants, who, it was felt, had not suffered from the rebellion to the extent of the farmer.   This wholly provincial revenue staved off financial disaster—at some cost to inter-regional trade. Foreigners objected to the transit tax on the grounds that it could undo the advantages of a fixed tariff, and special concessions were therefore made to foreign goods.   But further emergencies required additional funds, and the authorities looked to the foreigners for loans.   In the Imperial Maritime Customs, China found the basis for its foreign credit, despite the fact that this organization did not, as we have seen, actually handle the funds.   So foreigners saw in this provincial need a chance to encourage national financial outlook, but they succeeded only in requiring that provincial loans be approved and authorized by the Emperor.   Augustine Heard and Company, for example, hoping to make a loan directly to Peking failed completely in their purpose ; in similar fashion other "national" all-embracing financial projects failed, *e.g.* the Mitkiewicz scheme, fantastic from the outset, came to nought. Thus the provinces in the mid-nineteenth century found one further source—the *likin*—to prevent financial disaster. Otherwise they too had to depend on such measures as foreign loans and capital sums from rich merchants or officials.

Some degree of flexibility was given to the Chinese system by the movement of funds from one area to another as needed. Thus copper mines might be renovated to meet the needs of the coinage by funds from several provinces sent to Yunnan on imperial instructions. Li Hung-chang's "provincial" Hwai Army was financed from a diversity of sources, with the funds originating in several jurisdictions and pieced together by a combination of personal relationships among officials, but always with imperial sanction. These arrangements could not always be depended upon. The interprovincial transfer was subject to interruption when local requirements became too demanding. And again we revert to our analysis of the Ch'ing state ; such an interruption was not a denial of imperial authority. The governor would simply state that the transmission of the usual funds, say to Yunnan, was made impossible by such and such an event, but that the transfers would be resumed as soon as possible. An imperial edict would usually result in some of the funds actually being sent. This was not, however, a very sound basis on which to plan a modernization project. (For an exception, see Taiwan in Chapter VI).

Indeed, new projects were an addition to the functions of government and were treated as marginal. That is to say, the make-shift nature of the *additional* or marginal financing made the actual commencement of any new project excessively slow and its continuation constantly in doubt. A technical hitch in the construction, the transfer of an interested official, or the sudden demand for the funds elsewhere could delay or stop any scheme which lacked overwhelming support of a powerful official interest. Thus we must conclude with contemporary observers that the Ch'ing financial system, when considered together with the structure and traditions of the Ch'ing state, was a direct impediment to economic development. Initiative might, therefore, be taken by an official, but the financing would often come from the private sector, a basic reason—other than tradition—for the so-called "merchant undertakings under official supervision" (*kuan-tu shang-pan*). This government-merchant partnership had, however, its own unfortunate problems, as we shall see below. For the rest, the initiative was placed on the private sector, and here too there were problems which must be considered.

There were some state problems in which financing was undoubtedly a problem, although hardly the limiting one. Failure to maintain water controls, especially the Yellow River, or to keep the Grand Canal open—this was undoubtedly due both to the technical and administrative problems involved; financing was just one of many barriers.

With this background of the Ch'ing state and its role both as referee and allocator of resources, especially with reference to the monetary system and policy and the fiscal system and policy, we should consider the slow course of industrialization in China—at least through 1895. After this date concessions won by the Japanese at the Treaty of Shimonoseki and the allies at the Boxer Protocol permit the direct interference in the economy which provided the Chinese with the models they needed for their own industrialization. We should consider first the nature of the impact of the foreigners on the economy we have so far described.

THE FOREIGN IMPACT TO 1895

Early significance. In one sense the foreign impact on the Chinese economy was profound, even in the period before 1895. New crops for upland and dry farming and improved rice varieties were significant importations. Foreign trade with its favourable balance through the early 1830's brought to China her first real silver coin, and the dollar circulated widely, especially in China south of the Yangtze, even replacing the traditional *tael* with the *dollar* unit of account in many localities. The growth of the tea and silk traders must have affected the prosperity of the areas concerned, although we have little specific information and rely on such inferences as the disruption caused to that economy by the opening of treaty ports from Canton to Shanghai with the consequent change in the direction of internal trade routes. The trade balance turned against China in the late 1830's but in the 1850's was partially responsible for the silver drain from France where gold was relatively overvalued by the mint pars. Eventually, as we have seen, China adopted the dollar as the first coin to be minted under modern conditions and by the 1930's the *dollar* had completely replaced the *tael* as the unit of account.

Thus agriculture, trade, and the monetary system were affected by the foreign impact. Trade, too, had its impact on Chinese finances through the growing customs duties; foreign loans provided an additional source of funds. But all of this fell on the traditional economy; it was not a prelude to modernization. Until 1842 foreigners were effectively confined to Canton. The interior areas felt the inflow of dollars and the heightened demand for tea as something caused by that part of the *internal* trade with which they came in contact. The success of the foreigners in nineteenth-century conflicts did not change this—although it had its own impact, which we must consider below. So far as the important impact on the traditional sector is concerned, we must not confuse the importance of foreign contact with the importance of the influence of foreigners, much less foreign ideas.

Effects of foreign military success. The situation did not change significantly as a direct cause of foreign military success. Organizational changes were immediate, but even their political impact was limited in that many such changes could be fit into the traditional framework. Thus foreigners could trade at the new "treaty-ports" of Foochow, Amoy, Ningpo, and Shanghai, as well as Canton and through the newly ceded Hong Kong; they no longer had to deal with designated merchants as in Canton; and they could press their claims through consular representatives while enjoying extra-territoriality. But to the Chinese, this was still a barbarian problem on the frontier. To the average Chinese it must have seemed little

52 A Concise Economic History of Modern China

different. The foreigners were in more places but doing the same thing. Their inability to move into the areas of supply, into the tea and silk districts, rendered their other commercial gains illusory. Foreigners were primarily merchants, not interested in fixed capital investment, and concerned with making those high profits which each generation believe had been the standard in the "good old days". The attitude was changing; American partners at home might see greater opportunities in the American West and steadily withdraw their support from China ventures, but others became institutionalized and saw themselves playing a permanent role on the China coast. These foreign merchants strove for industrialization; they were concerned with projects beyond the clear approval of the treaty concessions; but they were hampered by lack of industrial experience and know-how.

But what of the tariff, what of extra-territoriality? These were surely factors which showed the Chinese that something very significant was occurring. Interestingly enough, this conclusion is erroneous—the concessions of the so-called "unequal treaties" made a more emotional impact on the Chinese nationalists of the twentieth century than on the Manchu dynasty. After all, changes in tariff rates had not been a traditional tool of Ch'ing economic policy; rather changes in extra charges and collection fees had been traditional methods of raising additional funds on an *ad hoc* basis. The treaty agreements to fix the tariff at an intended 5% *ad valorem* reflected both the foreign dislike of such changes *per se* and their belief in free trade. The significance of the loss of tariff autonomy was cloaked by the increasing revenues from the foreign customs. As for extra-territoriality, this was a formalization of a convention long in use between countries with differing legal concepts. China as an empire was not overly concerned; China as a nation would be.

If we must guard against the impression that the British defeat of China in the First Sino-British War and the Treaty of 1842 must surely have sounded both a warning of potentially greater dangers and a call to immediate reform and industrialization, we must not suppose that the Chinese regarded the changes forced upon them either as totally insignificant or merely an unexceptional extension of an existing system. The changes were stimuli to economic change at two distinct levels: first, at the official level the military defeats gave rise to the "self-strengthening" movement already mentioned earlier in this chapter; second, it gave rise to those day-to-day contacts and released those market forces which eventually produced economic change in the private sector. The two were not mutually self-exclusive. But the military defeats which brought about increased foreign activity in and influence on China also stimulated forces opposed to change in the sense of modernization. First, we must recall the traditional Chinese attitude to foreigners and thus the opposition to modernization as a foreign innovation—hence, of course, the many writings designed to show that Western engineering techniques were merely developments of originally Chinese discoveries and to attempt to support new economic policies by quotations, carefully selected and newly interpreted, from the classics. Secondly, those in favour of "self-strengthening" were equally anxious that the adoption of foreign methods would not in itself subject China to foreign control—a possibility which the Chinese Communist government found to be real even in dealing with the Soviet Union. To summarize: the impact of foreign contact on the rate of economic change was limited to the self-strengthening movement at the official level and to weak and uncertain market stimuli at the private level, but both were hampered by Chinese attitudes to foreign innovation and Chinese fear of foreign control. The Indian experience was not lost on China.

If we were to conclude that foreign contacts triggered the Taiping rebellion, we should be forced to a reassessment indeed. Certainly the Christian elements, however distorted, were foreign; less certainly, but arguable, the disruption of internal trade routes aggravated already existing economic troubles—and in this the new treaty ports were factors. But since the other factors of revolt were there, native to China, growing since at least the middle of the eighteenth century, we should be cautious in stressing the foreign role.

The "old Canton system". The original contact of China with the European powers came through the same gate as that of the minor sultanates and kingdoms of Southeast Asia: Europe was represented first by the Portuguese who, like the Norse traders before them, were always part viking. China knew how to deal with them. The tributary system continued satisfactorily through the eighteenth century despite the growth of trade and the frequency of contact because the East India Companies and the Canton merchants wished it so. Complaints were made and attempts to surmount the Canton monopoly undertaken, but they were never pushed to conclusion. The end of the British company's monopoly in 1832 and the opening of the China trade—by the British—to the "private English", represented by a consul, brought political relations under the same strain as commercial relations and the two joined to force the end of the old Canton system: with the Treaty of Nanking in 1842, the treaty system began. It was not to end until World War II, when foreign powers finally gave up their extra-territoriality.

The "Treaty System". But there were significant changes within the treaty system. The conflict of 1840-1842 was followed by a second round in 1858 ending with the treaties of Tientsin. These largely confirmed the privileges of 1842 and made technical improvements. The number of treaty ports was substantially increased and the Yangtze River opened to foreign shipping. While this brought the foreigner into the heart of China, he remained as before effectually confined to the treaty ports, his influence limited to matters of trade, to the generally fruitless advice given unsolicited to various levels of officialdom, and to specific services rendered under the self-strengthening movement. Efforts to extend the scope of economic relations were largely frustrated; ironically China felt too weak to seriously consider strengthening.

The Treaty of Shimonoseki in 1895, however, made possible the erection of factories in the treaty ports and foreign settlements; the aftermath of the Boxer debacle reinforced the foreign role, and the last years of the dynasty saw territorial concessions and the development of spheres of influence—both economic and political—which threatened the integrity of China itself. (See map on p. 12 for the location of such foreign encroachments. There were, of course, other treaty ports, ports-of-call, and frontier trading points—too numerous to indicate.) With the founding of the Republic many foreigners sympathized, and the changing attitudes of European and American States to the "new imperialism" gave increasing hope to China's rising nationalism. Thus, while the basis of the economic relationship remained unchanged, changes were being prepared. Furthermore, foreigners found a national government wishing for and capable of receiving advice. That it did not control its territory was, obviously, a limiting factor in the effectiveness of such advice! But the period after 1895, including the last few years of the Ch'ing, is better studied in Chapter IV.

Foreign trade development. With the foreigner excluded from the interior, supervision of the source of supply for both tea and silk had to come from the Chinese themselves. But just as merchants complained in the boom of the 1860's that Bombay cotton was too often mixed with trash, so foreigners reported on the deterioration of China's staple exports. In part, this was the fault of the speculative manner in which the trade was conducted, although the different varieties and taste of

Table 2. CHINA: TEA AND SILK EXPORTS, 1867, 1886, 1905 (1000 piculs)[a]

	Tea Leaf	Brick Tea	Silk[b]	Tea as a percentage of total exports
1867	1248	65	40[c]	59
1886	1846	370	64	43
1905[d]	839	530	80	11

a   I picul = $133\frac{1}{3}$ lb. av.

b   White and yellow raw silk.

c   But 67,000 piculs in 1860.

d   UK imports from China, 1905=49,000 piculs; from India=1,129,000 piculs; from Ceylon=670,000 piculs.

Source :   H. B. Morse.

Note :   See also Table 6a below.

Indian tea adds a significant factor to the analysis. In 1886 tea exports reached their maximum—they had already been declining as a percentage of total exports (See Table 2). The relatively less important brick tea for Russia continued to find an increasing market, but India and Ceylon replaced China as the principal source of Britain's tea leaf. As for silk, quantities exported increased during the nineteenth century, but they became less significant in China's total trade picture as Japanese competition began to play a more important role.

China's export trade became, therefore, increasingly dependent upon what the merchants had called in disgust the "muck and truck" trade—feathers, soya beans, hides and skins, bristles, straw braid, and other miscellaneous items. This change had some impact on the rate of growth of manufacturing enterprise, since most of these commodities had to be processed. And to this we now turn.

INDUSTRIALIZATION: THE RECORD TO 1895

In the early years the treaty ports were strictly places of trade where merchants lived in a "foreign settlement" and kept within the limitations of the treaty. By the early 1860's Shanghai was of sufficient size to warrant a good newspaper, to have enjoyed a real estate boom—induced at least partially by the proximity of the Taiping rebels and the refugees—and to have become sufficiently concerned with its role in China to have become involved in the rebellion itself, to have pressed for rights for a railway to Soochow, and to have begun the exploitation of the Yangtze trade. The Soochow railway project and subsequent foreign attempts to sponsor railways failed, at least until the 1880's; banking, land investment, insurance, and other financial-type enterprises accounted for almost all the non-trading activities of the port, and these, of course, were intimately connected with trade. Gas came to Shanghai in the 1860's; water, electricity and the telephone were there before the end of the century.

A stock exchange catered to these companies and the shares listed grew from 84,000 in 1877 to 1.3 million in 1895 while the *tael* value of shares quoted grew from 11.6 million to 57.6 million. Some of these shares, about 12% in 1890 and 5% in 1895, were those of companies operating outside China ; Shanghai capital was exported to finance mining and forestry in Southeast Asia before manufacturing in China. The reason is not hard to find; in colonial areas foreigners had access to the interior and to control of their enterprises. Foreigners could not reach the mines of Yunnan, and China tried to keep such enterprises under Chinese control. While this proved impossible in the next period, it successfully restricted investment before 1895.

Scope of modern enterprise. We have now to turn to very inconclusive figures, but ones which nevertheless give the general scope of Chinese manufacturing enterprise in this early period, say 1880-1895. A listing of some 74 companies using foreign machinery can be made for Shanghai; of these about one-quarter were Chinese owned. There were a few more scattered among the other treaty ports. It is hardly an impressive record. Of the Shanghai companies, about one-half were devoted to manufacturing—flour milling, furniture making, and textiles; another quarter were in processing— especially silk filatures. About 15% were in shipping and docks. Since these companies were small-scale enterprises, probably with less than 200 employees, it can be seen that few Chinese worked with or had experience of foreign equipment in this period from the private sector.

"Self-strengthening" enterprises. The public sector performance was more dramatic by comparison but did not really move beyond the pilot project stage. In 1865 the Kiangnan Arsenal was established, followed in 1866 with a shipyard at Foochow, in 1870 a machine factory at Tientsin, 1872 an arsenal at Lanchow, and 1882 a shipyard at Port Arthur. A naval academy in 1880 and a military academy in 1885 were all part of China's limited modernization under self-strengthening. To foreigners despairing of any concession to the times, each project seemed possibly the beginning of China's "awakening" and became the subject of considerable speculative

discussion. In fact, these had little impact on the economy; the "linkage effects" were minimal.

Joint enterprises. More significant were the joint merchant undertakings under official supervision. In 1872 a group of Shanghai compradores and merchants with close foreign associations and some experience with modern management techniques—such as they were on the China coast—bought out the American-managed Shanghai Steam Navigation Company and formed, with official sponsorship, the first of China's modern-type companies, the China Merchants' Steam Navigation Company, for trade on the Yangtze and between Shanghai and Tientsin. Formation of the company was preceded by less permanent steamship and trading ventures undertaken by Chinese merchants who were already investing in European-managed companies. The basic experience came from employment or association with the agency houses and their shipping enterprises.

Here we have a classic example of the impact of foreign investment and of the educational value of the foreign presence. Our thesis is, however, that such examples are limited. Steamships were an innovation which foreign merchants more or less understood and which could be readily accepted into the Chinese economy. Officials saw a Chinese company both as an alternative carrier of rice and as competition to foreign companies threatening to monopolize not just the coastal trade but also the trade up the Yangtze, into China's interior. Self-strengthening, the traditional requirements of the Ch'ing state, and the competence of Chinese and foreign merchants were all combined to enable the establishment of the China Merchants' Steam Navigation Company.

This is not to suggest that the company developed without problems—even if we omit the difficulties provoked by war with France. The merchant owners were not, after all, highly qualified managers and they were involved in heavy speculations on other accounts. But the official supervisors also created problems, the most serious of which was their tendency to appropriate, often for official purposes, the company's cash, leaving it short of operating capital. This is a common failing of successive Chinese governments, especially where such operations provide funds to conceal a budget deficit by forcing the company into the short-term capital market.

On a different level, the peculiar combination of circumstances under which the China Merchants' Steam Navigation Company was founded suggest that here too we have a sort of "pilot" project rather than the beginning of privately financed investment in modern-type enterprises. Other "merchant undertakings under government supervision" did, however, follow, but each a pilot in its own field and each serving some national as well as wholly economy function. In mining there was the Kaiping Mining Company, 1878, later to fall into foreign hands; the Imperial Telegraph Administration was formed in 1880; and the Hua-sheng textile mill, completed in 1891. It was on the tracks of the Kaiping Mining Company that China's first steam train ran—if the Woosung railway be excluded—and China's railway development began, under Chinese control, in 1882. Chang Chih-tung, the viceroy who sponsored the first modern mint, was transferred from Canton to Wuchang in 1889 and there began supervision of the Peking-Hankow line and of a complex of industrial enterprises, including an iron foundry, cotton mills and in 1894, the Tayeh iron mines. This was perhaps the most spectacular of provincial officially-sponsored enterprises, of which Tso Tsung-t'ang's Lanchow woollen weaving mill in 1878 is an early example.

Limitations of China's response. Yet these industrial pilots suffered from a complex of problems—poor administration, unsound financing, foreign involvement. The Kaiping Mining Company fell into foreign hands; the Hanyehp'ing Company with its iron foundry and mines ran into financial difficulties and fell eventually under Japanese control; the Huasheng textile mill simply took too long to get operating. This last story is significant. The first memorial dealing with a cotton textile enterprise was dated twelve full years before the factory actually went into operation in 1891. Then in 1893 it was destroyed by fire and, being uninsured, required new financing before being again in operation in late 1894. This time lag may have been excessive even by Chinese standards, but it is illustrative of the tentative nature of Chinese industrial progress.

Since the industrial revolution of the eighteenth-century, time has been compressed, and a country can fall quickly behind. Thus China could change from a "model for Europe" to a "semi-civilized" state in 100 years; the long-despised "little dwarfs" of Japan could overtake her even faster. By the First Sino-Japanese War, China had 174,564 spindles in operation, Japan 530,074. Statistics comparing such apparently diverse but actually inter-connected activities as naval ship-building and students training overseas tell comparable stories. China was reacting to the stimuli of foreign contact; China was adapting at both public and private levels. But as yet there was no sense of urgency and certainly no sense of central direction or planning. Yet time was both a theoretically significant economic factor and a political weapon. The pilot schemes were developed with sufficient deliberation that they could be fitted into the traditional economy with minimum linkage effects, a fact related to the concept of the critical level of investment. The political aspect is a reminder that Japan, already invading the Chinese market, presented both an economic and a military threat to the development of China.

The economic history of China from 1860 to 1895 is replete with examples of pilot schemes, individual attempts to introduce machinery in this or that small plant or mine. There is nothing to suggest modernization of management or control techniques: the machines—like the computors which merely replace older accounting practices—had a strictly limited impact. While some foreigners might see all this as a beginning, they could mean by this only the beginning of an awareness, not a preparation for sustained modernization.

The location of these various efforts depended upon the political centre of the enterprising official or, usually, a treaty-port, especially Shanghai. Whereas local officials did not always prohibit the use of foreign equipment, there is some general validity to the British Consul's report from Tamsui, Taiwan :

Why is there no machinery in Chinese mines? Supposing the proprietors have ever heard of it, they see it connected with increased outlay. Their want of capital would not allow of their purchasing it. But if they did this would mean employment of foreigners [as technical advisers and, possibly, as managers]—and mandarin interference with perhaps loss of life to the owner.

Hong Kong. Many of the problems encountered in investment on the mainland of China, even within the treaty ports, should have been absent in the British Crown Colony of Hong Kong. We should then stop to note briefly that the economic history of that colony does not seem extraordinarily different from the treaty-ports proper. In an overbursting of enthusiasm after the First Sino-British War the story is that enterprising merchants imported pianos from England in anticipation of the new China market. The vision of China as a market of 400 million customers capable of keeping the wheels of British industry turning for untold generations was never wholly lost, but it was quickly tempered by realism. Hong Kong merchants came to learn and to live by the slogan that Hong Kong could not lead China. They learned this lesson again with the failure of such ventures as the China Railways Company of 1865; and yet again with the closure of the modern Hong Kong mint in 1868.

An 1871 share list for Hong Kong shows a pattern similar to that of Shanghai, with banking and insurance, enterprises ancillary to the China trade, hotels, and a distillery. Hong Kong caught the fever of company promotion from London and Bombay and passed its own limited liability ordinance in 1865—in this it had an advantage over Shanghai—and sundry enterprises were forthcoming, especially docks. Indeed, the Hongkong and Shanghai Bank's first chief manager became too closely involved in this speculation and resigned in 1870. Too many of the enterprises had been hurt by mercantile attitudes inappropriate to industrial undertakings. There was a further crisis in 1874 during which Augustine Heard and Co., the representative American house, failed—its interests were taken up by the new Butterfield and Swire,

and even the Hongkong and Shanghai Bank itself was brought
low, although this was its last serious crisis.

A summary of industrial activity in Hong Kong in 1886 is
not impressive : manufacture of Chinese "hubble-bubble"
pipes and brass sheathing ; leather boots and shoes for export
to North and Central America ; tobacco, preserved ginger ;
and the remelting of old glass.   Even when these are coupled
with the shipyards and their ancillary activities, the enterprises
listed hardly constitute an industrial revolution or a model
for China.   Hong Kong fulfilled its original purpose and
little else : it remained a suitable location where head offices
could be subject to British company law as enacted in the
Colony ; it never became a guide to Chinese economic development.

In this the colony's merchants were realistic.   For them
the prize was China, and China had to be won on the mainland.   Later with China's regaining of tariff autonomy,
there was the additional reason to get inside the tariff walls.
The brilliance of the colony's post-1949 performance was its
reorientation to Southeast Asia and world markets, but that
story, though it is part of the accomplishment of the Chinese
people, is not properly part of China's economic history.

These then were for China's economic development the
lost years.   Hereafter China would have to develop, at least
in part, at a pace set by foreign investors and on their terms.
Not until the 1930's would China begin to take an initiative so
soon to be offset by war and revolution.   The pace begins to
change almost immediately after the First Sino-Japanese War
and its course to the end of the Ch'ing can be studied in terms
of governmental change, the foreign concessions, railway and
mining development, and industrial growth.   An assessment
of the economic elements will appear sounder in Chapter IV.

Chapter III

INDIA AND CHINA: A CASE STUDY

ANGLO-INDIAN BANKS ON THE CHINA COAST

The economic relations between India and China have historically been of varying significance. In the nineteenth century the pattern established during the days of the East India Company's trade monopoly at Canton continued as an important element in the Asian trade structure. The fortunes of silver and the changes in Indian currency had their impact not only on the trade magnitudes but also on the profitability of Chinese industry, especially textiles. But economic relations between the two countries have never been a leading factor in either's development. Even the vital importance of India to the Canton trade was of more significance to England than to China, although opium sales provided an important tax basis for the East India Company's administration in parts of India. Thus, a detailed study of India-China relations hardly has a place in an introductory economic history of modern China.

The present chapter then is a brief introduction to the study of Indian-Chinese economic relations, concentrating on one particular aspect—the spread of Indian and Anglo-Indian banking institutions to China in the mid-nineteenth century. (Students in search of doctoral research topics will doubtlessly find in the economic histories of the two countries similar opportunities for the case study approach. It is a relatively undisturbed field !)

Financing the China trade. The establishment of agencies and branches of banking institutions founded in India can be explained by reference to several contributing factors.

First, the European-China trade was from earliest times balanced in favour of China, and Europe needed a source of finance. India provided this with opium, but after 1840 the balances were not certain, and with the added complications of the Australian and Californian trade and bullion exports, a complex network of trade finance was required which continued, nevertheless, to be based on the Bombay, Hong Kong, London triangle. Secondly, this basic financial need had its institutional counterpart in the network of relationships between British, Chinese, and Indian merchant houses. At first these were European, but quite early the China merchants were representing Bombay houses and by mid-century Sassoon and Cama were familiar names on the China coast. As the financial resources of the merchant houses came to be supplemented by banks, it was not surprising that these banks should parallel the structure of the trade and the merchants they were financing. Thus we find banks reaching out to Canton and Hong Kong both from London and from Bombay. Those from Bombay went first.

Three banking enterprises—the Oriental Bank Corporation, the Commercial Bank of India, and the Agra and United Service Bank—comprise the mainstream of Anglo-Indian banking in China, and their histories are of considerable significance in themselves. After 1860 the field broadened considerably reaching a climax in the Bombay cotton boom of 1864, and continuing along more conservative lines after the crisis of 1866.

Anglo-Indian banks : origins. The period 1830-1866 may be briefly characterised, as far as Indian foreign-style banking is concerned, as one in which the Presidency banks dominated in a specific but restricted field and in which other banks attempted with more or less success to undertake aspects of the banking business which these government-sponsored banks failed or were unable because of their charters to undertake. Characteristically, therefore, banks were founded for a particular purpose—to serve a neglected area or portion of the community and provide internal transfer facilities, e.g. the Agra Bank, to deal in foreign exchange, e.g. the Oriental, to facilitate the financing of local trade, e.g., the Commercial

Bank of India. Founded in 1833 (Agra), 1844 (Oriental) and 1845 (Commercial), the banks were, in a sense, of the new generation, succeeding where the Union Bank of Calcutta and the old Commercial Bank (founded 1819) had failed.

The move to London. The foreign contacts of the three banks led in turn to the overseas expansion of the banks themselves. At this point they found their Indian base inadequate and each eventually sought and secured an "Imperial" charter and London headquarters. The reasons for this were manifold. First, the desire to play a role in the finance of foreign trade in competition with the already established merchant-cum-bankers of the agency houses forced the banks to depend upon low profit margins and, therefore, high turnover. For this they needed constituents ; and this, in turn suggested not only a London office for contacts with British firms but also British shareholders and even directors. This could best be achieved by moving to London. Secondly, as neither British nor Indian legislation provided for limited liability before 1858, this could only be obtained through the medium of a Crown charter granted after the bank had met the requirements of the Colonial Banking Regulations. (It is true that limited liability could, in effect, be achieved by inserting a clause into the Memorandum of Association calling for the winding up of the company when, say, as much as one-half the paid-up capital had been lost, thus halting further operations before losses could exceed the subscribed capital. But this was something of a makeshift, and *de jure* limited liability was sought.) Thirdly, although there were no restrictions on banking in several of the colonies, e.g., Hong Kong, a bank's profitability could be checked by refusal of a colonial treasury to accept its notes in payment of taxes. This acceptance was valuable in that it kept notes in circulation, and it had the additional effect of giving—or appearing to give—some government stamp of approval on the soundness of the bank, thus further facilitating acceptance of its notes. That the note issue was profitable both as a status symbol and as a source of interest-free funds is, for our period, unquestioned. Later the growing importance of current accounts, stamp duty on banknotes, and reserve regulations lessened the significance of the note issue which still remains, nevertheless, as a prestige symbol. Fourthly, the bank management felt that it could compete for funds more advantageously with a London head office—but this topic, which is complex, would take us too far afield.

The actual course of expansion pursued by each bank differed.

The Agra Bank. The Agra opened a London branch in 1846, moved into Canton in 1854 removing to Hong Kong in 1856, and established its head office in London in 1857. The Bank effected the move to London by securing letters patent under the Act of 1844 which required all English banks with seven or more partners, i.e. joint stock banks, to secure such a charter to permit them to operate in England. This made the Agra an English bank, still with unlimited liability, but apparently free to operate in the overseas territories where local legislation did not forbid it. Indeed, what started as bank primarily concerned with financial transactions with service officers in the Agra division developed first into an exchange bank and subsequently into a British bank with both local English and overseas interests. The English interest was confirmed by the Agra's merger with Messrs. Masterman, Peters, Mildred and Company to form the Agra and Masterman's Bank in 1865 ; the overseas expansion included an extension to Shanghai in 1858 as well as appointment of mercantile agents in other ports.

The Agra became a limited liability bank under the new legislation of 1858—and all subsequent revisions—but continued to be otherwise regulated by its letters patent. It was on this basis that the Agra became the only bank subject to the Companies Act of 1862 to be allowed the privilege of having its notes received by the Hong Kong treasury. Even then, it had to agree to abide by substantially the same rules as governed the note issue of the royally chartered banks under the Colonial Regulations.

The Oriental Bank. The Oriental Bank was actually founded as the Bank of Western India in 1842, a key function declared at its founding being foreign exchange transactions.

Moving to London as the Oriental Bank in 1845, the bank—unlike the Agra—remained an Indian institution while seeking Indian legislation of incorporation or a royal charter. Failing through the opposition of the Indian government to secure either, the Bank's management sought a charter for a "Bank of Hong Kong", while negotiating with the Bank of Ceylon to operate there under its already existing charter. These plans were scrapped in 1851 when the imperial government, neglecting its long standing deference to Indian views, granted a charter to the Oriental itself, providing for operations east of the Cape of Good Hope and, most important, the right to establish agencies in India without specific permission of the Indian government. Since the only significant difference between an agency and a branch was that the latter had the right of note issue and since the note issue was already a monopoly of the Presidency Banks in India, such permission to establish agencies was all the Bank had expected or desired.

The charter of the Oriental Bank Corporation established a precedent in that, for the first time, a bank was authorized to do banking business in India by an authority obviously not subject to the Indian government. Thus the activities of the bank within the scope permitted by the charter were not subject to Indian legislation. Other foreign banks had operated in India, but not under such conditions. In consequence, during the 1850's several other chartered banks were established with permission to establish Indian agencies, but only after consultation with the Indian authorities. With the passage of adequate Indian banking legislation, royal charters giving the right of establishing agencies in India without Indian government consent were not granted. The new banks established under the British Companies Act of 1862 operated in India subject to Indian legislation.

The Commercial Bank. The Commercial Bank of India was founded in 1845 to finance local Bombay trade, but by 1850 was operating a branch in Canton strictly for foreign exchange. The Canton agency moved to Hong Kong in 1857 in which year the bank was incorporated under Indian legislation. Influenced by the cotton boom, the Bank sought expansion through Royal Charter, which was granted in

1864, becoming the Commercial Banking Corporation of India and the East with operations extending from London to Shanghai and San Francisco—this last involving the sort of unfortunate speculative transaction which eventually brought about the downfall of the Bank.

The Chartered Mercantile. A similar history is noted in the Chartered Mercantile Bank of India, London, and China which was originally established as a Bombay bank of similar title in 1853. By 1855 it had agencies in Canton and Shanghai as well as London, and in 1857 was *de jure* wound up to enable a company to be formed with the defunct Bank of Asia under a royal charter. Thus India was responsible for three chartered banks on the China coast, banks governed by principles of double liability, a note issue limited to paid up capital and accepted at colonial treasuries, with a London head office, and with exchange and the finance of the Far Eastern trade as primary functions. In addition, the Agra and United Service Bank, legally an English establishment after 1857, served the Far East on principles similar to those of the royally chartered banks, and, since its paid-up capital was but one-half the subscribed capital, it, too, effectively provided its customers double liability.

Other Banks. In the boom years preceding 1865 several other banks of Indian origin reached the China coast. The Asiatic Banking Corporation was promoted in Bombay in 1865 and received its royal charter in 1864 with head office in London ; in late 1864 it had found mercantile agents in Hong Kong, the American Augustine Heard and Co., who promptly gave it the Chinese name of "Heard's Bank", later regretting the too close association. The promoters of this bank were closely associated with the Bombay Reclamation Company and the managers of the Bank of Bombay and the Asiatic were too close for sound business practices. The Asiatic, although not necessarily a "bubble company" itself, was too involved to escape the fate of Bombay joint stock enterprises in the crises of 1865 and 1866.

The Bank of India and the Central Bank of Western India founded in 1860 and 1863 respectively had both reached Hong Kong by 1864 and were under Indian banking legislation. They did not attempt a note issue in the Colony. The Bombay Trading and Bankers' Association and the Scinde, Punjab and Delhi Bank Corporation both had agencies in Hong Kong, the latter with Dent and Company, but there is no indication that their business was significant on the China coast. The Scinde Bank, founded in London under the Companies Act of 1862, was obviously railway related. Bombay Trading was a local bank.

By 1864 the Bank of Hindustan, China, and Japan, Ltd. had also reached Hong Kong along with the Chartered Bank of India, Australia and China, but these had their origins primarily in Britain. At the same time the Indian Peninsular, London and China Bank, the National Bank of India, the Royal Bank of India, the Alliance Bank of Bombay, and the Bank of Baroda were all Indian banks on record as intending to establish Hong Kong and China branches. While from England the Imperial Bank of China, India, and Japan, Ltd., the British and Netherlands India Bank, Ltd., and the Eastern Exchange Bank similarly declared their China intentions. Possibly they found the field too heavily exploited, or too few competent managers were to be had—in any case, these banks either failed to start business or at least failed to reach China.

California links. The Indian exchange banks had not only expanded to London and the China coast but had also been instrumental in the establishment of banks linking California into the China trade, especially in connection with the export of bullion across the Pacific. Thus the Oriental was involved in the founding of the British and American Exchange Banking Corporation in 1863 and with the English and American Bank, Ltd., in 1865, while the Agra was closely connected with the British and California Banking Company. The three companies were short-lived, and the Eastern exchange banks' subsequent activities in California were, in the nineteenth-century at least, through agents.

BOMBAY'S BANK OF CHINA, LTD., AND THE HONG KONG
AND SHANGHAI BANKING CO. LTD.

The prospects for still further banking operations on the China coast may have seemed poor indeed. Even the direct

French trade had financial backing in the Comptoir d'Escompte de Paris with its Bombay, Shanghai, and Hong Kong agencies. Nevertheless there was a glaring omission apparent to contemporaries—a bank with local Hong Kong management and with a concern for the growing interport trade, expanding as the full measure of the Yangtze trade was realized and the Taipings crushed permitted the growth of trade in the central rice plains of China.

Founding of the Bank of China. The chance was seized by a group of Bombay company promoters involved in the Financial Association of India and China, Ltd. In June of 1864 the Association sponsored the founding of a Bank of China, Ltd., to be established with head office in Hong Kong and under a board of directors resident in that colony. The Bank's original directors were Michael H. Scott, promoter of the Asiatic Bank and the Bombay Reclamation Company, Walter R. Cassels, sometime director of the Bank of Bombay, Richard Willis of Forbes and Co., director of the Bank of India and chairman of the Financial Association ; A. F. Wallace of Findlay Clark and Co., a director of the Financial Association ; Robert Hannay, sometime chairman of the Bombay Reclamation Company, promoter and Bombay advisory board member of the Asiatic Bank, sometime president of the Bank of Bombay; and Cowasjee Jehangeer, director of the Bank of Bombay and the Reclamation Company and a promoter of the Asiatic Bank. These were powerful names in Bombay not only for their long-time mercantile and financial associations but also for their new role in the first financial promotions of the cotton boom.

The prospectus reads in part :

The Bank of China is projected to occupy in China a position similar to that which the banks of Bengal, Bombay and Madras hold in India...the promoters will apply to H. M. government for a charter . . . the promoters will memorialize the British government in China to establish the same relation with the 'Bank of China' as exist between the Indian government and the three Presidency Banks.

The capital was declared in August to be set at 80 lacs of rupees in 40,000 shares of Rs. 200 each of which Rs. 25 only would be called up.

Allotment letters went out to applicants on August 9, 1864, but the shares of the bank were already at an 85% premium. Only one-sixth of the bank's capital had been reserved for China-coast applicants, and the inevitable conclusion must be that this was basically a speculative bubble company in which the shares had been staged for the benefit of insiders. It would, however, be unwise to stop the analysis here. The fact remains that the promoters had indeed detected a genuine deficiency in the banking structure of the China coast, which they intended the Bank of China should exploit. Proof that the purpose of the Bank would differ from the "exchange banks" is partly demonstrated by the close connection of the promoters with the Asiatic, which was designed as an exchange bank, and although merchants were often close to several competing banks it is too much to suppose that the Asiatic and the Bank of China were intended as competitors.

Yet how did the promoters in Bombay expect to operate a bank in China ? The answer is probably that they did not. The Bank of China's promoters undoubtedly counted on the inability of Hong Kong merchants to co-operate among themselves and on the assistance of Dent and Company with whom there had possibly been some informal contact, although not necessarily in Hong Kong. With a board of directors in Hong Kong, chaired for example by Dent and Co., the Bank might well have been a success. The Bombay shareholders could then have sold out with a capital gain leaving Hong Kong to carry on.

The Hong Kong reaction. Unfortunately for the promoters, this sequence of events was clearly seen by the Hong Kong representative of the P. and O. S. N. Company, the extraordinary Thomas Sutherland. On receiving the first news of the Bank of China from a P. and O. Captain, Sutherland, although with no banking experience, drew up a prospectus for a rival local bank to be called the Hong Kong and Shanghai Banking Company, Ltd., and within days had secured the support of the important merchant houses—with Dent and Co. in the chair and excepting Jardine Matheson and Co. and the American Russell and Co. The new bank was soon more than a reaction. It became a genuine, local effort into which considerable time and effort were put—these being much more important than capital in the Bank's initial development. Thus, although the Hong Kong bank had problems in securing its charter— in the form of a local ordinance conforming to the Colonial Banking Regulations—and although several founder firms were very soon bankrupted and the first manager and the London representative had, subsequently, to resign, the Bank retained the complete confidence of the business community. It served a real need and with all its difficulties the local management and direction preserved its integrity unscathed.

The "Battle" of the Charters. The reaction of the Bombay promoters to the news of the rival indicates that they did have some intention of actually going into operation, that they were not interested only in financial speculation. The Bank of China's London solicitors were urged to press for the charter ; a special representative, Neale Porter, a man presumably close to the Dents, was sent to Hong Kong. Both projects failed. No Hong Kong merchant was interested in co-operating with the Bank of China, and the promoters had to satisfy themselves in the false hope that the British government would deny the Hong Kong bank its charter while granting the request of the Bank of China. In fact, the reverse was the consequence. The British Treasury, having agreed not to sanction an Indian bank without Indian government approval, refused to grant a charter to a bank whose headquarters were to be out of England. The application of the Hong Kong bank was quickly approved in principle, however, since the objection to a non-English headquarters did not apply—a Hong Kong ordinance rather than imperial charter was being requested.

ANGLO-INDIAN BANKING IN CHINA : FAILURE AND RETRENCHMENT

After 1866. The period beginning in 1866 witnessed the reorganization of Indian banking on the China coast. The

Bank of China application having failed the promoters sought to wind up in October, but their attempt to withdraw the subscription money from the Asiatic Bank was the straw which forced this exchange bank to close its doors. Other banks failed to weather the financial crisis which followed the cotton and financial booms : the Commercial Bank Corporation fell victim to Shanghai, San Francisco, and Indian speculation ; the Bank of India and the Central Bank of Western India failed ; the Agra and Masterman's fell victim to the tight credit situation in London following the May 1866 crash of Overend Gurney. The Bank of Hindustan and the Scinde, Punjab and Delhi ceased operations. Thus three chartered banks survived—the Oriental, the Chartered, and the Chartered Mercantile, while the new Hongkong and Shanghai Banking Corporation developed not only local trade and financing but also standard exchange bank operations. An Agra Bank and a Commercial Bank, deprived of their English connections, were revived and again linked India with the China coast. Exchange banking was stabilized for some 25 years before another financial crisis saw the failure of the Agra and the Oriental and the reorganization of the Chartered Mercantile.

Contribution of the Anglo-Indian banks. Despite the need for additional finance in the China trade, it cannot be said that the role of the Indian exchange banks was wholly beneficial. The generally accepted consequence of the facilities provided by the new banks has been the growth of speculation, especially in the China tea trade, a speculation which caused mercantile disasters from 1864 through 1868. This conclusion rests, however, on the assumption that the speculation was the result of the activities of younger merchants— or possibly, the newer, smaller partnerships—which could not have acted so rashly without the financial support of the banks. The older firms, it is argued, had their own resources, and indeed we find merchant houses of the magnitude of the American Augustine Heard contending that they held more specie in their vaults than any bank. It is further argued that the established firms objected to the new banks on the grounds that they provided dangerous financial facilities.

These views cannot be accepted without reservation, however. One of the spectacular China-trade failures was that of Dent and Co. itself, which in 1868 promised to pay two shillings six pence in the pound. Secondly, the old houses had access to facilities in London ; it is not true that they operated on the China-coast entirely with "their own" resources. Thirdly, the example of Butterfield—later Butterfield and Swire—suggests that just as "old" was not synonymous with soundness, neither was "new" with speculation. Indeed, much of the above thesis may be derived from the opposition of Jardine Matheson and Company to the Hongkong and Shanghai Banking Company, Ltd. at its inception. But this opposition cannot be traced to any single factor and rests as much on disapproval of Dent and Company leadership and on Jardine's assessment of the speculative atmosphere than on the principle of the dangers of bank finance alone. The fact that the Hongkong Bank was both sound and successful does not in itself invalidate the reasonableness of Jardine Matheson's caution.

Certainly the combination of additional exchange and financial facilities combined with poor management, lack of central office control from the bank's side, and unwise commodity speculation on the other was disastrous both for bankers and merchants. The era in which new banks were needed was also an era in which it was unlikely that any but the most cautious would survive. In fact, the unwise activities of certain China branches were aggravated by speculative investments in both Bombay and London, and such business behaviour in any one of the centres was sufficient at that time to bring down the bank. The Agra Bank was fortunate in being able to disassociate itself from its worse activities—those in London and France—and thus revive as an Indian bank with China-coast activities. The older exchange banks— the Oriental, the Chartered, and the Chartered Mercantile— simply withdrew from the Bombay market. The Hongkong and Shanghai Banking Co. Ltd. never really attempted to become active in India until after the crises. But the others succumbed after playing a dramatic role in this interlude in China-India economic relations.

Chapter IV

CHINA'S ATTEMPT AT ECONOMIC MODERNIZATION, 1896-1936

THE CH'ING ECONOMY AND THE NEW IMPERIALISM

China's defeat by the Japanese and the terms of the Treaty of Shimonoseki alerted many Chinese at various levels to their continued weakness despite self-strengthening ; it alerted foreign powers to the possibility of the breakup of China at a time when the New Imperialism in general and Russian, French and German interests in the Far East in particular were a potential threat to Chinese sovereignty. Foreign pressure on the Chinese government was, of course, nothing new, but after 1895 it became increasingly unlikely that China, even if she were to survive as a political entity, could do so without accepting specific instruction from the Powers ; after the Boxer uprising this possibility became a reality.

The relationship between the treaty ports and the hinterland had a significant parallel with the port colonies of Africa and their interiors, which British Colonial Secretary Joseph Chamberlain had referred to as great undeveloped estates. What foreigners had done for the ports could also be done for the interior ; the European civilizing role would incidentally insure improvements at the sources of export supply and thus boost China's foreign trade, the basis of the historic foreign economic interests. But such a role would require railroads, and railroads in turn would permit development of mines and expansion of other economic activities, which it would be unrealistic to suppose would be undertaken to their full potential without foreign participation. In Africa this had led to indirect rule through existing native regimes by European countries operating within internationally recognized areas, whether protectorates or colonies. Developments in China stopped short of such international division.

The immediate impact of 1895 on China was contradictory. While on the one hand the defeat facilitated further, but still limited, government-sponsored economic projects ; on the other hand, it temporarily discredited officials like Li Hung-chang who had been powers in the self-strengthening movement. It fostered the 100-days reform of 1898, the abortive attempt to reform along traditional lines by edict from above, and the Boxer Rebellion, the fanatical reaction the failure of which forced China to, in effect, accept foreign tutelage. More accurately, the defeat was both a cause of subsequent developments and a watershed, an event marking the dividing of two periods. In this latter role, the initial impact of the event was continued and supported by the continuing activities of the Powers in China. But the final pattern was not the break-up of China ; rather the direct foreign consequence was the recognition of spheres of influence, countered by an apparently contradictory "open door" policy, plus the beginnings of China government reform, in which the centre attempted to reorganize its role into that of a national-type government.

With the exception of the Boxer reaction, all these policies fostered some economic development and modernization. While these economic consequences might have been more rationally executed, they could be rationalized subsequently and, as an inheritance of the Republic, they were undoubted assets. Two exceptions should be noted to these generalizations : first, the Manchurian sphere of influence did indeed lead to territorial separation ; secondly, the Province of Taiwan was ceded to Japan under terms of the 1895 treaty. The former we shall consider briefly in this section ; the latter does not belong to Chinese economic history again until 1945, and we shall discuss recent developments in Chapter VI.

China's modernization did not, of course, begin in 1896. As a conscious, effective policy and specific long-term goal one might argue that 1952 is more reasonable date. At the other extreme some writers have claimed that economic modernization began in the late Ming or in the eighteenth-century, only to be interrupted by imperialism. It is safer to be descriptive. On the eve of the First Sino-Japanese War China had a modern textile industry, the first few hundred miles of the Peking-Mukden-Newchwang railway, port cities with exemplary social overhead projects completed, an iron and steel complex in advance of Japan's Yawata, officials constantly broadening their understanding of the scope of the term "self-strengthening", a growing number of younger men conscious of the need for modern education and themselves with some technical competence. The financial resources of Shanghai, indeed of many country "gentry", were such as to permit industrial investment. An extensive native banking system, including the facilities of the Shansi banks, which provided transfer and exchange operations in many of the central and northern market centres, was supplemented by the foreign banks. The private sector was prepared to react to the new atmosphere caused by the impact of China's defeat—as well as to the opportunities offered by the depreciation of silver.

And yet this base was, as we have seen, very thin. In absolute terms the record, even compared to Japan, was not extraordinarily different, but the *per capita* record was insignificant. The foreigners who had seen in China the great market, the great source of mutual profit through free trade, were frustrated. With the tea trade down from its peak of 150 million pounds in the 1880's, with opium imports in the hands of Indian merchants and silk stagnant—it was soon to decline—the foreigners sought to break down the barriers which separated them, they were convinced, from the logical benefits of trade. As these frustrations mounted, China was defeated, and there was a hope that now at least something could be done in—or with—China. A study of this period naturally breaks down, therefore, into three headings: first, the development of the more active foreign role, especially in the establishment of spheres of influence; secondly, the Chinese government response in the form of Imperial government reorganization; and, thirdly, the role of the private sector, that is, foreign

TABLE 3: CHINA: INDICES OF EXTERNAL TRADE, 1864-1936a
(1913=100)

Selected year			Value	Imports	Quantity Exports
1864		..	9·7		
1867	..	..	11·8	24·7	31·9
1872	..	..	14·6	27·9	43·3
1874	..	..	13·5	31·5	40·1
1876	..	..	15·5	36·3	42·8
1881	..	..	16·8	40·8	43·5
1889	..	..	21·3	44·0	45·2
1899	..	..	47·3	69·2	62·5
1908	..	..	68·9	72·7	73·0
1909	..	..	77·8	77·1	92·9
1924	..	..	183·9	119·6	136·6
1931	..	..	240·7	129·9	136·5
1935b	..	..	98·6	83·6	126·7
1936b	..	..	108·6	77·9	125·6

a. Values in 1913 : net exports 403,306 *Hk taels*
net imports 570,163 *Hk taels*
Total 973,469 *Hk taels*
b. Excluding Manchuria
Source : Cheng Yü-kwei.

and Chinese investment in the modern sector. In the clash between government reform and private development, the Ch'ing dynasty lost further support, its reorganization came too late, and the boy Emperor abdicated. This not only marked a political transition, it also introduced new economic problems which we shall wish to consider in the next section.

Spheres of influence and railway development. In a sense, an increase in foreign influence came automatically. The indemnity payments to Japan had to be financed, as did the later Boxer indemnity. Secondly, China's recognition of the need for railways and the success of the initial line from Shanhaikwan on the Manchurian border, past the Kaiping mines, to Tientsin and Peking inevitably meant foreign participation. (See map on p. 12.) For, despite her best efforts, China proved unable either to raise the needed funds domestically or to borrow abroad without granting varying degrees of control over the construction and management of the railways. Given the political weakness of China and the concurrent foreign pressures, the government was unable to award financial and building contracts on purely economic or business considerations; the awards were to be partly the result of an international trade-off, and thus had to be satisfactory to the Powers, and partly a consequence of specific relations between China and each Power. But the consequence was "spheres of influence".

The tributary areas were eventually completely detached —this was a general pattern, e.g. Kedah from Siam, Korea from China, and, of course, the Vietnam area to the French. We are not here concerned with these countries, whose history is better considered separately, but it was from Annam that the French saw the potentials of those special concessions which marked the "new imperialism" and threatened the "old treaty system" which the British, principally, with the French and Americans, had built up. In 1895 the French gained mining concessions, special land-frontier tariffs, and railway rights in southwest China adjoining Annam. Another agreement in 1898 was instrumental in a railroad being continued up from the Red River delta into Yunnan, reaching the provincial capital of Kunming in 1910. Southwest China, Kwangtung-Kwangsi-Yunnan, was a French sphere of influence, and they leased a naval base to prove it. But in a sense the 1895 French demands were but a development of her previous aggression against China; the new pressures were initiated by Russia.

Russia's role in China led eventually to the separation of Manchuria, a topic to be discussed below. But to keep the historical sequence, we should note that Russia's renewed interest in the Far East was manifest in the construction of the Trans-Siberian railway, beginning in 1891. In 1895 Russian and French interests made a £15.8 million equivalent loan to China; in 1896 a Russian-Chinese secret alliance was established when Li Hung-chang visited St. Petersburg for the coronation of Nicholas II, and the Russo-Chinese bank, with French capital, and the Chinese Eastern Railway Concession were agreed to. Further concessions in 1897 and 1898 resulted in the Russian leasing of part of the Kwantung Peninsula where are situated the Port Arthur naval base and the port city of Ta-lien (or Dairen, Dalny). The South Manchurian Railways concession permitted the Russians to build a line south from Harbin to Port Arthur.

Germany secured a sphere of influence in Shantung, operating out of the leased territory of Kaiochow. Both the Russian and the German moves involved the need for naval bases as part of a world-wide political policy, but the immediate impact in both places was the establishment also of economic bases, similar to but never as significant as Hong Kong, with railway, mining and other economic rights in the neighbouring interior.

The British reaction was on the one hand to seek equality of treatment—they had after all four-fifths of the foreign trade of China, and "compensation" on the other, that is, the offsetting of concessions to other powers by similar grants to Britain. As Britain already had her base of Hong Kong and *de facto* control of the Internationl Settlement at Shanghai, her demands were less damaging to China's sovereignty. Refusing to accept the "old China hands" solution of military occupation of the Yangtze valley, Britain nevertheless secured recognition of this as her sphere. Then, too, she moved into southwest China from Canton and the West River, at least partially offsetting special French privileges there. But, more in keeping with the times, Britain enlarged Hong Kong by leasing additional mainland territory and the surrounding islands ; she also leased Weihaiwei as a second base.

In addition to these spheres, that is to say, areas open to general exploitation by a particular power, there were special concessions, especially in mining and railways. These might upset the "spheres of influence" concept, as the British financing of the Peking-Mukden railway in Manchuria, and lead to international complications. The Belgian Syndicate, which also involved Russia, for example, won the right to construct the Peking-Hankow railway, and Britain secured concessions for 2800 miles of which only a portion was in her "sphere".

While American interests became involved financially in various concessions and consortia over the next fifty years, official government policy supported "the open door", first to protect the treaty system and secondly to preserve China's territorial integrity. Grandiose schemes for a round-the-world American railway or for intimate links between American west coast and Manchurian lines came to nothing, given the exclusive intentions of Russia and later Japan in that area.

The logic of these developments is as inevitable economically as they were unacceptable politically. China could neither finance nor construct railways by herself; she could not expect to secure adequate financing without giving up management rights; since she was reluctant, given the international situation, pressure was applied. In consequence, railways were built, mines were exploited, the private modern sector grew, but there were disadvantages. First, growth was not as certain as if political stability had been achieved and yet, to offset this, China's growing sponsorship and acceptance of modernization was never checked, as in India, by special interests of an imperial power with direct political control—China's loss of tariff autonomy and consequent inability to raise a protective tariff is a possible exception, but there is no evidence that lack of protection was a factor in the slow development of China's industrial sector. Secondly, the demonstration and linkage effects were possibly not as great as if China had herself been able to develop her mines and railways. The dominance of foreigners in all important positions and the limited area of operation together with the association of modernization with imperialism, all limited the impact of projects within the concessional context. But certainly the physical plant remained.

As important as the railways, mining, sphere of influence sequence as a pressure on the Chinese government were the financial counterparts, including the finance of general government debt. Rivalry in international lending can be particularly serious. A nation can become loaned up before it has established any rational system of priorities, or the loans can be pressed without any clear purpose for their use. Competition in this field is not necessarily advantageous, and since in the end the competitors often must go to the same capital market to raise funds, non-price competition in the form of bribes and political pressure may be practiced. Despite China's ever-chaotic fiscal system and dubious political situation, she had available several sources of funds which were capable of capitalization. Most obvious of these was the revenue of the Imperial Martime Customs. To this was added the revenue of the salt gabelle, certain provincial likin administration revenues, and the potential revenue of the railways and mines themselves. But to assure these incomes for the purpose of debt repayment, while it proved unnecessary to take over China itself, the foreigners did insist on controlling the several income-generating administrations or, as in the case of several railways, they reserved the right to do so. There were certain administrative improvements which the foreigners created—including the Chinese modern postal service—but these and other concessions formed the basis for a growing anti-imperialist nationalism which also turned against the dynasty.

In the case of the all-important British, the construction and financial aspects of the concessions were in part combined by the formation of the British and Chinese Corporation, founded in London in 1898 by the Hongkong and Shanghai Banking Corporation and Jardine, Matheson and Co. Through this company the functions of a merchant banker and a contracting firm were combined. The firm's first venture was actually in Manchuria—completion of the Peking-Mukden railway—and it was awarded the contract in 1899. The company, of course, asked the Hongkong Bank to float the required loan of £2.3 million, for which the Bank received brokerage of 2%. The company also asked Jardine Matheson to act as contractors, and they were remunerated by the various commissions on purchases. Security for the loan, according to the Bank's official history, was the property of the entire line, including the Peking-Shanhaikwan section, then already in profitable operation. In the event of default, this would be turned over to the Corporation to manage until the debt was extinguished.

In 1903 the Corporation was awarded the contract for the economically significant Shanghai-Nanking railway against

Russian opposition. Again the Hongkong Bank was responsible for the loan, raising in the first instance £2.25 million in 5% sterling bonds at 97.5, principal and interest guaranteed by the central government with the further provision of profit sharing for bond subscribers for a period of 50 years. This combination made considerable economic sense. Investors were not prepared to buy into the equity of Chinese railways, yet they were unlikely to be satisfied with the normal rate of return for foreign debentures ; in effect, this was a parallel to financing schemes permitting conversion from debt to equity or giving equity rights, and a study of the present International Finance Corporation will show the continued need for such operation. The British and Chinese Corporation also contracted for the Chinese section of the Canton-Hongkong railway, accepting a fee of £35,000 rather than a commission as payment. In 1908 the British and Chinese Corporation contracted for the £1.5 million Shanghai-Ningpo railway, wholly in the British sphere of influence.

The Hongkong and Shanghai Bank was involved in other railway financing, including a 1907 loan for Manchurian railway rehabilitation, £4 million (5% sterling bonds at 97) to the then Japanese-owned South Manchurian Railway, and participation in a £ 5 million financing of the Tientsin-Pukow railway through a syndicate entitled Chinese Central Railways, Ltd., jointly with the Deutsch Asiatische Bank in 1905. This railway traversed a part of Shantung, a German sphere of influence. Another £ 3 million was floated in 1910. Significantly, the first loan for the Tientsin-Pukow (opposite Nanking) line was secured by the revenues of a provincial tax, the *likin* (transit tax) revenues of Chihli and Shantung and the Nanking Likin Collectorate. There is a suggestion that the Maritime Customs was loaned up, but there is also an element of provincial-centre conflict here. Railways were expensive, their routing was of national importance, and the Imperial government attempted, vainly, to keep control of railway development. The conflict with the provinces, going ahead with their own schemes and financing them locally with foreign groups, was one of the immediate causes of the alienation of the gentry from the dynasty which forced the final abdication.

Construction of railways did not lead to the full and rapid development of the Chinese economy, although there is evidence that they contributed significantly. There were, after all, several problems which railways *per se* could not solve. First, the railway mileage was strictly limited, considering the vast area of China and even allowing for that area served by waterways. Secondly, various practices, some necessary for a modern-type-undertaking, some holdovers from former Chinese business practices, made the lines relatively expensive to use. The railway "system" was not immediately integrated and rates were unco-ordinated. Finally, in the subsequent warlord period, physical hindrance of transport and other direct impediments, including bloody strikes fomented by the Communist Party labour activists under Liu Shao-ch'i, prevented the railways from fulfilling their economic role or, in some cases, paying off their debt. The story of the Hongkong Bank's participation has been cited in full, first, because their role has been studied thoroughly, secondly because while it was the most important single body in China-financing it was also typical of those chosen instruments which furthered the economic development of the less developed world in the days of imperialism.

Manchuria. The separation of Manchuria cannot be ascribed wholly to the wiles of imperialism. Although an "integral part" of China in international law, it had had a different history, certainly a different economic history. The Japanese act of detachment in 1931 came just at the point when this separateness might have been ended. After World War II, the Manchurian economy (the Northeast provinces) was not then fully integrated with that of the rest of China, and even in the post-1949 period the People's Government in Peking had to deal with the activities of Kao Kang. First, Manchuria is geographically different in resource endowment, in population density ; its area of some 300,000 square miles had a population of only 15 million in 1910 ; nearly one-fifth the area of China proper, it had about 4 per cent of the population, suggesting a potential for development of a less labour-intensive agriculture than that prevailed in China.

Secondly, Manchuria as the original home of the Manchus had been closed until late in the nineteenth century to Chinese immigration. As the regulations were relaxed, Chinese moved in, but so did others. Indeed, many Chinese preferred to migrate seasonally, a practice that continued from Shantung and the north certainly into the late 1920's when net migration averaged 400,000 annually. Thirdly, the post-1911 history of Manchuria continues the separate trend with the combination of Japanese power exercised through the concessions granted to the South Manchurian Railway, the naval base of Port Arthur, and the Kwantung Leased Territory coupled with the warlord-type authority of Chang Tso-lin. It was from this latter authority that the Japanese seized total power, before Chang's son, Chang Hsüeh-liang, the Young Marshal, could consolidate his pro-Nationalist moves.

The economic history of Manchuria involves, therefore, not only the story of railway concessions but also the rapid change which these lines brought to the country. As we have seen, Russian concessions resulted in the construction of the Chinese Eastern Railway, the South Manchurian Railway, and subsidiary lines were later constructed by the Chinese. With Japanese victory in the Russo-Japanese War, the railway from Changchun south to Mukden and Dairen, as well as to the Korean frontier, came into Japanese hands and its gauge was altered to conform to the Chinese system, a change financed with funds from the Hongkong Bank loan of 1907, already mentioned above. By 1931 (and we shall cover very briefly here the period up to the establishment of the puppet state of Manchukuo), there were some 4,300 miles of railway in Manchuria, of which about 40 per cent were direct foreign investments, then Japanese or Russian owned, 40 per cent financed, principally in the 1920s, through Chinese sources—this includes the British and Chinese Corporation concessions on the Peking-Mukden line—and 10 per cent of other railways, of which more than half were financed by Japanese loans.

The significance of these lines to the economy may be judged, first by the fact that, contrary to other Chinese experience, freight constituted the most important revenue item rather than passengers. Secondly, the abuses to which other Chinese rail-roads were subjected were not characteristic of Manchurian practice. Thirdly, the lack of alternative means of transport, especially the short coastline and lack of navigable rivers, and the heavy-for-value type of commodity which could find a market principally through being exported made the railways essential. The soya beans and bean oil, the coal, cement, salt, pig iron—these were the principal commodities composing the railway's freight, and their exploitation grew with the railways.

Of an estimated Ch $ 2.5 million of foreign investment in Manchuria in 1930, some 70 per cent was Japanese and 26 per cent Russian ; of the Japanese 33 per cent was in railways, of the Russian 76 per cent. Obviously, the principal basis of the development of Manchuria was railways coupled with Japanese capital. The most important single economic institution was the South Manchurian Railway Company, which S. H. Chou suggests was not only a system of railways, but a gigantic holding company with interests including harbour development, public utilities, hotels, and oil and mining industries, e.g., the Fushun coal mine and the Anshan steel works. Their control of land on either side of their concessioned line gave them political authority ; here was a state within a state. The rights of these diverse activities had been partly procured by Japanese pressure on the Chinese Government, especially the Twenty-one Demands of 1915 (see below). And from the Kwantung Leased Territory, from Dairen, a port second only to Shanghai, the trade of Manchuria was linked with Japan ; in the 1930's the link was forged stronger with the creation of the *yen* bloc. But it should be noted that from the first the development of Manchuria was co-ordinated with the needs of Japan, and that the other special factors present in this area make it a much less useful basis for understanding Chinese economic problems than, say, a study of the treaty ports. This link with Japan also explains why Russia, with its industrial base far to the west, was unlikely to find in Manchuria the same degree of economic success.

But as is the pattern with export-oriented economies, the development need not benefit the inhabitants of the area.

TABLE 4.   MANCHURIA : PRODUCTION UNDER THE JAPANESE

	1931-32	Percentage of production in China Proper 1944-45	1945
Electric Power, installed capacity, 1000 kW	250	1776	247
Coal, million tons	8·8	25·6	98
Iron, pig, 1000 tons	335	1159	847
Cement, 1000 tons	108	1514	949
Cotton, 1000 spindles	151	541	12
Railways, 1000 km	5·6	11·1	83

Source :   Cheng Yü-kwei from Pauley Mission reports and Yearbooks.

And, indeed, there is no evidence of the modern sector contributing significantly to Chinese standards of living in Manchuria, other than through, for example, electricity, and from the social overhead projects. The Chinese benefited as much from the differing factor proportions. But Japanese technicians manned the new industries and the railways, and the problem of integration was not seriously considered.   A glimpse at the fiscal problems of local Chinese administrations suggests much of the confusion of China proper.   Although there was continuity of government in Manchuria through Chang Tso-lin, this warlord also had ambitions in China, and military expenses were high, financed by such standbys as salt tax and fiduciary issues of banks controlled by the government.   Manchuria was not an "ideal" state or model. Furthermore, the serious and planned development of Manchuria occurs after 1931, and this is beyond the scope of this history.   However, sufficient has been said to show, first, how the base for industrialization was laid and, secondly, how the Manchurian example is of limited relevance for comparison with the history of China Proper.

Imperial reform.   Indemnity had become a custom ; this is the only explanation of the action of Powers which, complaining bitterly about China's backwardness and lack of development with side-glances at the growing power of Japan, should at the same time impose an indemnity of US $ 334 million equivalent (450 million *Haikwan taels*). There were remissions and a final cancellation beginning with Chinese entry into World War I, but this does not render the original attitudes so difficult to comprehend. Furthermore, the suggestion of Sir Robert Hart that the Chinese be somehow protected from the loss of gold value in their customs revenues to ease the burden of repayment was refused. The question foremost in the minds of the foreign negotiators was simply what could China afford to pay? In consequence, the Chinese government, even after increasing the remittances from provincial authorities, found itself with limited sources of funds. The customs revenues were hypothecated, the revenues of the railways were committed to loan repayments— how tempting, though unsatisfactory, a source of revenue that would have been—and the salt gabelle was also practically

TABLE 5. LATE CH'ING REVENUE, 1900's

(millions of *taels* per annum)

Land tax	25
Grain tribute	7
Salt excises	14
Likin	15a
Maritime customs	35a
Sale of office, etc.	6a
Total : as reported to Peking	92
Total revenue estimated, 1908	200
Total taxes paid by taxpayers	284b
Provincial assessments, Boxer indemnity	18

Note : The 92 million *taels* represents funds reported to be at the disposal of the Imperial government. Consider the implications of the difference between this and the sums at the disposal of the local and provincial governments and the sums paid by taxpayers. The Imperial government was able to tap 18 million *taels* of this—but only under foreign pressures. As a historical "might-have-been", suppose the 284 million *taels* paid had all been wisely expended towards modernization of China.

   a. For a comparable pre-1850 total, eliminate these items and subtract, say, 6 million from salt excises.
   b. Rough estimate quoted in H. B. Morse.

Source : H. B. Morse.

loaned up, although in the early republican period, its surplus was about all the central government in Peking could depend upon. The need for fiscal reform was urgent.

China had agreed to reform ; Chinese felt the need for reform. The Manchu dynasty was not a satisfactory instrument for that reform, and it failed. Nevertheless, the redefinition of the functions of the centre was attempted and the new organization activated. We shall state the change in economic ministries and related bodies, both to complete the record and to indicate the inheritance of the Republican administration. But we should note from the first that, despite the reformation of the boards, no cabinet was created (until April, 1911 !) and the co-ordination of ministerial policy and its relation to the Imperial authority was as confused as ever.

Our primary concern is with the changes in the two boards involved directly in economic affairs, the Board of Revenue (*Hu-pu*) and the Board of Works (*Kung-pu*). Imperial authority established in 1903 a Committee of Finance in connection with a proposed reform of the finances of the Empire and in accordance with China's undertaking to the Powers. This committee and the *Hu-pu* were amalgamated in 1906 to form the Ministry of Finance. (The Chinese term *pu* may be translated "board" or "ministry" according to its meaning, and our changed translation, i.e. "board" prior to 1906 and "ministry" afterwards is designed to indicate the intended difference in function brought about by the reform.) According to the study of H. S. Brunnert and V. V. Hagelstrom, the combined ministry was to be in charge of all financial affairs, regulating the levying and collection of duties and taxes, supervising transportation and storage of grain, arranging state loans, controlling mints, banks and financial establishments. The bureaus of the ministry were organized on functional lines in contrast to the traditional provincial designations ; that is, the assignment of duties within the ministry was now on a more rational basis. The Salt-Gabelle, which had become as important as the Imperial Maritime Customs as a source of credit, was centralized in 1909 and 1910 in close association with the Ministry of Finance.

Again in 1903, Imperial authority established a Board of Trade and this was combined with the long-established *Kung-pu* in 1906 to form the Ministry of Agriculture, Industry and Commerce. Its functions were to supervise agriculture, colonization, forestry, sericulture, tea planting, horticulture, fisheries, the building of wharves, bunds and dykes, and the conservancy of rivers and harbours. In 1906 a new ministry, that of Posts and Communications, was established to control navigation, railways, telegraphs, while the posts remained for the time being under the Inspector General of Customs. Significantly, the Maritime Customs, which was by now certifying revenues to be used on behalf of foreign creditors, was transferred from the Foreign Ministry (the old Tsungli Yamen) to the Board of Customs Control. There was some foreign protest to this move, and it is instructive to note that, even in this time of foreign domination, the Chinese were able to place this, to the foreigners, key governmental unit, under normal, economic administrative control. Other significant features of the reforms in the Chinese government are, first, the stress on training schools which form an integral part of the work of many ministries, secondly, the stress on provincial reorganization from the imperial ministries, thirdly, the clearer definition of the duties and functions not only of each ministry but also of the imperial regime, and fourthly, the involvement in both commercial and savings banking.

The very dates of these changes, 1906 and 1907, suggest that few, if any of the more drastic reforms, especially those involving direction of provincial affairs, ever had a chance of being implemented. The government was, indeed, very much in the training and research stage. In 1909, for example, a Committee for the Reorganization of the Financial Affairs of the Empire was established in the Ministry of Finance with branches in the provinces. Its purpose was to undertake studies prior to drawing up a state budget, and its first tentative efforts were published in 1910 on the eve of the Revolution. The stress on training can be seen, for example, from the list of schools, etc. under the Ministry of Agriculture, Industry and Commerce, which it is worth briefly listing :

agricultural schools in the capital and in the provinces, schools of craft and mining, metropolitan professional schools ; Industrial Institute at Peking and elsewhere ; commercial schools ; and agricultural guilds, exhibitions for the encouragement of industry, chemical laboratories, department to control Chambers of Commerce. The importance of these educational functions must be remembered in the context of the revolutionary change which the Imperial government's abolition of the old style, classical examinations had on the entire direction of education in China. So essential and basic a reform has not as yet been successfully carried out in Britain, where classics graduates are still preferred in the civil services ; in China, however, the change came in 1905.

Money and banking. The Hongkong and Shanghai Bank had already had one bank modelled after it—the Yokohama Specie Bank, now it was China's turn to imitate this most successful of Asian banking institutions. In 1896 Sheng Hsüan-huai (1844-1916), an official closely involved in the key merchant undertakings under government supervision (*kuan-tu shang-pan*), proposed the Imperial Bank of China, also modelled on the Hongkong Bank, as part of a scheme to finance the Peking-Hankow railway. The Bank was to have a subscribed capital of 5 million *taels*, half paid-up, with a guaranteed return of 8% on shares offered to the public. By the time the Bank was in operation, however, it was clear that China could not finance her railways internally, and Sheng then stressed the central banking aspects of his project. While keeping its constitution modelled after the Hongkong Bank, the Imperial Bank of China attempted to formalize its relationship with the government by having itself designated as the official depository, as the agent for effecting internal exchange operations, as a potential underwriter of government internal loans, and as an issuer of banknotes. The relationship with the government was that familiar with enterprises of the *kuan-tu shang-pan* type, but Sheng was never able to enforce the exclusive privileges which his institution had been rather tentatively assigned. The link with the government in fact deteriorated, especially after 1905, and the Imperial Bank became an ordinary commercial bank under the title Commercial Bank of China. Thus China's first modern bank failed to secure central bank status.

As Albert Feuerwerker has pointed out there was another scheme to establish a central bank in 1896 which Sheng's prevented. Nevertheless, the foreigners' conviction that a unified monetary system was necessary to China's modernization was a constant pressure on the imperial regime. And, as part of a general reform programme, such a reform made considerably more sense than the isolated demands for a standard, Empire-wide silver coin. Thus, in 1904 a memorial of the Board of Revenue was approved permitting establishment of a government bank, with half the shares offered to the public and with a subscribed capital of 4 million *taels*. The Bank opened for business in 1905, becoming a limited liability joint-stock company under the title Ta Ch'ing Government Bank in 1908 and a capital of 10 million *taels*. Typically, the bank operated a training school. The Ta Ch'ing, which became eventually the Bank of China, also failed to establish itself as a central bank, but evolved into the government's chosen instrument for foreign banking operations. During the Empire, it was responsible for supervision of the Peking savings banks, and other government banks where branches of the Ta Ch'ing had been established. Government banking plans also included creation of general banks, banks of agricultural and industry, and savings banks. In 1907 the Bank of Communications under the Ministry of Posts and Communications was sanctioned with the declared object of "assisting in the development of shipping, railways, telegraphs and posts". Although both the Ta Ch'ing and the Bank of Communications had specialized functions, they soon developed a general business along the lines of the foreign "exchange" banks, and these semi-governmental institutions came to be part of that important class of banks known as Sino-foreign, to distinguish them from the native banks on the one hand and the foreign exchange banks on the other.

Although the Ch'ing administration now took a more direct interest in banking and the monetary system, the currency was far from unified. Various types of copper coins, including both those with the traditional centre hole and those without, various dollars, including Chinese minted coins, and literally hundreds of varieties of banknotes continued to circulate. The depreciation of silver forced Indian monetary reform and brought the Straits Settlements and Siam on the gold-exchange standard, but the Chinese government was not prepared for so basic a reform and was rebuffed in her efforts to set up a gold unit of account for the customs revenues.

In the private banking sector, the old established foreign exchange banks were supplemented by the development of Sino-foreign banks, including the National Bank of China, Ltd., the last effort of the American trading firm of Russell and Co. before its failure. Then too the age of the new imperialism required national banking institutions several of which we have already seen at work in railway and government financing. Yet Shanghai, the principal monetary centre, was still dependent upon the native banks as a source of local funds and for the finance of internal trade. This weak link magnified the dangers from the speculation which was part of the cost Shanghai paid for its close connection with world trade and capital markets. The rubber boom and collapse of 1910, for example, illustrates this integration. Shanghai Chinese capital had, as early as the 1880's, been used for the financing of plantations and mines in Southest Asia; it was natural, therefore, that the Malayan rubber boom and Brazilian speculation should affect the Chinese market, but the speculative facilities provided by native bank funds resulted in financial panic when the crash came. A virtual collapse of the Shanghai money market resulted, and there followed a forced reorganization of the banking structure with funds supplied principally by the Hongkong and Shanghai Bank.

Private Sector. Statistics for the textile industry show that in the twenty years from 1890 to 1910, the number of spindles operating rose from 35,000 to 630,000, the number of looms from 530 to 2,316—the difference between spindles and looms being a comment on the labour-saving characteristics of each. Of 26 Chinese-owned textile projects only 11 were in Shanghai; of 12 such projects where the source of finance is known, five were financed by officials, six by compradores, and one by another merchant. A survey of 52 compradores in Shanghai,

1907, showed a wide diversity of investment interest from mills to banks and steamships. Provincial "gentry" became actively involved in the financing and construction of the Hankow-Canton railway line, securing a British loan in 1905, which replaced the American China Development Company's contract of 1898. In 1899 Chang Chien (1853-1926), top scholar of the Empire in 1894, was so impressed by the results of the Sino-Japanese War that he turned to industry, establishing his Dah-Sun cotton-spinning mill and continuing to become one of China's most important industrialists.

With the Empress Dowager suggesting that the "strong points of foreign countries" should be adopted to make up China's shortcomings, with leading officials of the stature of Chang Chih-tung and Liu K'un-i supporting modernization, beginning with basic education reforms, with the first Chinese-engineered railway, the Peking-Kalgan line, in 1909, and with the examination system discarded, Chang was correct in asserting that "popular feelings are not the same as thirty years ago." For these miscellaneous facts highlight an undoubted change in China, an acceptance of the need for change and a translation of this into economic action. The base was broadened from the merchant-compradore acting within the traditional scope of the *kuan-tu shang-pan* enterprise. Even as Sheng Hsūan-huai was attempting to weave together the various enterprises and railways of this category into a single industrial empire linked to the state—and to his own interests, Chang Chien was one stage away, seeking the type of patronage now accepted in undeveloped countries as part of the concessions needed to encourage new industrial undertakings. The scholar-official and "gentry" were, at another level, beginning to examine the possibilities of modern, manufacturing enterprise; while their projects were few relative to the population or needs of China, yet they made some successful beginnings. In Shanghai, of course, a modern, well-integrated economy had developed, complete with social overhead projects which facilitated on economic grounds alone the concentration of manufacturing enterprise there. The broadened base should not be interpreted as meaning that large-scale industry could be established with official support outside the treaty ports, but as the treaty system expanded, the number of such ports, broadly defined, finally totalled 90 in all provinces, thus even this limitation was not too confining.

Development of China's mineral resources had been difficult, first, because of the lack of specific information, secondly because of the Ch'ing government's reluctance to allow foreigners into the interior, and thirdly, because mines attracted "rowdies" and caused trouble. Mines, like railways, required concessions and, in the days of the new imperialism, were often linked with railways in spheres of influence. The British interest in Chinese mining potential dates at least back to the 1870's, but until the early 1900's foreigners had no sound legal basis for their exploitation. The Kaiping mines were operated as merchant undertakings under government supervision (*kuan-tu shang-pan*), and the important copper mines in Yunnan were operated by Chinese licensee companies. Some of these latter raised capital in Shanghai and employed some Japanese engineers, but the cost of transporting machinery to the site proved prohibitive. There are random examples of Chinese attempts to use foreign mining machinery which show mixed results. In the last years of the Ch'ing, the Kaiping mines, by then under British ownership (and managed by Herbert Hoover, later president of the United States), the Lanchow Mining Company, 1908, the Pekin Syndicate formed in London in 1897, Archibald Little's company at the Kiangpei mines in 1898, and German interests in Shantung in 1902, were the major examples of modern mining endeavours in China Proper. Although Little's enterprise was by 1908 a failure, the others flourished and were of significance beyond coal mining itself.

To generalize : the mining enterprises were sufficiently large to permit introduction of modern methods of accounting and labour management; they developed ancilliary enterprises, including the building of necessary railways to carry the coal, steamships for the same purpose, electric lighting, and technical schools for Chinese employees and apprentices. Their connection with railways gave an assured market. But mining is an emotional subject when nationalism is heard, and the mining syndicates found increasing local opposition—

although not necessarily from their employees. In some
cases mines came under Chinese management and continued
operations ; in the case of the Pekin Syndicate, operations
were suspended in the warlord period.

There were signs to encourage the optimist, but it was
difficult for him to argue away the basic fiscal and monetary
chaos, the lack of effective national economic policy, and the
ever-growing hostility to foreign participation in the economy
other than on terms of equality which the foreigner would
not as yet accept. In a sense all this was prophetic, for the
modern sector continued to grow, but the economic development of China was checked by just those politico-economic
factors which had plagued the empire from the beginning.
In the warlord period, of course, the situation was to grow
worse, and the National Government under Kuomintang
tutelage was unable to make corrections in time. The
People's Republic began again, but with a more advanced
base—though not as advanced as that of the Soviet Union
at the beginning of her first five-year plan—but the Communist Government had other problems, which we shall
wish to discuss in chapter six. Meanwhile, in the countryside, little had or could be done. All this activity was of little
immediate economic significance to the great bulk of the
Chinese people. Our interest in it reveals our prejudices
as economists as well as our concern with the longer-term
trends of the Chinese economy.

The Republic : Imperialism Distorted, 1911-1926

The heritage. The Republic inherited the economic
problems of the late Ch'ing, its incompleted reforms, and its
lack of financial stability. When Dr. Sun Yet-sen, founder
and first President of the Chinese Republic, resigned in favour
of Yüang Shih-k'ai in February 1912, the question of the
republic's survival was temporarily answered. It would
survive under its new strong man against internal dissension
and possible Manchu resurgence ; Japan was not prepared
to move : the other Powers wanted continuity and a central
authority. This the Republic provided. The next problem
was to keep it financially afloat until it could mobilize what

few fiscal resources were left to it after the debt service had been accounted for. Indeed, something had to be done quickly ; the official Hongkong Bank history states the foreigner's view of the crisis succinctly—payments fallen due on imperial loans amounted to £4.5 million, on provincial loans £2.87 million, shortly to mature another £3.5 million, back pay of troops £3 million, current expenses of the government £5.5 million, a necessary reorganization of the salt gabelle £2 million—or £21 million total. Foreigners had the choice of backing a strong central government or taking over the administration of China itself. They compromised. The Imperial Maritime Customs, still foreign run, took over for the first time actual collection of the revenues. The Hongkong and Shanghai Bank began advancing funds to the Yüan regime, and the Four-Power Consortium began negotiations for a Reorganization Loan.

It should be clear from all this that the Chinese government was in a sense dependent upon foreign financial support while the foreigners were also dependent upon a complying regime for the continued service of their debts. This latter fact was to give the Nationalist regime some leverage in recovering economic and administrative sovereignty. But during the period of warlordism from 1916 to 1927, the Peking government, which maintained China's international continuity while the Kuomintang established its Canton base and warlords controlled the provinces, was always in too precarious a position to take a long-term stand against the Powers. In any case, willingness to accept the treaty and debt obligations of China was one of the prerequisites of foreign recognition and sometimes, financial support.

Foreign support for Yüan Shih-k'ai. The need to supply financial assistance to the Chinese government was seen immediately upon the success of the revolution, and two groups entered the field in competition. First was the four-power consortium, formed originally in 1910 in connection with financing of the Hukuang railway, included French, German, and American (Morgan) banks under the leadership of the (British) Hongkong and Shanghai Banking Corporation. The second was inspired by the Eastern Bank, founded in 1909, on the British side and was combined with others into an Anglo-Belgian syndicate. This latter group did in fact reach an agreement with the Chinese government, but since funds had already been advanced by the consortium, especially the Hongkong Bank, foreign government pressure forced cancellation of the agreement. Chinese efforts to raise sufficient money more favourably elsewhere failed, and in 1913 the unpopular Reorganization Loan of £ 25 million, which netted China £21 million at an effective rate of approximately 6 per cent, secured on the salt revenue to be collected under joint Sino-foreign administration, was signed by the consortium—which by now had Russian and Japanese participation. The Americans had withdrawn under pressure from President Woodrow Wilson, who considered the terms would infringe on Chinese sovereignty—thus opening the way for a new Japanese financial role in China. China had, however, made one break-through ; it had secured £10 million—even if half the loan was subsequently cancelled—from a British group working with the Chinese minister in London. This, known as the Crisp Loan, was on terms which yielded the Chinese government £5 per cent more than the subsequent Reorganization Loan.

These loans and advances could not solve China's financial problems. Indeed, there is no evidence that the monies received were put to any purpose other than making back payments on foreign debts and, with the balance, paying off various political debts as a means of staying in power. When Yüan died in 1916, having vainly attempted to establish his own imperial dynasty, the financial problems were as acute as ever, the governments of the day depending practically on spasmodic and limited provincial remittances, the surplus funds of the salt administration, and loans from private Chinese banks—by "surplus" is meant over and above the amount needed to service foreign debts. This situation coupled with the focus of the European powers on the war in Europe, led to the imposition by Japan of a series of Twenty-one Demands practically denying Chinese sovereignty and, particularly important from our point of view, a series of loans, the Nishihara loans of 1917-1918, which Carl F. Remer has defined as :

a series of payments of Japanese funds to a group of Chinese officials—then in power—in exchange for agreements giving Japanese interests certain claims, particularly in Manchuria, and so advancing the policy of the Japanese government.

Nevertheless, as Chi-ming Hou states, railway loans to a total of £31 million and industrial loans for telephone and cable construction for £12 million were also made at this time.

The Washington Conference. By the time the foreign Powers were prepared to take a more constructive approach to the China situation, the credit of the country had been practically exhausted and there was little private financiers could do. The best solution, and the one arrived at during the Washington Conference of 1922 in the resulting Nine Power Treaty, ratified in 1925, was, among other things, to effect a holding operation until "something turned up", i.e. a government capable of ruling all China, should prove itself, meanwhile guaranteeing Chinese sovereignty, returning jurisdiction in Shantung from Japan (which had taken over during the war from Germany), and attempting to keep some international control on loans, consortia and spheres of influence. Tentative steps were then taken to return the administration of the customs and the salt to the Chinese and, in 1925-1926, to restore her tariff autonomy. An attempt to resolve the question of outstanding debt was hampered by Japan, with her Nishihara loans, and France, then as now concerned with gold. Given the internal state of China, it was not to be expected that anything would be done about extra-territoriality.

The new consortium—England, France, Japan and America—was established in 1920, partly in fear of what Japan might accomplish alone and partly to discourage international competition in lending to a Chinese government already unable to fulfil its foreign obligations and already bearing an unsecured internal debt of some Ch$800 million. The respective governments gave the participating banks their support, and the Washington Conference confirmed the spirit of the agreement. The inclusion of Japan made the consortium less than popular in China but Japan had to be kept working in co-operation with the powers lest she secure complete domination in China and so close the "open door". In proof of the new spirit of responsibility being attempted towards China, the new consortium resolved to lend only when the funds could, under supervision, be properly used. In consequence, the Consortium was inactive, turning down repeated requests for support from first this warlord and then another who temporarily secured power in Peking. At one point the suggestion was made that China be allowed to raise tariffs so that she could borrow ; that this suggestion made sense—could a reasonable purpose for the loan be found—is an illustration of the senselessness of the system. The inactivity of the consortium was necessitated by financial principles, but it also made it difficult for any government to secure its position, a situation pleasing to the Japanese. Further financial developments would have to await unification of the country under the Kuomintang.

Anti-foreignism and the economy. When the Powers turned their attention to the south, to Canton, they saw a Kuomintang-sponsored government becoming increasingly "left-wing" with Soviet advisers and Communist support. This is no place to assess this typical "old China hand" reaction, but certainly here the intellectual environment was anti-foreign. Boycotts were an old Chinese weapon, and they had been used in 1905 to damage American trade when the exclusive U.S. immigration laws discriminated against Chinese labour ; they had been used again to protest against the Japanese Twenty-one Demands of 1915, leading ultimately to that dividing point in Communist historiography—and, in any case, a key event in modern China—the May Fourth Movement. The boycott was used in 1925 against the British in Shanghai, protesting the northern alliance of imperialism and warlordism ; the subsequent 15-month strike and boycott against Hong Kong damaged British trade in South China.

Thus imperialism had turned from the development of Chamberlain's estates to the financing of corrupt regimes. There is evidence that foreigners and their governments remained genuinely concerned—for varying reasons, some naturally included a degree of self-interest—with the development of China's economy. Yet incredibly they devoted their time to insuring the repayment of a poorly conceived indebtedness and to maintaining rights which, acceptable possibly under the Empire, were not tolerable to a people awakened to nationhood. The Chinese too reacted in kind, devoting their energies to seizing and holding political power or to protesting against "imperialism" or the distorted form it had taken. In Lenin's writings some found a scientific explanation of the nature of imperialism, which tended to undermine even its more defensible aspects. In the neglected countryside, however, there were some political leaders beginning to take interest in the plight of the peasantry and in their needs, not for economic reasons alone, but as a path to power. In all this the foreigners were virtually powerless—at least in the political context of the 1920's.

The Powers could destroy China or dismember her, but they could not develop her. Dr. Sun Yat-sen was one political leader concerned with China's development, but he could not rule. The Chinese Communist Party was still not aware of its path to political power, but Mao Tse-tung was learning. Thus, when the Kuomintang came to power, they had the thoughts of Dr. Sun with all their imperfections, they had the heritage of financial chaos, of foreign pressure, of Communist extremism, and of Japanese military threats. In this atmosphere they were required to reorganize China and begin the development of her countryside.

THE REPUBLIC: POLITICAL LIMITATIONS TO ECONOMIC POLICY

Periodization. Students of China must learn first to scorn those who talk of "unchanging China". Secondly, they must recall the French saying, "Plus ca change, Plus ca la même chose" and reconsider. Although nationalists are reluctant to admit it, the visiting scholar may provide some shrewd insights which the native prefers left unsaid. Thus the British economic historian R. Tawney wrote of China :

......her peasants, who ploughed with iron when Europe used wood and continued to plough with it when Europe used steel.

The period of the Republic, 1911-1949, is a period of plans and frustrations, of real change and of economic stagnation, of critical analysis and political impotence. Even the most vague proponent of "unchanging China" would agree that dynasties came and went and that emperors succeeded and died. China was both changing and unchanging; the questions are rather, Which aspects changed, and Were they the significant ones? Even if we confine this sort of query to the economic sector, the task is formidable.

Although the entire republican period is politically inimicable to economic development in the current sense, the years 1937 to 1949, that is, the years of the Japanese War and its aftermath, are obviously even more so and are dominated by the great inflation. The discussion in this chapter will, therefore, end with 1936. Even the period 1911 to 1936 could be further divided—the "upsurge" through the war years, the reaction and partial recovery in the 1920's, the success of the nationalist revolution and the beginning of national economic policy from 1927, the impact of the world depression. The currency reform of 1935 and the beginning of new plans, 1935-1937, belong in the next chapter. Or we might devise another basis: the growing financial role of Japan, temporarily countered by other foreign efforts in support of the national government, the regaining of economic sovereignty, countered by the economic impact of Manchuria's loss and the *de facto* autonomy of provincial leaders with their paper economic plans. But both sets of divisions cloak an underlying unity.

For when we write of "upsurge," to what indeed are we referring? We are talking, apparently, of the modern sector and considering such data as the number of operating spindles or the tons of steel produced. And when we write of planning, we are considering government bureaucracy at work and not necessarily of accomplishments in the field. Those concerned with the theory of planning or with the history of economic thought in China will find this as important as gross national product statistics. But one thing is clear—we are not writing of the agricultural sector, which remained, after all, the most significant for the Chinese people.

Thus the unity of our first republican period comes from the unchanging nature of the agricultural sector and from the ineffectiveness of government economic policy, except in the most limited fields. This is not, surprisingly, intended as a criticism. Perhaps a majority of Chinese politicians and economists were concerned with the state of agriculture and the welfare of the peasant—as who in an agricultural economy would not be—and it is sometimes assumed that lack of sincerity or honesty of purpose prevented the government from doing something for agriculture. Doing what is never quite clear.

Now with grain production in 1966 at the level of say 1957 and with *per capita* availability of food grains declining, writers have begun to recognize that the management of China's economy is a difficult task, not one whose solution is prepared ready for application by those sincere enough to apply it. The success of Taiwan's recent agricultural development has a mixed message: growth in the agricultural sector can be fast enough both to raise *per capita* real income of farm families and to provide a surplus for transfer to other sectors. But what is possible for one province of China may not be possible for all—at least, not yet. The intensity of the technical effort, the initial cost, and requirements in trained scientists, agricultural technicians—even agricultural economists—and extension workers are overwhelming. They are unavailable on an Empire-wide basis and (there was something of the Empire still about China; the analysis of the chapter two is not totally irrelevant here).

The limits of change. The choice of the phrase "unchanging nature of the agricultural sector" was deliberate. Obviously there were changes, if only famines and floods were not yearly occurrences. But beyond this, there were new cash crops, e.g. tobacco, new techniques, including the manufacture and application of fertilizers. Manchuria was developed on large-scale agriculture. There were co-operative movements, rural education programmes, and extension work. Each event required a considerable expenditure of resources and made a local impact. But when the change is divided by the Chinese population figure, the percentage impact is slight. Thus Tawney was able to write in 1930:

> Backward methods of cultivation, scattered holdings, lack of systematic planning, absence of capital in the hands of farmers, complete lack of knowledge as to how to maintain the quality of tea in less favoured years, unwillingness gradually to improve quality, all this has contributed to the rapid disintegration of the tea trade in China.

In the silk industry he noted that 75 per cent of the silk-worms hatched were killed by germs. This is an old story for tea and silk (as we saw in chapter two), but it is relevant for the republican period and for the whole agricultural sector.

Limitations of policy. As for economic policy, the cynic might suppose that it was geared simply to the immediate needs, usually personal, of the government in power. Or at best that government policy was wilfully misdirected. There are two features of the period that appear to support this view: first, the growth of China's external debt; secondly, the growth of what came to be called "bureaucratic capitalism", one of the primary targets of the Chinese Communist Party. Yet, in both cases, the policies had an economic rationale; like the Ch'ing fiscal system they were not *per se* corrupt, but they were dangerously susceptible to corruption. If we couple with this these very fiscal traditions inherited from the Ch'ing and add the cumulative frustrations which soured the young reformed and rendered the opposition subject to agreement by incorporation, we begin to understand why, given the practically insurmountable problems of the agricultural sector, the economic policy of the republic was less than inspired.

The change of government which occurred in 1911 is to some a revolution, to others a "revolution that never was". Despite the changes we noted during the last years of the

Ch'ing, the Chinese still, in Tawney's comparison, acted like the European hunter in Africa who wanted to learn from the native tracker—learn the tricks of his trade—but did not want to change his mode of life.   The Chinese would have accepted this judgement, some still sought a solution which would preserve the basic Chinese cultural values to which would be added Western technology.   For some this meant revival of Chinese values rather than survival, and we find political leaders within the Nationalist Party, or Kuomintang, espousing a reactionary neo-Confucianism in which nationalism in its narrow sense was combined with a defense of political absolutism and an emphasis on the virtue of obedience—filial piety, respect for Chinese traditions, i.e. the social structure degenerating into belief in the wrongness of any opposition. Another approach was to redefine traditional values in terms of some Western author and to suppose that such redefined attitude or policy thereby became "modern" and likely to be useful in the solution of China's problems dimly understood.   In either case the basic philosophy would be authoritarian.   The impact on the economy would be strongest in the recovery of lost economic sovereignty, but would lead also to autarkic concepts and government intervention in the private sector.

There were others, of course, who thought that by turning to Marxism and thus rejecting both the Confucian past of China—at least as interpreted by reactionary political leaders —and the liberal traditions of the "West", China's people and her economic forces would be liberated.   Attractive as this solution must have appeared to those suffering the abuses of the old system and frustrated both by the slowness of economic change and by what they considered the "betrayal" of the West and the imperial aggression of Japan, the economic history of China since 1949 suggests that it is just as important to select the right development philosophy as it is to break down and cut loose from the old.   Economic development policies have since World War II been most successful in properly motivated conservative-style governments.   While there is possibly no verifiable generalization to be made from this observation, we must conclude not that socialism in any of its various forms *cannot* work but simply that to date it has not.   The proposition that highly motivated, self-sacrificing officials will better serve the people's needs than the profit-seeking businessman is an appealing one. The economic history of modern China provides evidence, first, that officials may not be properly motivated—even under a so-called Communist government—and, secondly, that the private sector, although wasteful and to some motivated by forces which cannot be considered "moral", often succeeds. But the Chinese, having overthrown the alien dynasty and finding China's position but little changed thereby, struck about for a solution and eventually found none. To some economists this has been considered a deliberate trick of a reactionary clique, stagnation as a policy to preserve the social and economic *status quo*. Such an explanation, or condemnation, is quite unsatisfactory and must be discarded.

The Kuomintang. Although the Kuomintang dominates our concept of pre-1949 China, we must remember several limiting facts. First, the party's National Government was not recognised as such until 1928; secondly, the National Government lost control of Manchuria; thirdly, in some provinces its control was nominal, either because the "governor" was *de facto* virtually autonomous or because dissidents had control in the countryside. Naturally, therefore, the government's economic policies, to the extent that they involved work on the ground, e.g. extension work, or control of provincial finances, could never be more than partially effective. With foreign powers still able to exert direct pressure on policy, with extra-territoriality and other privileges, with the virtual independence of the International settlements, especially Shanghai, with the survival of enclaves and spheres of influence, it is hardly surprising that the government was nationalistic and anti-foreign, not so much subordinating economic development to national unity as seeing the latter as a necessary prerequisite to the former.

Economic Policy and Dr. Sun Yat-sen. Nevertheless, there is a thread of underlying unity in this period of confusion to be found in the economic thought of Dr. Sun Yat-sen, founder of the Chinese republic. If his efforts as a politician in government were abortive due to the usurpations of Yüan Shih-k'ai, his influence on the later role of the Kuomintang, and through the party on the Chinese government, is sufficiently important to warrant consideration. We shall consider this influence in the form of two works, his 1921 *International Development of China* and his lectures in 1924 on the "Principle of People's Livelihood" (*min-sheng*). Neither work contains, of course, profound economics. Their importance rests mainly in the fact that they—especially the *min-sheng* lectures— became the basis of Kuomintang economic philosophy and the authoritative text to be quoted in support of any economic policy advocated by members of the party. It is said that the lectures served to stifle independent thought and action, but that is perhaps attributing them with too significant a role. Sun's lectures remain the official doctrine of the KMT and in Taiwan today university students are required, as they were on the Mainland, to include a full course of study of Sun's thoughts, and yet growth has not been stifled there. Perhaps a more balanced assessment of Sun's impact would be to suggest that his economic thought reflected the weaknesses of the science of economics at the time. Sun's particular exposition expressed rather than caused the lack of effective policy in the republican period.

Sun's development plan. In one sense, however, Sun's *International Development of China* was some thirty years before its time, for it is nothing less than a plan for the development of China with foreign capital on a government-to-government aid basis. This is more than a plan in that it combines specific projects with Sun's own economic philosophy and with a certain degree of what Lenin is said to have called his virginal naivete about the attitudes of foreign governments to the plight of China. In fact, even though Austin Chamberlain had referred to British colonies as undeveloped estates and called for their development, even though this change of emphasis marked the transition from the imperialism of free trade to the New Imperialism, yet the colonial powers were hardly thinking in the comprehensive terms and in the magnitudes involved in Sun's plan—indeed, is that not perhaps the problem today?

Specifically, Sun called for an international consortium to "make capitalism create socialism in China" so that the two economic forces of human evolution would work side by side in future civilization. This is Sun the idealist ; this is obviously a call which would not be heeded. But if we ignore the plea for socialism, we find in much of the rest of the text the blue-prints for the type of capital overhead project so essential for development. Sun himself was particularly concerned with transportation, and the plan is heavily weighted, in terms of wordage, in this direction. Sun wrote most fully about those economic phenomena with which he had had most experience. This does not mean to suggest that his specific projects were sound in the sense of being economically or technically feasible. When specific criticisms were made, Sun accepted them, stating that he never supposed himself to be making a final allocation of resources. His plan becomes then either a jumble of ill-conceived projects to be immediately rejected by the practical man as the typical impractical output of a dreamer, or a statement of the *type* of project needed, combined with a plea for external assistance. Naturally, governments unprepared to accept the basic concept of total development assistance efforts interpreted Sun's writing in the former and less favourable light. In fairness to Sun himself, the latter interpretation is more consistent with his own evaluation of his contribution.

When Sun's "plan" is stripped of its detail, we find we are left with certain valid points. First, China needed external assistance of sufficient magnitude to require an international effort. Secondly, the aid should be granted in conformity with a plan for construction of evaluated projects. Programme aid, i.e. general budget support, would have been wasted, subjecting China further to the political pressures of her creditors. Thirdly, Sun, and the Chinese opinion he reflected, had still not realized that modernization could proceed most easily only if the Chinese government accepted the leadership in a vast educational campaign designed to prepare people for such change. Furthermore, Sun had not yet settled on what he meant by "socialism", nor was he apparently aware of the total unacceptability of the concept to the capitalist powers from whom he sought aid. Thus a careful contemporary reader of

International Development of China should have seen that the problem was not the imperfection of Sun's plan but the unwillingness or inability of others thinking in the same vein, on the same grand level, to produce something more substantial, more acceptable to both the Chinese and the foreign powers. Although lip service would be given to planning, there was nothing comprehensive until possibly the end of the Communist government's first five-year plan, 1956-1967. Piecemeal planning, small-scale aid—these proved totally inadequate for rapid development in the sense of significant *per capita* as opposed to aggregate changes in output.

Sun's economic thought. If the *International Development of China* was, as Sun admitted, a layman's thought supplemented by the very limited technical materials at his disposal, it was nevertheless a pioneering statement of the *magnitude* of the task. Its inadequacies should have helped statesmen to a realization of the urgency of beginning. In contrast, Sun's lectures on the Principle of People's Livelihood offer a set of economic principles, sometimes mutually conflicting, with general proposals but without a specific plan for action. Chinese politicians, unable themselves to evolve a course of economic action, stressed the principles until they became dogma and an end in themselves. In the more (paradoxically speaking) hopeful atmosphere of Taiwan, the dogma could be broken through ; the *min sheng* principle was not necessarily a bar to constructive economic thought nor to the creation of effective development policy, especially if it were properly interpreted.

The lectures on *min sheng* were the third part of a series entitled "The Three Principles of the People" (*San Min Chu I*), which became the basis of Kuomintang dogma. The first two dealt with nationalism and democracy. The third is an attempted rebuttal of Marxian socialism, Confucian in spirit, but with a terminology based on the writing of an obscure American dentist and socialist thinker, Maurice William, and with overtones of Henry George. In part, Sun is arguing with his former more Marxian expression in that, although accepting the untenable thesis that the industrial revolution led to unemployment and misery, he rejects with William the necessity of class conflict. "Society progresses," writes Sun, "through adjustment of major economic interests rather than through the clash of interest." In his rejection of "surpus value" and a materialistic interpretation of history, Sun provides a somewhat ambiguous "social interpretation." With this he couples specific proposals. Sun advocates social and industrial reform, public ownership of transportation and communication, the direct tax, and socialized distribution. While the call to public ownership is clear enough, the remaining platforms are susceptible of several interpretations and can deteriorate into slogans.

The approach Sun chooses illustrates a point we made earlier, *viz.* that some Chinese reformers tended to develop their ideas based on traditional thought and then cast about for a Western writer whose terminology might be borrowed to give these ideas a new garb. Thus Sun conceived his economic programme in terms of *min sheng*, a traditional goal of the Confucian state. He attempted to express this in Marxian terminology but, finding this unsatisfactory, he grasped the words of an American few had heard of. We must not, then, think of Sun blindly following some obscure scribbler, mistakenly supposing him to be a "great socialist", but rather that Sun, in the work of William, found a terminology suitable to his already formed ideas.

> The energies of mankind have been spent largely in trying to solve the question of subsistence . . . Livelihood is the centre of government.

William and Sun emphasize consumption ; Marx, they claim, stressed production. This is, of course, a shift in the focus of ultimate interest, not a comment on the importance of production *per se*. But it is, quite naturally, with Sun's view on production and its organization that we are primarily concerned. And it is here that the practical difficulties begin.

Some 50 per cent of China's imports were agricultural products, including cereals, and for Sun this served to emphasise the importance of agricultural production. His solution : land reform, i.e., "equalisation of land-ownership" with compensation to landlords with appropriate incentives to peasant owners to encourage maximum output. Sun stated the importance of a programme of irrigation, fertilizer utilization, crop rotation, pest eradication, suitable processing and transportation services. While stating the problem is far from solving it, Sun was obviously right in supposing that here was the key to China's development. But his solution was in conflict with his other social aim, socialized distribution. Food production, he wrote, must *not* be for profit. Distribution of income must *not* be through the market alone.

The demand for "socialized distribution" presents problems in itself; it is not a precise concept and can be, and has been, variously interpreted. If the market is ruled out as the final arbiter of resource allocation and income distribution, some other criteria must be substituted. Having discarded Marxian slogans, Sun was left with nothing better than vague concepts of social justice. This could, and did, quickly degenerate into a Confucian paternalism impractical of specific application and offering merely an opportunity or excuse for indiscriminate government interference. Land reform was impractical as outlined by Sun for two reasons: lack of financial resources and lack of political control. When both were available in Taiwan, land reform on Sun's principles was accomplished.

From Sun's call for social and industrial reform provided the basis for the transition from merchant undertakings under government supervision to the bureaucratic capitalism of the 1930's. To Sun the involvement of the state in business was simply a corollary of his socialism, as was his more acceptable call for the nationalization of transportation and communication. And in conception this involvement is similar to the principle behind the Japanese government's early role in industry, for there is certainly a large risk factor involved in pioneer undertakings which no private entrepreneur may be willing to undertake.

The presence of this high risk component provides one of the standard arguments for the involvement of government

in the industrial sector of a mixed economy.   The problem of
China lay in the possible abuses of an otherwise acceptable
policy.   In the period of war-time and post-war economic
controls, the nature of these abuses is obvious.   But even in the
1930's the involvement of high ranking officials in industrial
concerns in which the government *per se* also held an equity
investment could mean unfair competition for government
contracts, high and unnecessary fees to the party members on
the Board, or, at the other extreme, an unsound financial
policy to meet temporary government fiscal needs.   The
enmity of the Communist Party, however, was based on
the dominant position and political creed of the bureaucratic
capitalists and they were singled out and distinguished from
the "national bourgeoisie" who, the Communists thought
(apparently over-optimistically), could be reoriented.

The Economic Consequences of Dr. Sun.   Sun's "Three
Principles" found subsequent expression in the conservative
"New Life Movement", in such writings as Chiang Kai-shek's
China's Destiny, and in rural reconstruction efforts.   Diverse
as these listings appear—diverse in the inspiration of their
sources and in their specific targets—they all picture a paternalistic state in continuity with the virtues of China's past
battling with the tide of imperialism, and actively participating
in the economic activities of society.   It is fair to ask what
else could be expected.   Economic planning as it developed
after World War II was then unknown, and the magnitude of
the development problem gave rise to the vague, all-embracing
economic platitudes which could be variously interpreted.   The
state had not the political power to apply a totally dictatorial
economic solution ; its role was more experimental and was
unevenly effective.   The general political situation was not
conducive to spontaneous growth, and the economy was
subjected to such negative forces as the world depression of the
1930's.   We should, therefore, expect some progress in the
modern sector, especially in the Treaty Ports, but little if any
recognizable growth in the living standards of the people.   We
should now check this impression with accounts of China's
economy through the mid-1930's.

THE STATE OF THE ECONOMY, 1928-1936

The government. The eight years of relative control by the National Government show, as has been suggested, a mixed record. Considering first the activities of the government, we find such contrasts as, for example, that, while tax collection relative to excise taxes in the cities and coastal provinces was improved and rates raised, the basic land tax was alienated, that is, granted by the centre to the provincial governments. The central government presumably had no choice, but in consequence budget deficits were normal and financed by borrowing at unnecessarily high rates through a banking system dominated (eventually) by four government banks. Nor is it clear that *likin,* or its equivalent, was actually abandoned as a *quid pro quo.* The opportunity this provided for private profits from political influence was supplemented by the activities of, for example, the China Development Finance Corporation, which forged a lasting relationship between officials and capitalists—institutionalized bureaucratic capitalism.

On the foreign front, the government secured tariff autonomy, but, given the aggression of Japan and the still unsettled condition of the countryside, was unable to eliminate other special rights and privileges. From an economic point of view, what was needed was full control of currency and trade and a moratorium on foreign debt unconnected with growth of foreign exchange earnings—the other matters are political. The Nationalists obtained their control, but not, of course, the moratorium. And foreign businesses, while standing by their extra-territorial rights, often came to agreements over tax matters which were economically satisfactory to the government.

But development, despite the paper work of the National Economic Council (established in 1933), could not be given priority. Railway construction recommended and the Canton-Hankow and the Chekiang-Kiangsi lines were completed. 60,000 miles of motor roads were constructed. Nevertheless, a list of the military campaigns which the National Government led against the Communists and against dissident elements of the Kuomintang and warlords confirms that military expenditure continued to absorb too great a proportion of the nation's resources, depleted as they were by the loss of Manchuria.

Rural sector. Tawney described China as belonging to the pre-capitalist period. Writing at the break of the great depression, he saw the development prospects of China as slight. For him China was overwhelmed by chaos, by lack of government, and by poverty. There were provincial tax barriers, costly transport—therefore, hundreds of little markets. War and famine crushed the peasant who was constantly on the verge of actual destitution. The peasants were, he thought, "propertied proletariat", saved only by their admirable ingenuity, family communism, and by "roughing" like European livestock through the winter. Thus with no reserves, they were helpless against calamity. Since in an agricultural nation there is a temptation to seek a surplus from the peasants for transfer—either for productive or unproductive purposes—to other sectors, the peasants were victims of official and unofficial exactions. They formed leagues to keep out bandits, Communists, and government soldiers with fine impartiality.

With some 30% of all farmers tenants and another 25% part-owners, at least part of the economic, social and political problems of the peasants was ascribed to the system of land tenure, and the government has been severely criticized for not implementing Dr. Sun's land programme—or one interpretation of it. Indeed, land reform became a catch-all policy which, in the words of T.H. Shen, would (1) improve the economic condition and welfare of farmers, (2) secure political and social independence, and (3) encourage the tiller's interest in improvement of land productivity. Since Shen himself proved to be a successful and practical agricultural reform administrator, one must question his thesis with caution. It is, however, possible to suggest that agricultural reform in the Chinese situation could be successful *despite* land tenure reforms. As his significant study, *The Agricultural Resources of China*, points out at the end of each chapter, each feature of the rural scene needed careful analysis and scientific improvement, the nature of which was intricate, requiring years of planning and a well-trained staff to implement. Without these concurrent advances, land reform must be little more than a political sop ; indeed, the land redistribution under the People's Republic was but the first step towards collectivization and the proletarianization of the peasantry. This is not at all what the liberal reformers, including Dr. Sun, had in mind.

Although agriculture is the basis of the rural economy, other economic activities are involved. Thus in a survey of 515 families in Ting *hsien* (county) made over the years 1926-1936, the following occupational survey was made of 1282 males over 14 years of age: 933 farming, 64 hired farm labour, 48 students, 40 unemployed, 25 merchants, 19 education, 17 skilled labour, 15 military, 13 unskilled labour, 11 government, 7 pedlars, 7 home weaving, 6 store employees, 4 apprentices, 2 doctors, and 11 others. This, of course, shows the dominance of agriculture, but the level of living might rather depend on the fortunes of secondary employments : home weaving was most important with 112 out of 389 listings. This in turn would depend upon size of markets, competition from modern factories both foreign and domestic, and other conditions of trade. Obviously, cheap factory-made goods could undersell those of domestic industry at certain times and places, and some have ascribed to this the major explanation of rural poverty.

While it is not clear, *prima facie*, how the advent of cheap goods would be harmful to a peasant community, the situation becomes more plausible if we posit special conditions. Thus if the peasants were, in their spare time, producing for a market and exchanging their products for other manufactures, the loss of that market would be serious to income on the supposition that the peasants were not able to do anything further with their free time. But the economic problem is not the advent of cheap goods but the failure to readjust the rural regime or to reorganize agricultural production sufficiently to enable labour to be taken from the land and used elsewhere, in the pattern, but not the consequences of Communist mass labour projects. This type of readjustment requires the sort of co-ordination that central planning facilitates and which the situation in China—political, social, cultural—made extremely difficult.

The pessimistic view of the agricultural sector is not universally accepted, perhaps—and this may be unfair—for two reasons. First, if we can show a sound agricultural base, the failure of Communist policies under the People's Republic is an even greater condemnation of their record. Secondly, if we say no progress was made in agriculture during the Kuomintang, we apparently condemn both the regime and those capable and dedicated men who devoted their lives to the improvement of Chinese agriculture. If, for example, we turn to a 1966 publication of John Lossing Buck, so long a leading foreign expert, we find a compilation which comprises the "inheritance of agricultural advances from the previous regime". And he concludes : "Thus, at the time of the Communist takeover, there was a good foundation for increasing production rather rapidly." Buck's compilation includes the institutions for agricultural education, research and extension; rural credit institutions, co-operatives; well-trained men ; improved seeds ; established disease and insect control methods ; land reform laws ; a fertilizer factory ; river control projects. We can see at a glance—the rural credit and the co-operative items are good signals for anyone with development experience—that this list, though well-meaning, reflects both accomplishment and wishful thinking, And of what was done, much was again lost in the period after 1937.

Modern Sector. If we turn to the modern sector, confined generally to the now widely distributed treaty ports as far as large-scale manufacturing enterprises were concerned, we find irregular progress. Here, too, the impact of government action was mostly felt, and the new problems of industrialization, including a politically orientated labour movement, were manifest. If the government could not reach down to the peasant, to reform either the method of production, the collection of taxes, or the extension of credit, in the modern sector the government was able to participate directly, from here it obtained its funds, here was the impact of its foreign negotiations, here went the benefits of such improvements as modern banking, railroads, and social overhead investment. The government's "successes" were not all favourable to economic growth, however, this being but one aspect of total policy.

The recovery of tariff autonomy in 1928 enabled the government to raise the level of both import and export taxes, probably on balance to the detriment of modern industrial growth. Reform of the monetary system, including the almost exclusive official use of a *dollar* unit of account from 1933 and the elimination of the old *tael* unit, the establishment of government banks with rationalized but overlapping functions, and the control of that paper money issued by Chinese institutions (banking notes of foreign banks were, of course, subject to the protection of extra-territoriality), did much to assist business, but the problems of silver as a standard were sufficiently great to minimize the impact of these reforms. A "Central Bank of China", established in 1924, reorganized in 1928, supplemented the work of the Bank of China and the Bank of Communications. Though none achieved the status of a functioning central bank—in the European sense—some check on the co-ordination of the monetary implications of government policies became possible. Control and inspection of note issue is one example. In 1933 the Farmers' Bank was founded, but it hardly met the needs of truly rural credit.

A new index constructed by John K. Chang gives 9.2% as the average annual growth rate of China's modern industry between 1912 and 1936, and 8.4% during the government of the Kuomintang, 1928-1936. This was not stagnation ; but, given the small base in 1912, neither do the figures indicate a satisfactory rate of growth if a modern Chinese economy were to be created. Selected statistics show growth after 1896, followed by an easing during the 1911 period. Manufacturing pushed ahead during World War I : manufacturing and railroads developed again in the period just before 1930. Thus, there were 12 cotton mills in 1896, 28 in 1939 but 118 in 1925. The number of spindles increased from 417,000 in 1896 to 4.2 million in 125 mills in 1930. The number of factories with over 30 workers was, however, only something over 2,000 in 1930 and 47% of all workers in such factories were in the textile industry. Furthermore, China was becoming increasingly subject to Japanese economic and political pressure. Railroad mileage increased from 250 miles to 9,500 in 1930 and pig iron reached 433,000 tons in 1928. The important fact which emerges, since the actual figures are as absolutes of not much meaning, is that Tawney's description of the economy, even the modern sector, as in the pre-capitalist or early capitalist state is not unreasonable. Little significant progress had been made.

The growth of modern industry, however limited, spotlighted two increasingly serious problems : the difficulty of popularizing the corporate form of enterprise needed if sufficient capital was to be raised, and the need for some more rational form of labour representation. These problems occur to the student simultaneously not only because their solution was a prerequisite to growth if the private sector were to be responsible for manufacturing and mining enterprize, but also because provincialism and traditional attitudes hampered those solutions. However, it is with the labour problem that we are concerned here.

An estimated 1.5 million Chinese were employed in modern factories in 1930. Their conditions, despite laws and regulations which date to the Ch'ing, were as might be expected. Long hours in poor and unsanitary conditions, low wages, few holidays would be typical, although there were model exceptions. These were the visible consequences of industrialization, but, of course, as in eighteenth-century England, the rural and handicraft conditions these workers left behind were as bad or worse than those in the modern factory. The Chinese problem was aggravated by exploitation through contract-labour systems, so-called apprenticeship schemes, secret society terrorism and extortion, and a recruiting system which left especially women workers in a powerless position. To correct these abuses, labour combinations and strikes were organized spontaneously at first, but workers returning from France, where they had served during and immediately after World War I, student and professional organizers involved in such anti-foreign demonstrations as those against the Japanese in 1915 and, of course, the May Fourth Movement (1919) activists gave a more continuous and professional basis to labour agitation. Successful strikes were noted in the early 1920's. By 1927 the All-China Labour Federation's fourth congress, meeting under the auspices of the leftist Kuomintang government in Hankow, could report a total of 3 million organized workers—undoubtedly an exaggeration.

The labour movement did indeed grow significantly after 1925, and M. N. Roy and other activists visited China in 1927 to preach world revolution. It was apparent that the Communist Party had given the movement an almost wholly political bias—the leadership was no longer primarily concerned with industrial relations but had political goals. Thus it was the Shanghai General Labour Union which, in 1927, called a general strike in that city in support of the approaching Nationalist forces. But the political orientation of the so-called "Red" unions was to be their downfall, and within a month of the occupation of the Chinese areas of Shanghai a purge of labour agitators had been ordered. In the months that followed both the Red Unions and the Communist Party went underground, the latter eventually joining forces with Mao Tse-tung in the countryside. The Kuomintang was not, certainly on Dr. Sun's teachings, opposed to industrial unionism *per se*, and the Party encouraged formation of rival (Yellow) unions to replace the purged. China joined the International Labour Organization, and a model labour legislation was drafted. But the economic pressures on the labour force were such as to make improvement of workers' conditions largely up to the decision of individual employers and to organizations such as the Y.M.C.A. We are not, of course, suggesting that workers in the modern sector are entitled to wages commensurate with their higher rate of productivity, and this for reasons which should be obvious to any student of economic development problems. We are suggesting that the National Government's policy towards the labour movement was theoretically sound but, as too often, most effective where it was most repressive.

On the international account, it should be briefly noted that although balance of payments statistics are inadequate, it appears that China characteristically had an unfavourable balance of trade, aggravated by the service of foreign loans, an import of bullion, and payments to Chinese diplomatic missions and students abroad. This was offset by an import of foreign capital, foreign expenditures on missionary activities, armed forces, and educational institutions, and the

TABLE 6A : CHINA SELECTED TRADE STATISTICS, 1882-1931

(*annual average*)

	1882-1886	1892-1896	1907-1911	1912-1916	1927-1931
Net imports (*Hk taels, millions*) of which (percentages):	80	165	433	517	1244
Machinery and electrical equipmeet	0	a	4	4	6
Cotton manufactures	32	35	30	31	13b
Opium (including tobacco)	33	18	11	10	4
Net exports (*Hk taels, millions*) of which (percentages):	69	124	328	406	946
Tea	46	24	10	10	4
Silk	34	34	28	24	17
Bean cake and beans	0	a	11	13	21
Trade Balance (*Hk taels, millions*)	—11	41	—105	—111	298

a.   less than 1%.
b.   Raw cotton imports had risen to 9% of total net imports.

Source : T. R. Bannister. *A History of the External Trade of China,* 1834-81, Shanghai 1931.

remittances of overseas Chinese. This last-mentioned item has been called probably the most remarkable item in view of its persistence to very recent times. (See Table 15 at the end of chapter six; but read the notes carefully and take the *caveat* to heart).

Although China's trade as calculated in *taels* increased significantly during the Republican period, this was at least partly the consequence of the depreciated value of silver in relation to gold. (See Table 3 on page 78 and Table 6B below). The foreigner was far from satisfied with developments, although his position was influenced as much by the decline of traditional exports as by the total export figure; as much by the failure of China to import more machinery as by the total import figure. As for exports, Table 6A shows the decline in the relative importance of tea and silk. (See also Table 2 on page 55.) In addition to the bean products shown in the table, egg products, vegetable oils, and skins and furs were of growing relative significance. Import statistics show the early importance of opium, but the decline in this import was partly offset by the increase in tobacco and partly by Chinese production of both opium and tobacco. The decline in the importance of cotton manufactures is the consequence of the growth of the Chinese textile industry, also revealed in the growth of raw cotton imports.

TABLE 6B. INDEX OF VALUE : TRADE OF CHINA'S LEADING PARTNERS
(1912 = 100)

	U.S.A.	Japan	United Kingdom	Germany
1920	295	254	195	20
1930	511	372	188	263
1935	280	101	104	239

Share of China's Trade, 1936

Exports	26	15	9	5
Imports	19	16a	12	16
Total	22	16	10·6	11·5

a. Excludes smuggled goods. If these had been included, Japan's share would probably have been greater than that of the U.S.A.

Source : *China Yearbook.*

In Table 6B China's external trade is related to her major trading partners, and we should note the less important role played by Britain in this period. China's tea trade to Britain had dwindled practically to insignificance and had only partly been replaced by the trade in eggs and egg products. Then too Japan was able to compete for China's imports of machinery, iron and steel, and, of course, fisheries. Japan also exported woollen and cotton goods, paper, and sugar in significant quantities. Britain's exports to China were headed by metals, machinery, and vehicles. The United States, apparently China's most important trading partner in 1936, led with tobacco leaf, motor cars, raw cotton, and timber as well as kerosene, gasoline, and machinery. Germany's exports followed a pattern similar to that of Japan, although the high rate of growth stemmed, of course, from her position as a defeated nation in World War I and, hence, the low initial figure. Shanghai accounted for 51% of the exports and 59% of the imports of China's 1936 trade, excluding Manchuria.

Prospects on the eve of war. When, however, we move forward to 1937 on the eve of the Second Sino-Japanese War, we can become for the moment more optimistic. Although the National Government of the Kuomintang had lost Manchuria, it was gradually consolidating its political control of China Proper. True, the fiscal situation continued basically unsound. The national government depended too heavily on customs and other excise taxes whose incidence lay principally on the modern sector, the land tax was wholly controlled by provincial and local governments, and tax collection costs were excessive. Furthermore, the monetary reform, which we shall consider in chapter five, had not been wholly successful, and extra-territoriality remained. But on the credit side, a gradual increase in rural development activities was discernible, the reorganization of banking and the stability of the government permitted sale of government bonds domestically—although this was subject to abuse when used to finance current expenditures and was, in any case, expensive. Railway and road construction had revived, manufacturing enterprises continued to grow—but still in the Treaty Ports—and government planning by the National Economic Council provided at least a platform for nationwide thinking on the important subject of economic development. It may even be argued that the remaining special rights of foreigners marked a mutual bond of interest against Japanese pretensions, both political and economic, in China.

We must be careful to qualify this optimism and to point out that we are dealing in any case with an historical "might have been," for the Japanese war introduced the final and tragic stage of the republican economy. If we consider the pioneering national income statistics of Ou Pao-san, we are led to the conclusion that foreign investment declined, industrial output in the modern sector was approximately constant, and investment inadequate to maintain the industrial plant. Ta-chung Liu, on the other hand, although he estimated total agricultural output as constant—and therefore declining *per capita*—estimated industrial growth at about 1% per annum. Although Liu's figures are generally more optimistic than Ou's, they both describe what Douglas S. Paauw has designated a period of stagnation.

What evidence is there, then that the situation in 1937 was in any sense different? First, we must recall that the figures cited are for the period 1931-1936, that is, during the Great Depression. At a time when world trade and production were at low levels, perhaps it is not helpful to describe, say, a constant level of production in China as "stagnation", which, though a fair dictionary description may not be analytically sound, may not, that is, tell us what was going on. Secondly, if we relate the unsound fiscal policies of the National Government—especially the reliance on excise taxes on the modern sector—to political necessity, we can suggest the possibility of change as the political control of the government became more certain. Thirdly, we must notice that foreign powers were coming to accept the stability and national role of the Kuomintang's government and, anxious of Japan's role, were beginning to take a constructive interest in China's development. This was, we must remember, in the days before the techniques of government-to-government aid were even attempted—they are still uncertain and generally ineffective. But in their support of large-scale efforts, from the work of the Famine Commission to banking support for the monetary reform, foreign governments staked their fortunes in China on economic development under the National Government. The significance of this attitude became apparent during the Sino-Japanese War when foreign aid took on a new status— although its purpose was then to insure China's survival rather than economic development.

By 1937 certainly China had committed itself to economic development in the sense of modernization, industrialization, growth of output—all the generally accepted criteria marking accomplishment of this goal. Yet there remained barriers. Although the Boxer Rebellion had forced even the Empress Dowager to reassess the formula which attempted to graft Western techniques onto a basically unchanged Chinese society, we have cited Tawney's observation that such an approach remained typical in the 1920's. We have seen too that in the 1930's the official emphasis on traditional Chinese values, sometimes referred to as neo-Confucianism—although this term also refers to a philosophically sounder trend of Chinese thought—found a basis in the accepted dogma of Sun Yat-sen. It was the philosophy of a government urging patience on a people suffering much and promised much by other political groups—especially the Communists. As a defense, this traditionalism was not likely to appeal; during the demoralization of the war-time inflation it became a cloak attempting to prevent a critical examination of the government's shortcomings and as such hindered the type of thinking likely to produce economic development. On the other hand, the official acceptance of traditionalism can be at least partially accounted for by the lack of success—lack of reality—of Western trained economists and businessmen who sought to apply Western remedies directly and immediately to the Chinese economy. Just as the early factory managers in China found that a turn-key operation based on a Lancashire factory would run into difficulties in the new Shanghai environment, so would-be economic administrators and policymakers found that their learning needed modification.

THE ROLE OF FOREIGN INVESTMENT

Criticism of the foreign role. Whatever the Chinese might think of the West, it is certain that the stimulus and example for modernization came from the West and to some degree forced China to change, however slowly, however reluctantly. Yet this same West, which demonstrated the need for modernization and obviously had to set the example for it, may also have prevented China from modernizing effectively. That is, the West has been accused, on the one hand, of forcing China to betray her culture for "progress" and, on the other, to have made it difficult if not impossible for her to achieve that "progress". Lenin's "Theory of Imperialism" was a popular pamphlet in China.

In stating that the West interfered with China's hope for "progress", we should here eliminate the political arguments as outside our scope. We may note that the threat to China's political sovereignty arose from European desires to insure a role in the capital development of the country. The international disputes over spheres of influence, financial consortia, and treaty rights were often part of a conflict over participation in China's development. Chinese nationalists would contend that the foreign role in China prevented the Chinese from taking advantage of the economic modernization by limiting China's economic sovereignty, by direct investments against which the Chinese could not compete, by preventing tariff protection for Chinese industry, by burdening China with foreign debts for non-productive purposes at high rates of interest, and by the long series of so-called unequal treaties with damaging terms. Our concern now is to consider the merits of the arguments concerning the foreign economic role in China with special attention to the role of foreign investment.

The effect of the treaties on the Chinese economy was, first, to give a special status both to foreigners and to specified areas of international settlement. Both would tend to permit that investment which would have been made but for the political and legal situation in China. The existence of an international settlement with special privileges would also

tend to encourage concentration of this same type of economic enterprise, limiting the demonstration effect of foreign-
type enterprise by confining it to a very restricted area. Furthermore, to the extent that these treaty provisions gave some
protection to the Chinese in the settlements, their effect would
be to extend to them the advantages of exclusion from Chinese
political and legal control and to enable them to establish
foreign-style enterprises. This could also be done by Chinese
investment in foreign registered companies. To the nineteenth-century free trader the advantages of the Treaty System
to China would, at this point, have been proved.

We must question further, however. The treaties, in
permitting foreigners to establish factories, may have made it
impossible for the Chinese to compete, or the economic gain
may have been negated by the destruction of native handicrafts
industry, or other provisions may have offset the gains from
foreign investment, e.g. the limitations on protective tariff and
the special privileges foreigners were granted with regard to
transit taxes or *likin* . Actually, on this last, foreign rights were
largely disregarded by the 1920's and Kuomintang fiscal reform
minimized their impact after 1933. But in general the questions are legitimate. The definitive answer has yet to be given,
but we may, following the pioneering work of Chi-ming Hou,
examine the scope of foreign investment in China and its impact on the economy. At the present stage of analysis, this
must suffice.

Statistics. Foreign investment in China, including Manchuria and Hong Kong, rose from $787 millions, United
States currency, to $1610 million in 1914, $3242 million in
1931 and $3483 million in 1936. The inclusion of Hong Kong
must be justified on the grounds that it was, in fact, not much
different from the Treaty Ports, that its economy was closely
integrated with China's, and that, if anything, once China
regained tariff antonomy, its position would be less inviting to
foreign, China-oriented investment. These arguments would,
of course, be invalid for figures dealing with China post-1949.
As for Manchuria, Japanese investment there in 1937 was of the
magnitude of US $830 million. Of this foreign investment in

China, the largest proportion was for direct investment (64%
in 1902, 77% in 1936), the balance being obligations of the
Chinese government. The percentage of direct foreign investment in manufacturing increased but in 1936 was still only
20% of the total, compared to 25% in transportation, 20% in
banking and finance, and 17% in trade. The growth of investment in banking and finance from negligible in 1914 to 20%
in 1936 illustrates the changing and increasingly important
role of foreign banking institutions. There were significant
changes in the contribution of various countries to total foreign
investment: Great Britain, with 33% of the total in 1902 was
then in first place, but slipping to second with 35% in 1936,
while Japan's share rose from less than 1% to 40%. In 1902
Russia had the second largest stake with 31%, but this declined
to 8% in 1931 and to nothing in 1936. Germany with 21% in
1902 lost heavily in World War I and by 1936 had not recovered the same absolute figure. American investment, despite
such institutions as the International Banking Corporation
and efforts to participate in various loan consortia, lagged
significantly behind the leaders with 25% in 1902 and 9% in
1936.

When the aggregates are compared with the total outflow
of investment capital from Europe, we recall that the bulk went
to "areas of settlement" and that after this colonial territories
had preference. China, it has been said, suffered from colonialism without the benefits of colonialism. (For 1938 total
foreign capital in China was US $2557 million or US $5.7
per capita; for India, Burma and Ceylon US $3113 million or
US $9.6 *per capita*, compared with, say, Uruguay's US
$118.1 *per capita*.) But the criticism that China did not get
sufficient foreign investment seems to contradict the proposition that such investment was somehow detrimental to China's
growth. The reconciliation lies in the desire of the nationalists
to enjoy the benefits of foreign resources without the implications of foreign control, either by a colonial government or by
direct investment. This certainly lay behind the financing
plans for Sun's ambitious development proposals.

Chinese government borrowing. Between 1861 and 1937
the Chinese government borrowed externally the sum of £257

million at current prices (£275 million in 1913 prices), of which
some 60% were for military, indemnity or administrative purpose and the balance for railroad and industrial, principally
railroad.   Since foreign debt is in itself an economic burden,
these figures suggest a real basis for the Chinese nationalists'
complaint of "imperialism" or "imperialist aggression."   But
the complaint is properly a political, not an economic one.
Given China's defeat in, say, the First Sino-Japanese War, she
had to face the payment of 250 million *Kuping taels* in indemnity and other expenses to Japan.   This is the point of complaint; the foreign financing of the payment was necessitated
by military defeat, internal resources could not be mobilized,
and China borrowed on the supposed security of her customs
revenues at rates of interest comparable to the market rates
of the day.   Only the Japanese Nishihara loans made during
1917-1918 to finance the military activities of the Peking
government in return for economic concessions to the Japanese
can be considered pure examples of financial exploitation.
During the European speculative mania of the mid-1860's,
for example, considerable efforts were made by a French
consortium, and possibly by others, to involve the Chinese
government in large borrowings for unspecified purposes.
These came to nothing; the Chinese government, as we have
seen, chose to borrow through provincial authorities and then
only for specific projects.   Later foreign financial pressures
came in connection with railroad and other economic development projects or, as in the Re-organization Loan of 1913, from
the desperate needs of the Chinese government itself.

We have added "military indemnity, and administrative"
into one category on the assumption that sums borrowed under
these headings did not contribute to economic development.
Under other circumstances a loan for administrative purposes
could be for the "programme" as opposed to "project" financing of a development plan.   Considered by periods, China's
unproductive foreign debt was contracted as follows : before
1893 to finance internal military operations and the Sino-
French War, from 1894-1898 to finance indemnity payments
and other costs of the Sino-Japanese War, and from 1912 to
1926 to finance the general administration of the pre-Kuo-

mintang republican government of China. Of the £34 million equivalent borrowed between 1927 and 1937 only 23% was for "non-productive", *i.e.* administrative purposes; the balance was £24 million for railroads and £2 million for industry.

The rates of interest were fortunately not high, averaging 8-9% if the borrowing were done from funds competing in the Eastern money markets, and 5% or 6% if in Europe. Since Chinese bonds were sold at a discount from par an additional fractional percentage must be added to these rates to obtain the effective rate of interest. Since a great deal has been written about the "high cost" of Chinese government borrowing, this has become one of the myths of China's economic exploitation. The cost is naturally "high" when compared to the rate of interest on U.S. treasury bills or savings bonds, it is low when compared to, say, the rate of department store finance in the United States (18% per annum). Both these rates are irrelevant. Chinese officials are on record as complaining of high rates, quoting London market rates to support their arguments. But the rates they quote are often for some past period of exceptionally low rates and usually for short-term British government securities. At a time when the Hong Kong government found itself borrowing in London at 10%, Li Hung-chang was quoted as citing 3% rates in London and requesting similar facilities. The rates at which the Chinese government borrowed were only slightly higher than those at which other governments, usually considered better risks, were able to borrow. This is not a source of exploitation.

Had China been in a position to make use of the exceptionally favourable credit standing—that is, considering the general nature of her government—which was brought about by the foreign supervision of such revenue sources as the customs and, later, the salt gabelle, it is true that much might have been done. If the £80 million for military and indemnity purposes and the £28 million for administrative purposes had rather gone to economically productive purposes—but this is one of the tragic might-have-beens of history. That these funds were not devoted to economically useful purposes is not, however, the fault of the foreign lenders or an example of foreign economic imperialism—with the exception of Japan noted. The criticism of the foreign role lies elsewhere, partly, of course, in the whole concept of "indemnity" payments. This was the price China paid for her slow and uncertain reaction to the impact of the West. Given her weak international position, China was never able to develop an independent, rational policy of foreign borrowing. International pressures and Chinese fears, legitimate under the circumstances, of foreign control gained under the provisions of various loans, both these were important factors in dissipating the potentially favourable impact of sound foreign finance. Finally, the burden of debt repayment in the days of depreciating silver exaggerated an already serious economic burden.

Impact of direct investment. In his national product study, Ou Pao-san estimated that of the total output of factory industries in China (including Manchuria) for 1933, i.e. Ch $2186 million, some 65% was from Chinese-owned factories, 35% from foreign. Yen Chung-p'ing's estimates for 1930 show a somewhat more important role for foreign investment in shipping (83%), coal (76%), and iron ore and pig iron (99% each). A less easy to interpret figure is the 74% (for 1931) of mileage of Chinese railroads either owned or financed by foreigners. By any interpretation, however, these figures indicate a significant role for foreign direct investment even in manufacturing. Professor Hou examined the role in terms of its catalytic effect, oppressing effect, destructive effect, drain effect, and instability effect.

Although heavily weighted towards the finance of foreign trade and towards enterprises ancillary thereto, as we have seen, the range of foreign direct investment was broad and its impact on Chinese modern-type industry was affected by the "linkage effects". Thus the Chinese response to Western example, like the foreign response itself, moved from trade to dockyards, to shipping itself, and from shipping to coal mines to railroads to transport the coal for the use of the ships. These logical flows explain the foreign diversity, but why did the Chinese follow, and why in the amounts recorded?

China was motivated by ideas both of retaliation and imitation. In the nineteenth-century foreign methods proved themselves militarily and provincial officials supported by the Court retaliated by attempting to adopt a limited number of the new techniques in the "self-strengthening" programme. After 1895 with the example of foreign manufacturing enterprises in the Treaty Ports, private Chinese, sometimes aided by the government, sought to imitate successful foreign enterprises. Textile and processing plants are, of course, the prime examples. The existence of foreign enterprises in China would be helpful in supplying trained Chinese personnel and working models actually adapted to Chinese conditions. All this, stemming originally from foreign trade and the foreign institutions financing it, had a catalytic effect on the modern sector, which, as we have seen, grew significantly during the period of "stagnation" prior to 1937.

But as China did not fully modernize, we must ask whether, despite the effects stated above, the presence of foreign direct investment did not both set an example of what might be done and at the same time make imitation impossible by unfair competition, by largeness of resources, by the overwhelming background of technical know-how. The facts quoted above suggest that in manufacturing at least the Chinese held their own with 65% of total output by value. This can partly be explained by the specialization of production within the industry, with, for example, high quality textiles being produced in foreign factories for urban markets while the Chinese firms produced coarser goods for the rural markets. Such an explanation would be consistent with the fact that Chinese merchants continued to control the internal trade of China, excluding only the river trade open to foreign shipping. As for know-how, there is evidence that the Chinese could draw on this from Western enterprises and had the ability to adjust it to local conditions. Little reliable data are available on reinvestment and other financial policies, but there is no evidence to support the fact that Chinese enterprises were less inclined to reinvest or to allow for depreciation than their foreign rivals. Analysis of China's share in shipping is complicated by the existence of cartel-type agreements to which the China Merchants' Steam Navigation Company was an adherent. It is, of course, obvious that China was prevented by the treaties from exercising a monopoly over the coastal and river trade. The figures for mining reflect the limited sources from which ore could profitably be mined by modern methods, *given* the state of transportation and prospecting. But there is nothing in this record which suggests foreign economic inhibition of Chinese-owned, modern-style enterprise.

It is possible that growth of the modern sector, both Chinese and foreign-owned, took place at the expense of traditional handicraft and domestic industries. This is, of course, the Marxist position. Again the figures do not support this position. Ou Pao-san's estimates show that native-style industry produced 72% of the value added by manufacturing industry, ranging from 95% in wood working to 11% in electrical industries during 1933. The modern sector proved more important in coal, pig iron and iron ore production (about 80%), in banking (66%), but was relatively smaller in transportation (42%), exports (23%) and shipping (14%). Significantly, in textiles, so important to the modern sector, handicrafts accounted for 63% of value added. With these figures we show the survival of the native sector, they do not indicate absolute growth. Chi-ming Hou suggests, however, on the basis of his study of shipping, mining and textiles that an increase in both external and domestic demand for Chinese products probably meant growth on the balance for the native sector. This is consistent with the theory of the dual economy in which the growth of the modern sector is limited to certain areas and processes and is fed and supplemented by the traditional industries. They, too, show improved techniques until they become absorbed in the modern sector—or such, in part, has been Japanese experience. The process did not go so far in China and the figures available require further analysis. Tentatively we conclude that foreign investment had on the balance a stimulating effect on the Chinese economy through 1937 and that without it, little if any modernization of the economy could reasonably have been expected.

Nevertheless, in 1937 China's economy was incapable of supporting a modern-type war against Japan. In considering the dislocation and disruption which accompanied the war, we shall be concerned primarily with measures which the Chinese government took to secure resources for that war and with the severe consequence which resulted from these measures. In the final chapter we shall examine first how the new Communist regime effected economic recovery before beginning its first five-year plan.

Chapter V

THE GREAT INFLATION, 1937-1949

The period from 1937 to 1949 is dominated by the generation and development of a great inflation. At a time when the government of China was subjected first to foreign invasion and then to civil war, its financial and economic collapse could be prevented only by that sort of thorough-going reform which had proved impossible in easier times. At no point did the government undertake—or even for the most part propose—measures approximating in their impact those needed for economic stability.

This failure was not a wilful one; it cannot be ascribed solely to corruption and incompetence. The problems were complex and the future not as certain or as obvious as it appears in retrospect. Foreign exchange resources were used to bolster the external value of the Chinese dollar; it is now apparent that such measures, unaided by trade and exchange controls, were impractical and wasteful—indeed, they may have been totally unnecessary. Foreign aid programmes were an innovation and each step had to be discussed, each technique debated. And, as usual, the war lasted longer than expected. The Chinese equivalent of "bring the boys home by Christmas" encouraged short-term policies. The undoubted spirit of the early years could not be sustained, and corruption made impossible the administration of effective post-war controls. The basic problem of public finance was never solved. Currency manipulation and finally police power were resorted to where reform proved impossible, while the civil war prevented the physical reconstruction of the economy. The economic collapse came in the winter of 1948-1949. The modern sector ceased operation awaiting a change of government.

THE 1935 CURRENCY REFORM

The stage was set by the currency reform of 1935 by which China went off the silver standard and established a managed currency. In itself this reform was totally unconnected with the Japanese situation; it had its own logic and necessity. Nevertheless, historically China's move off silver provides a foundation for our discussion. In the following account we shall, therefore, begin with a currency history, proceeding later to describe the course of the inflation and the most obvious causes thereof, emphasising, of course, the impact of government fiscal policy.

The history of currency—with passing reference to exchange rates and to banking—provides more than a background against which to tell the story of the inflation. It is illustrative of the great diversity which continued to exist even within that part of China under control of the national government; a "national" reform was still not nationwide. Secondly, the history illustrates the tendency to tamper with economic factors which can be effectively manipulated, whether or not this will secure the goal desired. There is always the hope that it will, and since the Chinese experience was sufficiently new and complex, no economist or banker appeared to have a monopoly of sound advice.

China and silver. Following the Franco-Prussian War, Germany went off silver: Japan followed the same pattern after the First Sino-Japanese War. Meanwhile with silver production in the United States increasing, the gold price of silver fell from an average of five shillings (sterling) an ounce to one shilling ten-pence in 1915, a fall which closed the Indian mints to free coinage and took the Straits Settlements and Siam off the silver standard. Because of United States silver export policies, the price rose by 1920 to seven shillings and five-pence halfpenny, after which the price declined irregularly— but severely after 1927—to one shilling and five pence by 1933.

136   *A Concise Economic History of Modern China*

TABLE 7. SILVER-GOLD EXCHANGES: SHANGHAI ON LONDON, 1890-1936
(STERLING s/d PER *Shanghai Tael*. TT RATES)

Year[a]	High	Low
1890	5/3⅛	4/2⅝
1897	2/11⅛	2/3¼
1898	2/8⅞	2/5¾
1900	2/11¼	2/8
1902	2/6½	2/1
1906	3/2	2/9½
1908	2/7	2/2⅝
1909	2/5¼	2/3½
1910	2/6⅜	2/3½
1911	2/5⅞	2/4
1913	2/10¹¹⁄₁₆	2/6¾
1914	2/7⅝	2/1⅞
1919	7/10	4/6
1920	9/3	3/11
1923	3/4¼	3/0
1924	3/5¾	3/1¼
1926	3/1¼	2/3
1927	2/8	2/4¾
1928	2/10	2/6¾
1933[b]	1/3¾	1/1⅝
1935[b]	1/8	1/2⅜
1936[b]	1/2½	1/2¼

a.   Years selected are those in which direction of movement of exchanges changed.

b.   Chinese dollar.

Source :   *Chinese Yearbook.*   See also, Table 1, Page 20.

We have stated the adverse effect this fall had on the real burden of China's external debt. Since, however, the debt was largely serviced from the customs revenue, part of the problem of depreciating silver could be solved by paying these duties in gold, a proposition possible after China had regained her tariff autonomy. The 1930 *Kemmerer Report* proposed that China adopt a gold standard, however, with a unit of account to be known as the "*Sun*" to value 60.1866 centigrams of gold. While China did not go on gold—and, as Japan learned shortly thereafter, the great depression would in any case have disrupted such a policy—she did restate duties in a gold unit of account the *Customs Gold Unit* (CGU) valuing an amount of gold equal to the abortive *Sun,* and exchanging with the *Haikwan tael* in which the duties had been denominated at the initial rate of one *tael* to CGU 1.5, a rate which by overvaluing the *tael* compensated for the depreciation of silver which had occurred since the tariff rates had been established the previous year.

The CGU/*tael* rate, that is, the gold/silver rate was changed with movements in the gold market price of silver as reflected in the Shanghai-London exchanges. Traders, hedging against further declines in silver before their duties were payable, opened accounts with the Central Bank of China denominated in CGU. In 1931 the Central Bank began issuing banknotes denominated in CGU, backed 100% in silver, but as their value fluctuated in terms of *taels* (after 1933, the national *yuan* or *dollar* unit of account) and since large customs payments were made by cheque or CGU accounts, few such notes were actually issued.

China had solved one problem caused by adherence to a silver standard. Nor was this reform adversely affected when, from 1933, the price of silver began to rise—to one shilling and seven pence by April 1935—in response to American silver purchase policies. The treaty powers had after all abandoned the gold standard. But the appreciation of silver had other and serious consequences for China. First, there was a drain of silver metal which a Chinese export prohibition failed to check —some 112 million ounces may have been smuggled out in 1935 alone and in Manchukuo the Japanese co-operated with the smugglers. In consequence the Shanghai price index fell from 120 in 1930 and 132 in 1931 to 100 in 1935. A crisis was precipitated, however, by the fact that the silver backing for Chinese banknotes was being exported and by 1934 cash redemption of notes had been suspended. The first proposal to solve the crisis, once the export prohibition was seen as a failure, was a large foreign loan, but the problem proved too great.

China goes off silver. The eventual solution was to confirm the *de facto* situation and to go off silver. Thus China followed the advice of Sir Fredrick Leith Ross, sent at their request by the British Treasury, in setting up a managed, foreign-exchange backed currency. (Hong Kong followed China's lead in December 1935.) The value of the Chinese *dollar* was set at US $0.30 or 1s/2½d sterling, representing at 20% depreciation from the rate at which the Chinese government and the Hongkong and Shanghai Bank had managed to keep the exchanges since 1934; the new rate was some 40% below the silver par. In 1936 the Shanghai price index reflated to 112, in 1937 to 124. Beyond this lay the wartime inflation, but the initial price rises were part of the intended reform and recovery programme.

The assumption of the British-sponsored reform was that the Japanese intentions to China were basically peaceful and that they would co-operate in assisting the stability of the new currency unit. The move to a managed currency assumed also that the currency issue would be centralized in the three government banks—the Central Bank of China, the Bank of China, and the Bank of Communications; that the Central Bank should become independent of the Ministry of Finance and have effective control of the note issue; and that the government should reorganize its finances to eliminate the need for annual inflationary borrowing for current expenses. The reform was to be effected by the surrender by the public of all silver. This silver would be sold to provide an exchange fund in foreign currencies to support the external value of the Chinese dollar. Drastic as the currency reform may seem, it was assumed correctly that the people would accept the measures; they already held *Chinese national currency* (CNC) $453 million in notes of the government banks. And these had, as we have seen, been inconvertible since 1934.

Fiscal policy—latent problems. There was, however, a tradition of inflationary fiscal policy, principally through the sale of government bonds, at considerable discount, to the government banks. These bonds were allowed to stand as backing for the note issue. Although the government banks had been successful in defying earlier government attempts to raid their cash reserves directly, the government's need for funds was supplied in this indirect way. In the event, the Central Bank did not become independent and the government was not able to reform its finances. Budget deficits were at least partially responsible for the subsequent note expansion from the CNC $435 million in November 1935 to CNC $1477 million in June 1937—for only about half of this increase represented notes issued for surrendered silver.

THE CURRENCY UNDER ATTACK

Foreign exchange. Although the mechanics of the initial reform appeared to have been carried out successfully, there were minor inconsistencies. The existence of the *customs gold unit*, provincial note issues, and various units of account still kept China short of her goal of a unified currency. We shall consider this in detail below. But equally significant, the failure to carry out parallel reforms had led, even before the Japanese invasion, to a note issue potentially inflationary. The actual invasion triggered a run on the government banks which marked the beginning of the currency war, countered by the efforts of Chinese to save the external value of their dollar and thus their external credit. By March 1938 agreements with foreign banks to limit exchange transactions had proved inadequate, and the exchange rate fell to almost half in the next 12 months, despite heavy support in the market from China's foreign exchange reserves. In March 1939 the Sino-British Stabilization Fund was established with funds advanced by the Bank of China, the Bank of Communications and two British banks—the Hongkong and Shanghai and the Chartered Bank of India, Australia and China. With £10 million at its disposal the Fund could still not prevent the value of the Chinese dollar sinking to 4.5 US cents in May, 1940, although the German successes in Europe caused a capital flight from Hong Kong *to* Shanghai, driving the rate up to six U.S. cents by April 1941. At that time the Americans entered a reorganized Stabilization Board which operated until 1944, with initial loan funds of US $50 million and $5 million plus additional US $20 million of Chinese government exchange. In July key foreign governments froze Chinese and Japanese funds and instructed their nationals to co-operate with Chinese regulations. The new Board did almost succeed in eliminating black market operations but only at the cost of a further loss of foreign exchange and a lower support price for the Chinese dollar. The outbreak of the Pacific War moved the centre of Chinese international operations from Shanghai to Chungking and marked the beginning of a *de facto* policy of official rates for certain government operations, *viz.* five US cents, and an unofficial or open market rate which by mid-1945 had reached 0.0586 US cents per CNC dollar.

This is, of course, but an outline of a highly technical series of operations designed to meet the foreign-exchange impact of the unexpected events of the Sino-Japanese conflict. But it is illustrative of the sort of economic problems facing war-time China, of the strength of the modern sector, and of the limitation of the Chinese economy. For notice that we discuss this exchange rate problem in completely modern terminology—we do not ask about Confucian philosophy or the Chinese family system. Then too, we are provided with an example of the Treaty Powers—Great Britain and the United States—in an entirely new role of active supporter of China at the government-to-government level. Not for the first time the treaty ports and their separate jurisdiction provided a sanctuary for the legitimate operations of the Chinese. Nor was the currency support operation solely for prestige; a large proportion of the foreign exchange made available was to meet the obligations of the Chinese Government and the import requirements of the Shanghai economy and its hinterland. But as executed the operation was wasteful, for the administrative machinery was inadequate to devise a scheme by which that portion of the demand for foreign exchange arising out of the Japanese currency war or the flight of capital could be identified and checked. Much less could the Chinese government work out a plan for the more rational use of exchange for imports. And the political situation still required China to meet foreign obligations which had arisen from indemnity-forced loans; China's external position was basically weak considering the accumulation of foreign debt contracted originally for non-productive purposes—or for economic facilities fallen into the hands of the Japanese.

The Japanese currency war. The references to the Japanese "currency war" are to the efforts of the Japanese to undermine the Chinese economy through the issue of paper money which would, first, secure them real assets, secondly secure them *fapi*, that is, Chinese legal tender banknotes. The *fapi* were then used to purchase foreign exchange in the supported Shanghai market, in which way the Japanese secured foreign assets at the same time threatening the external value of the Chinese dollar. As we have seen, short of comprehensive controls which the government had no facilities for establishing or administering, there was little the Chinese could do. The Japanese established a Federal Reserve Bank in Peiping (Peking) in March 1938 and its operations were one factor forcing the Chinese to abandon across-the-board support of *fapi*, which, in consequence, depreciated.

Wei-wah money. The Chinese did, of course, attempt to counter this Japanese threat. Typical of the sophistication of the modern sector was the technique used to establish a money in Shanghai which would not lead to a foreign exchange drain. This was effected through the creation of "wei-wah" (*hui-hua*) or transfer money which was made legally unexchangeable for either legal tender or foreign currency. The cash orders of native banks when credited to a customer's account had been traditionally payable the day after maturity, until which date the order itself was negotiable—although at a varying discount. The August 1937 order of the Chinese government in effect blocked both the cash orders, which then circulated as bank-notes, and the accounts they created. Blocked deposits could be drawn out in *wei-wah* instruments but not in *fapi*, and *wei-wah* money could not be exchanged for *fapi* through the banks. New funds, however, could still be transferred from the interior of China and deposited in legal tender accounts and thus used to buy foreign exchange. In June, 1939, the Chinese Ministry of Finance blocked all bank accounts but permitted withdrawals in *wei-wah* orders. Thus, there developed a money usable within Shanghai but under the control of the Chinese authorities. Supplementing this control, remittances into Shanghai were controlled and remittances to Chungking, the war-time capital of Free China, were facilitated. While unable to prevent the depreciation of their currency, the Chinese were by such methods able to keep some controls of the use of their external resources within the context of their overall economic policy.

POST-1935 CURRENCY HISTORY

The customs gold unit. The currency war and the monetary policy of the Chinese government may also be examined through a brief survey of the history of the *customs gold unit* (CGU) already referred to. We have seen that this unit of account valued a fixed weight of gold and its relation to *fapi* after the 1935 monetary reform was determined initially by the market. From March 1938, however, the government allowed a discrepancy to arise between the open market rate and the official rate of exchange, i.e. the rate at which the Bank of China was willing to conduct authorized foreign exchange dealings. CGU continued to be valued according to the official rate and in 1939 was arbitrarily fixed at 1:2.707, thus overvaluing the *fapi*. But the important point is that the CGU, being now in fixed relationship with the standard Chinese unit of account, had lost its purpose, although customs duties and gold movements continued for a time to be stated in CGU. This chain of events also illustrates how a policy to transact business at the open market rate can slide without announcement into a policy of doing business at what the authorities consider the open market rate "ought" to be, i.e. the establishment of a *de facto* official rate, which may result in "other" open market rates being declared "black market" and *de facto* becoming *de jure* ; the government then becomes involved in the enforcement of complex controls in the specific market with, in the Chinese case, disastrous results, including the establishment of a new open market policy and a repeating, at a new and less favourable rate, of the steps just outlined !

In September 1939 the Japanese established their Hua Hsing Bank and issued banknotes at an official exchange rate of one to six pence sterling. To the extent that their control of the coast and the Shanghai area made possible, the Japanese required customs duties to be paid in Hua Hsing accounts or notes, which, of course, resembled the original CGU except that the foreign exchange paid came under the control of the Japanese rather than the Chinese authorities. This effort was not successful in undermining Chinese foreign exchange control measures. In December 1940 the Nanking puppet regime also entered the field with the notes of its Central Reserve Bank, but not even the Japanese welcomed this addition to China's monetary confusion.

The CGU's new role. The theoretical gold content of the CGU was changed for the first time in April 1942 to parity with the U.S. dollar. At this time the official *fapi*-US dollar exchange rate was 20: 1, and, thus the *fapi*-CGU rate was 20:1 at which it remained until the end of its history in the currency reform of August 1948. Although the CGU was now but a multiple of the *fapi*, *viz.* a CNC $20 note, there was apparently popular assumption that there remained some connection between CGU and gold. Accordingly some issues of government bonds were denominated in CGU to make them more attractive. Gold operations, denominated in CGU, continued to be part of the government's anti-inflationary policy. Indeed, had the CGU continued to be tied in value to a fixed quantity of gold, savers might have been induced to deposit funds in CGU accounts as a hedge against depreciation of the *fapi*, but this real role was denied it; instead the government traded on its name, a policy which had been rendered totally ineffective by 1943. Subsequently, the governmen sold gold to absorb *fapi* and to give the people some accepted commodity of accepted stability in which savings could be made. For a brief period only, May to June 1945, the government attempted a gold deposit system; otherwise it depended upon the name rather than the reality and on exchange rate manipulations which remind one of the cash silver manipulations of the Ch'ing and were a prelude to the events of the post-war monetary policy.

With the return of the National Government to east China, the final period of CGU began. Until 1942 circulation of CGU notes had been, as we stated previously, quite limited, and they had been backed by 100% reserves in silver and foreign exchange held by the Central Bank of China. When the Chinese officials came from Chungking to Shanghai, they brought with them new American-printed notes of CGU 1000; these proved more popular than the *fapi* notes and commanded a higher exchange rate with the puppet Central Reserve bank notes—as with dollar coins, the Chinese were still showing preferences apparently not warranted by intrinsic factors, but which were, nevertheless, explainable. The belief in a gold-redemption clause continued. The outcome was that the national government fixed the exchange with the Central Reserve Bank notes on the basis of the market rate for CGU at CGU I : 4000 and, therefore, CNC $1 : 200, a more favourable rate for *fapi* than might have been expected by comparison of prices. This gave to incoming officials a considerable financial advantage but had the effect of raising price levels in Shanghai and contributing to the already serious inflation.

But the main role of CGU in this post-war period was that of second legal tender currency used in the same way as *fapi* but worth in terms of CNC twenty times the face value printed on the CGU note. In the hyper-inflation of 1947 and 1948 these CGU notes could be issued in large denominations, yet worth twenty times their face value in CNC; psychologically this appears to have been important. In 1947, for example, when the Central Bank issued its first CNC$10,000 note, it was the excuse for a panic in the money market, but the contemporary issue of a CGU 10,000 note, actually worth CNC $200,000 seems to have provoked very little comment. Encouraged by this, the Central Bank ceased new issues of *fapi* in

1948 and instead issued large denomination CGU notes, the largest, introduced just before the August 1948 reform, was for CGU 250,000, that is, CNC $5,000,000. With the reform the CGU ceased to exist, but in March 1949 customs duties were again denominated in a separate unit of account, the value of which, in terms of the rapidly depreciating *gold yuan*, successor of the *fapi*, was to be constantly changed to insure that the duty paid would represent the same purchasing power implied when the tariff was established. Still another unit for payment of taxes existed and this was, like the original CGU, linked to gold. Neither of these 1949 units were represented by a money for circulation.

This account of the Customs Gold Unit and the 1949 units illustrates how close the Chinese government came to initiating the fixed-value unit, that is, a unit of account which has a constant purchasing power—at least to the extent that gold has this quality. Later the new Communist government was to use such a unit, tied however to a bundle of consumer commodities, as part of its initial stabilization policy. The National Government could not bring itself to admit the logic of the CGU, especially (as the Hungarian experiment with the "tax-pengo" warns) when fiscal reform was impossible. Instead, the government used the CGU as a psychological trick, which hardly stemmed the tide of inflation.

Exceptions to the 1935 reform. The history of the CGU also illustrates the fact that the Chinese monetary system could still not boast of a single, unified unit of account with monies directly linked to it—and only to it. We would expect, of course, that puppet currency, Japanese military currency, notes of Communist banks, banknotes from border regions, and certain foreign banknotes protected by extra-territorial privileges and circulating because of Chinese confidence in them should exist on the mainland of China, especially in areas not under Nationalist control. Obviously Taiwan and Manchukuo had their own note issue. But, and this is significant, even in China itself there were various units of account and monies circulating after the unification of 1935. The following account may be taken as illustrative of the problem of economic unification in Republican China, even to the end of the Nationalist regime.

Other post-1935 monies in China. First, there were after
the unification of 1935 at least three main units of account :
the national *yüan*, or CNC, represented by the notes of the
government banks, i.e. *fapi* ; the customs gold unit, already
discussed ; and the subsidiary standard in which the notes of
Kwangtung and Kwangsi provinces were denominated. This
last may be divided into silver subsidiary and copper subsidiary
units.

Secondly, there were the various monies. The government intended that all notes should be *fapi* issued by the
three government banks—The Central Bank of China, the
Bank of China, and the Bank of Communications. Later the
continued issue of the Farmers' Bank was admitted. These
were all to be controlled by the Ministry of Finance and a
Currency Reserve Board as part of the scheme to put China on
a managed foreign-exchange standard. The continued issue
of notes by the Farmers' Bank is a significant story. It had
issued notes since its founding in 1933 and in November 1935
had CNC$30 million in circulation. In 1936 the Bank was
given permission to circulate CNC$100 million in rural
areas where the Central Bank had no branches, but by 1937,
the year in which its entire issue was to be retired, this limit
had been exceeded. At the end of 1942 its note issue had
passed CNC$5 billion (1 billion = 1,000 million), and,
despite the fact that official note issue was, after this year,
limited to the native-style banknotes, i.e. notes signed and
dated at the time of issue, the Bank's note were still circulating
in the rural areas as late as 1945.

The noted American numismatist, the late Edward Kann,
estimated that there had been over 30,000 different issues of
banknotes in China since 1900, and it would be unreasonable
to suppose that the currency reform of 1935 suddenly swept
them all away. In the case of the Farmers' Bank, even a
government-owned institution continued in the old ways.
After the reform native banks and foreign-style commercial
banks did continue to issue notes, but, for the most part, they
were notes of the government banks which they obtained on
deposit of reserves, including up to 30 per cent in government
bonds, a provision which was, of course, potentially expan-
sionary and lessened central bank control of the currency sup-

ply.   Nevertheless, from 1935 to 1937 such issues declined significantly in Shanghai, although some remained in legal circulation until 1942. But these were all legally approved exceptions to the unification plan.

The real problem came with the issue of such provincial banks as the Central Bank of Kwangtung, the Provincial Bank of Kwangsi, the New Fu-Tien Bank of Yunnan, and the Provincial Bank of Hopei, which continued their own note issue. The Kwangtung and Kwangsi notes were denominated in "small money" unit of account and passed at a 20 per cent discount against *fapi*. The "small money" unit arose originally from the over-issue of subsidiary coins which had to be used for sums larger than one dollar and passed at a discount against the full-bodied coins when so used—for subsidiary coins contained relatively less silver. As these notes depreciated further, the national government attempted to have them redeemed, but they lasted until the Japanese occupation. The Kwangsi issue persisted until the 1942 reform ; circulation of the depreciated issue of the Fu-Tien Bank also lasted until 1942.

The Provincial Bank of Hopei presents a slightly different situation, for it played a role in the Japanese currency war. In May 1936 the Hopei-Chahar Political Council declared the bank to be government fiscal agent and the note issuing bank for the area and to it commercial banks turned over two-thirds of their silver currency reserves. Thus this bank usurped central banking functions, but in late 1936 the national government repudiated the legal tender status of its issue. Eventually the Japanese took it over, and the silver was alloted to the puppet Central Reserve Bank in Nanking.

Other provincial banks continued, with permission, to issue and at the end of 1942 some 19 such banks were circulating a reported CNC$788 million. Finally, the varying but widespread need for subsidiary monies to replace the copper coinage, now melted down, resulted in decentralizing the responsibility to "local financial organs", which were authorized to issue subsidiary notes against deposits of government bonds and commodities with the central bank. The area of circulation of each issue was intended to be confined to the immediate political jurisdiction of the local body responsible for the issue. These were under the general supervision of the Currency Reserve

Board.   At the same time, the Central Mint issued subsidiary coins which apparently passed at par with *fapi*.   Still another money comprised a subsidiary note issue of the Ministry of Finance itself.

The 1942 currency reform.   Another effort at currency unification and control was made in July 1942.   The main provisions were that note issue was to be concentrated in the Central Bank of China and all other issues were to cease.   As a consequence the provincial issues and the Ministry of Finance subsidiary issues apparently were withdrawn, and the currency of China consisted of *fapi* and CGU of the Central Bank with subsidiary coins and locally issued subsidiary notes under Central Bank control.

Credit control, however, was not centralized in that the Bank of China and the Bank of Communications had authority to borrow from the Central Bank without adequate controls and, therefore, had the same inflationary powers as before. Uniformity was also diminished by the Central Bank's expedient of issuing cashier's cheques in Chungking during 1944 and 1945 when *fapi* notes were in short physical supply—they had to be flown over the Hump from India—and the Fu-Tien Bank followed suit.   On the Burma frontier troops were using three new silver coins denominated in *taels* and minted especially to finance interfrontier operations.   It cannot be said that the unification was complete.

Post-war monies.   With the defeat of Japan, new currency problems presented themselves, problems which were partially solved by abandoning the principle of monetary unity.   In the former Manchukuo, the National Government issued Northeast currency notes at par with the notes of the Bank of Manchu ;   a similar solution was effected in Taiwan where a new issue of the Bank of Taiwan was made legal tender.   These currencies fluctuated in relation to *fapi* and transfer of funds from China to the North-east and to Taiwan was controlled.   The decision to isolate the monetary systems of these areas was sound ;   the Chinese government had decided to change their own monetary unit and meantime wished to prevent the spread of inflation from China to the two relatively stable areas. In fact, the postwar currency reform was postponed until August 1948 and was, as we shall see below, a failure.

Meanwhile, as inflation worsened in China proper, the use of silver, foreign banknotes, and U.S. dollars became more common, while as the Communists gained control of more territory and circulated their own notes, the area of circulation of *fapi* was severely restricted and some elements of the Japanese currency war were repeated. Even prices came to be quoted in foreign units of account, especially the *Hong Kong dollar* and the *U.S. dollar*. Since the government could not keep the market supplied with *fapi* as prices rose in exponential fashion, the local banks issued bank cheques which were echoes of the pre-war *wei-wah* monies. And, finally, *fapi* notes were over-stamped *"Customs Gold Units"* thus increasing their value twenty times. In August 1948 the Central Bank stated that CNC\$600 trillion worth of *fapi* and CGU banknotes were in circulation. The reform of that month was the final effort of the government to prevent complete economic chaos.

THE COURSE OF WAR-TIME INFLATION

Before considering this reform, however, we must return to 1937 and learn the history of the Chinese inflation. Statistics for the money supply are difficult to interpret because of the varying geographical areas of coverage—and this is especially true of the changes in 1945—nor can the figures be as meaningful as those in countries with a more integrated economy. With currency issues totalling CNC\$1.6 million and current accounts at CNC\$2 million at the end of 1937, the rise to CNC\$189.5 million and CNC\$85.6 million respectively by 1944 indicates an almost doubling of the money supply annually with 1942 and 1944 years of exceptionally serious growth. By the end of 1945 the money exceeded CNC\$1.5 billion (billion = 1,000 million) ; 1946, CNC\$9.2 billion and June 1948, CNC\$399 billion. There must be no surprise, therefore, that price levels rose at a rate which can be described as hyper-inflationary (See Table 8). With a 1937 base of 100 Chung-

TABLE 8.   FREE CHINA :   MONEY SUPPLY, 1937-1948
(BILLIONS OF CHINESE DOLLARS)

End of Year	Currency Issues	Current accounts	Total
1937	1·6	2·0	3·6
1938	2·3	2·5	4·8
1939	4·3	3·2	7·5
1940	7·9	4·3	12·2
1941	15·1	7·7	22·9
1942	34·4	16·4	50·8
1943	75·4	24·8	100·2
1944	189·5	85·6	275·1
1945	1,031·9	474·7	1,506·6
1946	3,724·1	5,455·5	9,181·6
1947	33,188·5	27,777·1	60,965·6
1948	196,520·3	202,571·3	399,091·6

Source :   Kia-Ngau Chang.

king prices had reached 569 in 1940, 13,298 in 1943, and
156,195 in 1945.   With the end of the Sino-Japanese War we
should turn to economically important Shanghai, where prices
rose on the same base from 160,315 in January 1946 to
287,700,000 in July 1958, that is, just before the August reform
(See Table 9).   At the end of the war the *fapi* appreciated to
1,222 : 1 U.S. dollar, but by August 1946, the *fapi* dollar rate
was 8,683,000 in the market.

It takes little understanding of economic theory and only
a minimum imagination to recognize that no meaningful reorganization of an economy can take place under such circumstances.   The type of behaviour necessary for this sort of price
increase in the post-war period may be characterized as follows.
Those having goods tried to hold them, selling reluctantly and
only against need even when in the selling business.   Those
with money literally ran or bicycled from the place of payment
to the various markets to exchange money for goods ; in turn,
those in the market attempted the same.   Those wishing to
save attempted to purchase gold or other precious commodi-

ties or foreign banknotes and exchange. There remained an exchange market which did, indeed, fluctuate but its trend was, of course, heavily against *fapi*. There was a flight from money, and prices were rising at a faster rate than size of the money supply, indicating an increase in velocity of circulation and a decreasing real value of the total money supply, a truly hyper-inflationary situation.

The statistics cited are not necessarily accurate, but they indicate magnitudes. All-China figures are available, but errors are minimized by using those for a single city. In the post-war period when the cost of living index determined the wages of Shanghai workers, there was an effort on the part of city officials to show a minimum increase. The index was subject to negotiation with the workers for it was, after all, as significant as a wage negotiation itself, and there was consequent distortion.

Origins. The inflation was generated in "Free China", that is, China under control of the Nationalist Government during the war period. From all that has been said before, it is obvious that this area must have excluded the treaty-port centres of the modern sector, and this is reflected in the figures for manufacturing output : cotton yarn reached a peak of 127,000 bales for Free China in 1943 compared to 2,582,000 for all-China in 1946 ; flour 239 million pounds in 1942 compared to 3,782 million in 1946 ; cement 353 million barrels in 1940 compared to 3,268 million barrels in 1947 ; and other commodities show the same pattern.

Free China, with its industrial requirements for modern warfare, was pushed into the undeveloped interior of China. Electric power, which totalled 3,624 million kwh in 1946, was limited to 196 million kwh in Free China during 1945. That production reached the levels stated during wartime is due, first, to the policy of removal of both government arsenals and private factories from the coastal areas to the interior, to imports of new equipment over the Indo-China railway, and, for scarce but critical equipment, by air over the Hump from India. Some of the reorganizational feats undertaken reached the heroic and might better be told saga-fashion than in an

economic history.   In the key agricultural sector, Free China
controlled some 50% of rice production, 40% of wheat, 18%
of cotton for a fourteen-province area.   Thus there was potentially sufficient to meet her food needs but inadequate transportation and a shortage of cotton.   As the war progressed
Japan tried to reach key food areas and to block still existing
trade routes and in this they very largely succeeded, despite
Chinese efforts.   Both real hardship and lowering morale
resulted as the war continued ;   both had an important impact on the tendency to inflation.

Real shortages may be stated relative to ideal requirements
rather than to demand in the sense understood by economists.
That is, it is possible to have shortage of food in the sense that
average *per capita* consumption is below 2350 per day and yet
not have inflation, providing aggregate demand is suitably
adjusted.   We have yet to consider the basic inflationary
engine in Free China, namely government finance.   The
government's plan to reorganize its finances and operate without continuing deficits was the basis for the anticipated success
of the 1935 move off silver; and indeed a modest surplus was
achieved in 1936-37, but with the loss of revenue involved in
the Japanese invasion and the subsequent increase in expenditures, each year in excess of that planned, the deficits grew
to CNC$133 billion in 1944 and an extraordinary CNC$1106
billion in 1945.   Despite significant efforts to increase revenue,
which reached a low of CNC$315 million in 1938 and rose to
CNC$38 billion in 1944, CNC$1241 billion in 1945, the
government obviously had to depend on borrowing to finance
its operations, and the bulk of this was inflationary in impact
since the government was unable to tap the real savings of the
people—beyond the relatively modest sum of CNC$69 million
(compared to a total expenditure of CNC$2626 billion and
inflationary borrowing of CNC$1316 billion during the
1937-1945 period).

1937-1939.   The course of the Chinese inflation has been
divided into three periods by Professor Kia-Ngau Chang, a
former governor of the Central Bank and an economist.   In
the first period from 1937 to 1939 the Japanese overrode the
most productive areas of China and by the end of 1938 occupied

regions producing 40% of China's agricultural output and
92% of her prewar industrial capacity. The loss of some economic facilities did not, of course, mean that the production
was unavailable to those Chinese people who lived in the
occupied areas—although food became very short before 1945
—but it did mean that the national government lost this tax
base and that goods it wished to purchase were in particularly
short supply. Nevertheless, the government resolved to
counter the Japanese invasion and increased its expenditures
to assist the development of industrial capacity in Free China
and to provide alternative transport routes to the still existing
outlets for foreign trade. Professor Chang sees these additional expenditures as the key to the deficits which generated
the inflation. The national government had neither the power
nor the staff to review its overall programme and cut unessential
while it increased emergency expenditures. Military requests
for funds were apparently granted uncritically, but judgement
on this issue would presumably involve us in an analysis of
military strategy and tactics. Certainly these expenditures
are vital to the economic analysis since they eventually reached
nearly 70% of central government expenditure.

Despite the seriousness of the economic dislocation, the
first two years of the war saw the price rise lagging behind the
increase in the money supply : indeed, prices rose relatively
slowly until the last months of 1939. There were, in fact, off-
sets to the adverse developments. Of the 50 million refugees
who settled in Free China, for example, there were 50,000
trained factory workers and large proportions of the others
could be absorbed into the military services and into the high-
speed construction tasks which kept China linked to the outside world. Thus, production in Free China could show a
significant increase. Secondly, morale could remain high,
meaning in the economic field that demands for wage increases might be temporarily waived, greater exertion than
usual might be expected on war-connected tasks, and the
resulting confidence would permit savings. The role of
government spending was not yet as overwhelming as it
would become. The failure of the Japanese to take the rice-
important area of Changsha had real and psychological impact. With agricultural prices slow to increase and with

government deficits sufficiently under control in a period of high morale and saving, China's economy appeared successful in its heroic readjustment.

1940-1941. The inflationary surge was triggered in 1940 by poor crops, resulting in hoarding and speculation in food. It was supplemented by a drastic increase in government military expenditures and by the continued success of the Japanese in denying outside sources of supply. This included sealing the Indo-Chinese frontier, temporarily closing the Burma Road, and preventing the smuggling of goods from Shanghai into Free China. The outbreak of the European War suggested that no help would be forthcoming from that direction, and the initial patriotism began to be subjected to severe strains. Economic man emerged more conscious of real wages, less willing to save in a currency which was rapidly depreciating. With the index of locally produced Chungking goods at 100 in June 1939, prices had risen to 1303 by the end of 1941 ; the government deficit had increased from CNC$2 billion in 1939 to CNC$8.7 billion in 1941. By the end of this second period (1940-1941), inflation was China's major economic problem ; one which the government would not give high policy priority. When faced with the issue of survival, such monetary matters may seem inconsequential— the government must be permitted to secure the real resources necessary to wage the war. Yet this understandable position ignores the problem of determining which resources are necessary by abandoning the criterion to judge necessity, and, in the case of China at least, military victory in inflation-bred economic chaos proved but temporary. The national government was defeated only four years after victory.

1942-1945. During the third period of war-time inflation the supply situation was crucial. Poor crops were typical of 1942 and 1943, and the improved harvests of 1944 were offset by renewed Japanese military activity in crucial agricultural areas. The Burma Road was again closed, this time until 1945, and materials for industrial production became scarce despite the increasing capacity of the airlift from India. The government deficit continued to increase but at a slower rate, an achievement resulting from both the military situation and new fiscal measures. This generalization does not, however, hold true to the first six months of 1945 when renewed military expenditure and loss of important agricultural areas resulted in a growth of the deficit from a level of 1,532 (December 1941 = 100) to 9,123 ; the index rose to 12,772 by December 1945. Prices of imported goods in Chungking rose on the same base to 198 by June 1942, more than doubling in the first six months of 1944—also a period of extraordinary government deficit—and from 2,940 to 8,610 in the first six months of 1945. Other indices show the same pattern.

The seriousness of the inflation encouraged the government to take drastic steps, short of actually cutting military expenditure, to minimize the government impact on the monetary sector and to keep prices stable by direct interference in the market. Since a large proportion of the budget was directed to the purchase of food supplies, and since food was a significant item in any cost of living or household budget, the government's attention was directed to the necessity of insuring adequate supplies both to the army and to the civil service in the cities. Thus came the June 1941 decision to take back the land tax which had been assigned to the provincial authorities in 1928 and to revert to the Ming dynasty practice of land tax in kind, supplemented by compulsory purchase at arbitrary prices. By "arbitary prices" we mean prices which would have prevailed in the market if they hadn't risen—hardly a sound economic principle.

The securing of tax in kind was the most important single fiscal reform during the war period and was responsible for the slower growth of the government deficit after 1941. The government used its foodstuffs received by taxation and compulsory purchase not only for military purposes but also for "stabilization" of prices and in support of price ceilings imposed by local authorities. Since the government had insufficient supplies to achieve its purpose by periodic selling in a rising market, an undesirable pattern of behaviour developed which was to plague the regime until the end.

To generalize: the authorities would set a ceiling price on, say, rice at about the then market level and would be prepared to support this with government rice purchased compulsorily at this or a lower price ; supplies in the market would prove inadequate and pressures would develop and there would be hoarding ; the government would run out of rice and, unable to support the market, would engage in police measures to force sales of hoarded commodities and to preserve the price levels ; these measures would fail, either through corruption of officials, by the standstill of trade, or by recognition of the facts ; and the government would let the market go for a period, setting a new ceiling and renewing the process. While the ceiling price was in effect, the cost-of-living contribution of, say, rice would not be increased even though effective private transactions were in the black market at a different price ; wages would thus lag. This eventually forced the providing of rice to civil servants, adding a new distribution problem and increasing the number of government officials. At the supply end farmers and landlords were reluctant to part with grain at official purchase prices when black market operations would bring a significantly greater reward ; the cost of collection and prevention of evasion thus rose. This dreary and obvious routine has been stated in full because it is symbolic of the increasing arbitrariness of government economic policy and points to the source of corruption and to discontent of wage earners, especially members of the civil services ; we have here the basis for wholesale demoralization. Furthermore, the government under such neo-Confucian slogans as the New Life Movement and the New Austerity Programme—even Officers Moral Endeavour Association— attempted to substitute traditional morality and patriotism for market realities. This barely operated in the first years of the war and became less so as official philosophy became more paternalistic and arbitrary.

Foreign aid. The record of foreign aid for Free China during the period 1937-1945 is a complex story of countries feeling their way into a method of international finance which has now become commonplace—if not successful. The Soviet Union led the way in 1938 with two loans of US $50 million equivalent each for Russian military supplies. Before the end of 1941 the United States, Britain, France, and the Soviet Union had announced credits totalling US$513.5 million of which, according to estimates of the former Financial Advisor to China, Arthur N. Young, some US$371 million were eventually utilized. American aid to China under the US $500 million credit, of which US$414.3 was utilized from 1942 to 1945, was supplemented by lend-lease totalling US$1309 million. British aid consisted of a £50 million credit, of which some 5% only was used, and lend-lease amounting to US $44 million equivalent. Considering the problems of transporting real goods to China, these sums may well represent the maximum which could be handled—they certainly financed the key items which permitted China to continue the struggle on a national level. The aid was obviously not adequate to offset the inflationary impact of excess demand, for which government fiscal programmes, inevitable as they had to be in wartime, were mainly responsible.

THE FAILURE OF POST-WAR ECONOMIC POLICIES

When the war with the Japanese ended, the Chinese may perhaps be excused for supposing that there was cause for optimism, but it proved an unfortunate indulgence. The temporary dismantling of price controls and emergency government transportation of facilities and the opening of the economy, still under inflationary impact, to the free market were also natural actions considering the inadequacy and abuses these measures had shown. But the facts can now been seen more clearly, and the Chinese had nothing in their economy about which they should have been optimistic. They faced, first, the effects of wartime inflation ; secondly, the effects of wartime real dislocation of resources ; and, thirdly, the continuing "war" situation—this time, civil war.

Redistribution of income. The inflation and government anti-inflationary measures gave rise to excessive corruption and profiteering. Although this was to some extent exaggerated by foreigners who did not understand that traditions of "squeeze", which remained as they were in the Ch'ing, there were, nevertheless, abuses. These abuses were magnified by their ostentation—for example, the importation of luxury foreign items for high officials at great cost over the Hump— by contrast to the privation in which many classes were living, and by the very fact of China's struggle for survival. The inflation first of all eliminated the personal savings held in the form of *fapi* or bank accounts. Arthur Young tells the story of the family who had saved to put their son through college; when his eighteenth birthday came they found their savings just sufficient to buy a cake. In contrast, farmers with rents fixed in CNC or with agreements including the right to purchase their land at a fixed price tended to benefit—at least at first. They later found that their rents were restated in grain, taxes were payable in kind, and they were further subjected to compulsory purchases and excessive tax levies without recourse.

Perhaps the most significant impact from the political point of view was that on the real income of salaried groups, especially teachers and government officials. Skilled workers had to be bid for, employees of private business would do well or poorly depending on the fate of the business. But college teachers, for example, with incomes of 100 in 1936-37 (and cost of living, COL, on the same base) found that by 1940, although their salaries had risen to 224, the COL index was 1,180 ; in 1945 salaries were 1,799 compared to COL of 18,300. Government officials fared about as well, although school teachers fared better. The actual seriousness of these figures would be modified somewhat by availability of rice at fixed prices, but even allowing for this adjustment, the situation was serious. Corruption was a necessity, but while legitimate squeeze can be explained and excused, the excesses alienated the intellectuals, rendered government action uncertain and inefficient, foreshadowing the sort of cynically resigned attitudes which eventually acquiesced in the Communist take-over.

State of the economy in 1946. China's national product in 1946 may have been as much as 20% less in real terms than in 1936. This is hardly surprising if we add to the toll of wartime destruction the severe famines in 1945-46. Wartime destruction accounted for half the locomotives, one-third of the freight cars, and 40% of the passenger cars of the Chinese railways. One-half of China's fishing fleet was destroyed. In the industrial sector there had been severe depreciation, so that statistics of numbers of surviving factories do not tell the true story, mineral production was slow to recover, coal production was but 75% of pre-war, and the stock of farm animals was off at least 20%.

War and famine had dislocated the farm economy, with many able-bodied men migrating to the cities to escape conscription and other abuses. The report of the Joint Sino-American Agricultural Mission submitted in 1948 states the heritage of rural problems which confronted a victorious nation: density of population in relation to soil resources, periodic floods and droughts, poor communications and transportation systems, uneconomic land tenure plans, and high cost of credit, inequitable taxes, lack of improved breeds of stock, lack of farm machinery and fertilizer, ravages of plant and animal pests, unsympathetic state and local administrations, excessive exactions of middlemen and the poor health and educational facilities. This report also contained the first recommendation for birth control to be approved by a Chinese government. If it is true that the National Government could survive only by solving the rural question, it was obviously doomed !

To this list of problems we must add the inflationary exchange rate at which puppet currencies were transferred into *fapi*—this has been discussed above. The threat of civil war decided the national government to keep the military on a war footing, and thus the most significant of expenditures was little affected by the end of the Japanese War. The political uncertainty in north China also prevented the reconstruction of damaged lines of communication, although this task was given priority by the Joint National Government, Communist Party, United States Executive Headquarters established in Peiping (Peking) in early 1946. Production in the modern sector especially in east China, was hampered by the labour dislocation caused by the expulsion of Japanese managers and technicians from China ; production in the Northeast, i.e. Manchuria, was hampered by the removal of equipment by the Soviet Union, by the division of the area between the Communists and the national government as well as by the evacuation of the Japanese.

Despite these obviously unfavourable factors, V-J Day did bring respite, the Chungking cost-of-living index falling from 179,500 in August to 122,600 in September. Prices of gold fell even more significantly. But by October prices were rising again in Shanghai and were double the August level by the end of 1945.

We have now to outline the events to the final effort of economic stabilization in August 1948. To do this we concentrate on Shanghai, and not only because statistics are most readily available for this city. We are, after all, stating that a monetary phenomenon, namely, inflation and then hyperinflation, was so severe that it not only dislocated production but demoralized the body politic. This combined with conventional military defeat in the field caused the disappearance of the national government. But the inflationary impact was on the modern sector—on wages and production, on savings and investment in the great cities, of which Shanghai was typical and most important. It was in Shanghai that the government was put to the economic test and failed.

But as we consider developments here, we must remember that China was still primarily an agricultural nation and that real production depended upon the hazards of nature and war. During the war China had followed a "scorched earth" policy, e.g. the opening of the dykes on the Yellow River which flooded three million acres of land in Honan. Post-war aid of the United Nations Relief and Rehabilitation Administration was instrumental in effecting the resettlement of farmers, and the reestablishment of production in such areas. Again, it must be emphasised that few in China underestimated the importance of the agricultural sector, and with all the efforts of government and international agencies in the immediate post-war period, agricultural production returned to or was a little in excess of the pre-war peak. Then the disorganization provoked by civil war and inflation set in, rehabilitation in north China had practically to cease, imports of foodstuffs forced the terms of trade against the domestic agricultural producer and proved a disincentive to increased production, taxation was excessive and collection erratic. With the exception of embryo projects of the Joint Commission on Rural Reconstruction (China and the United States), an organization to prove so vital to the successful development of Taiwan after 1949, the countryside, i.e. China, had to be left largely to itself.

TABLE 9. HYPERINFLATION : SHANGHAI INDICATORS, 1947-1948
(Jan. 1947 = 100)

		Wages	COL	Banknote Circulation	CNC per US $ 1·00
1947	January	100	100	100	100
	June	339	366	220	741
1948	January	1,450	1,679	1,027	2,370
	June	10,610	8,542	5,667	51,851
	Octobera	679,631	897,458b	106,356	444,444

a. Gold yuan converted to CNC equivalent.

b. November.

Sources : China Weekly Review, Monthly Bulletin of Statistics.

Inflation renewed. In January 1946 Shanghai's cost-of-living index (1937 = 100) had reached 89,924; a year later it was 1,145,000 ; in January 1948 it had reached 11,293,000; and in August, just before the reform, it was 317,152,000. When plotted, the COL trend—and the trends for the price of rice, workers' wages, U.S. dollars and gold—will be found most accurately described by an exponential function, i.e. one which describes an accelerating rate of growth. This is confirmed as reasonable by noting that the government deficit, the most important factor in the inflation given the failure of supply to increase, was four times higher in 1946 than in 1945, 6 times higher in 1947 than in 1946, and 30 times higher (considering the first-half of the year) in 1948 than in 1947 —all estimates are Professor Chang's. A similar relationship exists for government expenditures and the note issue.

We have already written of inflation *and* hyper-inflation, by which distinction we simply refer to the accelerating conditions of an inflation in which the real value of the money supply decreases as psychological factors dominate the income velocity. As Alfred Marshall wrote,

The total value of an inconvertible paper currency therefore cannot be increased by increasing its quantity ; an increase in its quantity, which seems likely to be repeated, will lower the value of each unit more than in proportion to the increase.

Calculating, for example, from the black market rates for U.S. dollars and the estimates of *fapi* notes in circulation, the increase in *fapi* during January and February of 1947 resulted in a decrease in the aggregate value of the currency from US $666 million to US $405 million—and by November 1947 to US $154 million.   In true historic form the greater the issue of *fapi* the greater the outcry against a "shortage of funds", indicating that a public, increasingly reluctant to hold money, was underestimating its needs for liquidity and demanding additional facilities.   Also in classic form, the later stages of the inflation saw depreciation of the currency as a serious obstacle to production and the increasing use of foreign currencies and money substitutes.   Those who experienced the German hyper-inflation following the First World War would have felt at home in the Shanghai of 1947-1948.

Anti-inflationary policies.   The actual course of the inflation was not, of course, as smooth as a formally drawn trend line.   There were periods of relative stability followed by unusually sharp increases in the indices, in a sense bringing the series back on trend.   This reflects Chinese economic policy and should be briefly considered.   Given the failure of the government to eliminate its deficits and of production to increase significantly or of imports to offset the inflationary significance of these two elements, economic administrators could only play for time—hoping that something would turn up, the civil war would end perhaps.   Given the police powers of the government and its ability to stockpile limited key supplies and to schedule imports, it was possible for, say, the mayor of Shanghai to mount a campaign designed to stabilize prices by a combination of operations in the market plus police action against hoarders, speculators, and others.   And this would be especially successful if supplemented with promises of over-all economic reform and good news from the war front.

With equal certainty, the government supplies would eventually run out and it would be forced to withdraw from the market, bad news would come from the war front, or the promised economic reforms would prove impractical. The police action would then become less effective—or bribes more effective—and the inflationary spiral would recommence. Such pauses and their inevitable sequence can be observed following Chinese New Year in 1946 and 1947. Economic reform proposals in early 1948 in connection with efforts to secure U.S. aid—in fact, U.S. $400 million was voted by Congress, probably a maximum given China's absorption capacity—had no lasting impact.

The course of inflation was also affected by specific events, e.g. the famine in early 1946, army interference with rice supplies intended for Shanghai in May 1946, and subsequent orders that the supplies be released. In the immediate postwar period a check on inflation was secured by sale of government property obtained from the Japanese as well as sale of gold and foreign exchange. But these could be but once-only solutions. The combination of adverse circumstances, police action, varying price and banking policies, erratic control of supply could lead eventually only to economic chaos. As Shanghai became in consequence a city of speculation, funds flowed in from the interior, there was a serious flight of capital to Hong Kong and, especially, Thailand, while the level of political discontent mounted with the opportunities afforded "insiders" with advance information on new regulations to make speculative gains. By May 1947 there were at least 300,000 unemployed in Shanghai and workers were urged to show "patriotism and social discipline", a cry which can only be understood in the context of China's history. Summarizing the first half of 1948, the *China Economist* wrote :

> The unprecedented deficit in the Government's budget, the astronomical proportions to which currency inflation has reached, the geometric ratio registered in the soaring of commodity prices, the acceleration of rural bankruptcy, the increased depression suffered by trade and industry, the growing weakness of the financial structure,

and the steady deterioration of the foreign trade situation, were the principal phases of the gloomy picture.

China's foreign economic relations reflected domestic problems and are illustrative of the confusions which were created
by inability to tackle the basic economic problems of government deficit and rehabilitation. Then, too, China faced
a specific problem with regard to the increasing use of the
U.S. dollar both as a unit of account and as a money. The
existence of a gap in purchasing power between two currencies is fatal to that currency deemed to be unstable, and the
actions of the market will increase this instability. This was
China's experience not only with the U.S. dollar but also with
the Hong Kong currency and with the silver coins dug up
from hoards.

Foreign trade policies. More conventional problems also
existed. By 1947 China's external reserves had fallen to the
equivalent of four months' imports and the capacity of her
ports and transportation facilities from the coast further limited the size of her import programme. China's policy was
therefore directed towards discouraging unessential imports
and encouraging exports—which called for a low external value
of the *fapi*—towards keeping the Shanghai COL to a minimum
by cheap essential imports and encouraging remittances of
overseas Chinese—which called for a *high* external value of the
fapi. To achieve this contradiction several combinations of
measures are possible; while supporting the value of the *fapi*,
the Chinese established import controls, a combination which,
if permitting sale of essential imports at a loss, might have
achieved all policy aims except encouragement of exports.
This last was attempted through subsidies, which would have
run against foreign import regulations, but other measures,
e.g. subsidized transportation of foodstuffs into Shanghai, had
the same effect.

Such a foreign trade and exchange policy is, however,
likely to break down into one of multiple exchange rates.
Since the exporter is unwilling to sell his foreign exchange
earnings at an unfavourable rate and since importers denied

licences or official exchange are willing to pay a premium, a black market is created. Since it is almost impossible to control this development, the Chinese wisely accepted it *de facto* and from time to time re-adjusted the official rate. But the changing rules and the licensing and the use of reserves for luxury imports, all these added to the possibility of corruption and to the discredit of the regime caught in so classic a dilemma. That the Chinese were able to finance a continuing and sizeable import surplus in view of the decline of overseas remittances, the burden of foreign debt service, and flight of capital is explained by the fact that exports exceeded the prewar level, by the expenditures of the United States and of Americans in China, and by the funds made available by UNRRA and the United States under various relief and rehabilitation programmes. Finally, in 1948 there was the new U.S. aid programme.

THE LAST CHANCE, AUGUST 1948

Commenting on the introduction and success of the *rentenmark* in the post-World War I German inflation, Bresciani-Turroni wrote :

> Whoever studies the recent economic history of Europe is struck by a most surprising fact : the rapid monetary restoration of some countries where for several years paper money had continually depreciated.

That this monetary restoration did not follow the introduction in August 1948 of the new *gold yüan* is symbolic of the economic tragedy of Nationalist China. The story of this new unit of account and its money can be briefly told, and this will end the economic history of pre-Communist mainland China.

The *gold yüan* was introduced as the sole, legal unit and currency of China, valued at U.S. $0.25. It was to be exchanged with the *fapi* at a rate of 1 : 3,000,000. This currency change was but part of an economic reform package, but before considering this, let us examine the case of the hypothetical Mr. Chang who had CNC $1 million in 1937 and perhaps some notion of the impact of this latest reform can be learned from a very simple example. In 1937 Mr. Chang's savings were worth US $ 333,333. When the Japanese occupied Shanghai, Mr. Chang, who had resolved to hold his savings in the form of notes, was forced to exchange his *fapi* for Japanese puppet Reserve Bank notes at the rate of 2 : 1, so he had CRB $500,000. At the end of the war he changed his money back into *fapi* at 200 : 1, he then had CNC $2,500. Now with the new change, Mr. Chang had, after exchanging at the rate of three million to one, some GY $0.00083 in his pocket, and we might suppose that his support of the national government by now lacked enthusiasm.

There is evidence, however, to support the thesis that many Chinese still supported the regime sufficiently to obey instructions to turn in gold, silver, and foreign banknotes in their possession. The stringent police measures taken in Shanghai in support of the anti-inflationary drive were temporarily successful and superficially there appeared to be grounds for hope. But statistics now available indicate that the promise of the government to restrict its expenditures could not be fulfilled once the Communists renewed their military offensive, as they did in September, 1948. And there is no reason to suppose that many were influenced by the complex currency-backing regulations designed to give the appearance that the *gold yūan* was "fully backed". As with the *customs gold unit*, the use of the word "gold" no longer had economic meaning.

The fight for the *gold yūan* and for stability had been lost by mid-October. Although prices had been temporarily checked in Shanghai they had not in other cities or at the sources of supply. Real shortages began to develop. By mid-September the Chinese began to recollect that, with their savings now wholly in the form of paper money—to the extent that they had obeyed the regulations—they had nothing to fall back on in the event of renewed inflation. In consequence a buying spree developed. Commenting on a wave of coffin buying, one Chinese stated : "A coffin may not be backed by gold reserves, but at least it is worth its weight in wood."

By November the cost of living index for Shanghai (1937 = 100), which had stood at 317 million in August, had reached 6035 million. The note issue in September was already twice that needed to withdraw outstanding *fapi*, and it continued to grow. The currency "reform" had turned out to be currency "substitution". Price controls were lifted in Shanghai, October 31, new regulations were issued, but the hyperinflation continued at accelerating rates.

As the Communist armies approached the Yangtze, the economic focus of Nationalist China moved south to Canton and new currency measures were attempted. Gold was sold by the Central Bank at open market rates from December 1948, a move which emphasised the failure of the August regulations and made a mockery of those who had sold their precious metals to the government at that time. A silver *yüan*, looking something like a U.S. dollar note, was issued in Canton and other fiscal "gimmicks" were instituted—some, no doubt, with temporary success where police or military power was adequate for enforcement. Meanwhile, a new political power was asserting itself, and the People's Republic of China eventually replaced the Nationalist Government in all provinces, with the important exception of Taiwan. Developments both on the Mainland and in Taiwan are the subject of our final chapter.

Chapter VI

ECONOMISM AND CONTINUOUS
REVOLUTION, 1949-1961

After some eleven years of the People's Republic, estimates of food availability in the winter of 1960-61 suggest that the calorific intake was at a low of 1790, where minimum requirements are 2350 or, more conservatively, 2000 per day. (See Table 10.) With disease flourishing because resistance was

TABLE 10. MAINLAND CHINA: ESTIMATED NUTRITIONAL INTAKE
(per person, per day)

	Minimum requirements	1931-37	1958	1959-61
Calories	2350	2200	2200	1790
Protein (grams)	60	71	65	48
Animal and pulse	20	26	21	10
Animal	10	7	6	3
Fat	40	40	32	20

Sources: U.S. Department of Agriculture as quoted by Marion R. Larsen in U.S. Congress, *Economic Profile of Mainland China.* For 1931-37, T. H. Shen, *Agricultural Resources of China.*

low, many were suffering from swelling brought on by nutritional deficiencies. The government has since responded by restoration of private plots and used other means to stimulate production not only of crops but also of poultry and other livestock, with the result that by 1965 calorific intake was up to 2000 per day, with about 80% being supplied by grains and potatoes. *Per capita* production of grains in 1965 recovered from a 1960 low to equal 1957 production.

China has become under the People's Republic one of the potentially great industrial powers of the world. At the end of her first five-year plan in 1957 she ranked third among the nations in the production of cotton yarn, fifth in coal, seventh in pig iron, eighth in cement and paper, ninth in crude steel and metallurgical coke, twelfth in electric power. She has mastered the techniques of nuclear devices ; and she has achieved rates of growth in selected sectors for limited periods which compare favourably with other developing nations.

Has the government of China since 1949 been a success ? The first two paragraphs present a contrast in points of view —if we may accept the validity of the information presented— which make the answer to this question exceedingly difficult. From the point of view of the Chinese government we may ask what her priorities were and whether the policies adopted were suited to their achievement. From a foreigner's point of view we may ask what China ought to have been attempting, but this is not particularly satisfactory. Perhaps we can phrase it differently. There are generally accepted criteria by which an economist might evaluate the performance of a developing nation, and, judged in her performance against these, how does China fare ? Growth in the sense of gross national product is, of course, too simple a criterion. Perhaps it can be extended to read, growth of per capita net national product consistent with reasonably rising standards of living of the people on the average, with achievement of a minimum growth rate for each cultural and geographical region, and with sufficient investment properly planned to permit continuation of the growth. Yet it is quite apparent that even such a qualified set of criteria cannot alone be allowed to establish the answer as to the success of the regime. When Confucius asked a man sorrowing over the depredations of a tiger why he did not remove to another place, he was told, "Here there is good government." Although we study *economic* history, we cannot ignore the non-economic goals of the government.

Yet it is difficult to conclude other than that the policy of the Chinese government on the mainland since 1949 has been, on the whole, less successful than expected or than it should have been, granted the extreme difficulty of ruling China and of devising plans to make significant impact on the agricultural sector. While the constant impinging of non-economic factors on economic policy—politics takes command—may suggest that the government's policies were not primarily concerned with economic goals at all, this would be quite false. The assumption underlying Communist policy has been that correct political policies will liberate the productive force of the people and will result in economic growth far surpassing that which would result from "economism", that is, from following the more generally accepted approach to economic planning.

Thus China's economy cannot be understood without reference to political ideals and goals, but the performance of the government can be measured by the performance of the economy. If the People's Livelihood has any basis as a criterion, the present government has failed ; if a more generous standard is allowed, we can conclude that the government's experiments in development have not been without some reasonable basis but they have been wasteful of resources and have cost China some ten years in legitimately expected growth. Given China's levels of living, this is a high cost. Time has since 1840 been precious in China, yet time has always been wasted at critical periods in the nation's history.

But we must be more specific. The economic history of the People's Republic can be periodized in several parallel categories. From the point of view of predominating macro-goals we can say : 1949-1952 was the period in which the new regime wished to gain control of the "commanding heights' of the economy and reestablish production prior to initiation of a five-year plan in a roughly Soviet model. 1953-1957 was the period of the first five-year plan during which the government sought in conventionally planned ways to achieve a high rate of growth for gross national product, stressing investment in industry, i.e. transferring resources through a real surplus in the agricultural sector. The second five-year plan, 1958-1962, based on similar assumptions was stillborn. It is at this point that the economic history of China takes on its peculiar features. As Walter Galenson has written concerning the problems confronting students of China's economy today :

> In order to qualify as a specialist on Communist China, some degree of immersion in the history and culture of China is essential. Many of us used to argue that a good knowledge of economic theory and statistics, plus an introduction to the institutions of communism, were sufficient background. There may have been some warrant for this view in the fact that during the first decade of their regime, the Chinese Communists were following the Soviet development model quite closely, and adopted many Soviet practices. The Great Leap Forward and its aftermath, plus the break with the Soviet Union, dispelled all illusions about the uniformity of world communism. It became clear that the Chinese style was unique, and that Chinese Communist policy had to be read in the context of the cultural milieu.

From 1958 to 1960 is the period of the Great Leap Forward—and its immediate aftermath—in which the Chinese people attempted to develop an economy which "walked on both legs", attempted, that is, the simultaneous development of agriculture and industry through mass labour-intensive projects while continuing investment in the modern sector. The dislocations which such a policy caused are in an historical sense too intimately connected to be separated. 1961-1965 is the period of recovery in which agriculture was to be taken as the foundation of the national economy, and estimates suggest that recovery in agriculture may have come in 1965, but in industry not until 1970. Since peaks were in 1958 and 1960 respectively, we have the accusation of ten lost years, a period which does not take population growth fully into account ! The stated existence of a third five-year plan (1966-1970) would not affect this periodization or analysis.

Continued recovery would be its theme. Another big-leap has not been scheduled.

From the point of view of economic organization we should add that the period 1951 to 1957 saw the socialist transformation of the countryside ; 1954 to 1957 the transformation of the private sector in both modern and handicrafts industry. Then with the Big Leap Forward came the premature attempt to establish "communism"; in the period of recovery came the retreat to decentralization of the commune and the reestablishment of the peasant's private plot. The outcome of the present (1967) "cultural revolution" may decide the legitimacy of these moves and so the future of the Chinese economy. Until 1958 the political line was not inconsistent with economic planning by experts ; from 1958 to 1960 "politics in command" meant a downgrading of the expert and assertion of the "mass line"; after 1961 the "mass line", while not formally abandoned, was in practice modified, and this modification was a target of the 1966-67 Cultural Revolution with its espousal of the "continuous revolution". Thus policy has veered from compatibility with the Soviet line to a new, almost desperate attempt to disprove the law of diminishing returns and to achieve, by the will of the people, an unprecedented rate of economic growth, hence the title of this chapter, "Economism and Continuous Revolution". Taiwan has, of course, chosen the former.

People's Republic : Years of Growth, 1949-1957

The presently embattled Chief of State Liu Shao-ch'i has stated the traditional Chinese Communist position thus :

> The road we are taking is the road traversed by the Soviet Union. The Soviet road is the road all humanity will eventually take, in accordance with the laws of development of history. To bypass this road is impossible. We have always believed that Marxism-Leninism is universal truth.

If we take this as the underlying principle of the period from 1949 to 1957, we have a certain unity of approach which permits assessment. While the government made mistakes during this period, its overall record was such as to permit it to exalt in such publications as *Ten Great Years* (including the first years of the Great Leap Forward) and to provide a model which was seriously considered by developing countries. Some economists compared Chinese and Indian growth as if the applicability of communism or democracy was being weighed in the balance. And although we cannot accept China's own estimates of her growth, net domestic product (NDP) did grow at an average 6% per annum during 1952-1957 and there is evidence of some (1.9%) growth in *per capita* consumption. When this was compared to the postwar record of the Nationalist Government, the communist achievement appeared all the more significant; when judged against the background of the successful social revolution which was proceeding concurrently, the future of the People's Republic seemed assured. Nevertheless, there were within the economy itself seeds of conflict which, when combined with political doctrine, were to cause the party to chart a new and dramatic course.

Statistics. But before examining this record, we should state briefly one or two problems of interpretation. First, this was not necessarily a period of centralized planning, Soviet style. Alexander Eckstein concludes that central planning in any operative sense was restricted to the years 1956-1957, that is, for only two years of the People's Republic. In a sense the first years of the plan were years of annual estimates not centrally directed. And, given the limitations of the statistical system, this is not surprising.

Secondly, what of the statistics ? Certainly the coverage and professional quality of China's statistical services developed significantly after 1952 ; certainly also no attempt was made to keep two sets of books, i.e. to present intentionally, false figures to the public. But changes in coverage present a problem and have been interpreted either to mean that the statistics became gradually more accurate or that, while early errors were subsequently corrected, later figures are subject to the distortion of reporting under the pressures of plan-fulfilment, despite improved technical quality of the statistical service. Under either set of circumstances, however, growth would be exaggerated, either because the early years were understated or because the later years were overstated.

How then is it possible to write of rates of growth of, say, 1.9%? Why do we quantify aggregates in this period but reject practically all those for previous periods—indeed, we have been reluctant to provide statistics for the Ch'ing and early Republic in this introductory study. The answer may well be that we are mistaken to do so, that the statistics continue to be misleading and that a qualitative, non-quantitative judgement of contemporary China is required. We find it difficult to accept this conclusion. We consider that, unlike previous periods, a mass of detail collected on mainland China has been subjected to the most critical analysis by highly-trained professional economists and that their results, qualified as they themselves have done, must be studied. Any qualitative judgement is dangerous which does not take these economic and statistical studies into account.

Thirdly, for those more concerned with the Chinese than with China, there is the population problem. Population statistics, too, have been subjected to analysis by experts but the results are less satisfactory. While an official estimate for 1968 was 750 million—although this may have been little more than an uncritical political announcement—foreign observers had assigned a 1965 total exceeding 750 million with a growth rate of 2.5 per cent. The difficulty is both with the 1953-54 enumeration and with subsequent follow-ups, which have proved inadequate for demographic analysis. For even the 750 million figure is considerably less than the *maximum* model projection of 875 million! John S. Aird's projections for 1965 vary from 715 million to 875 million depending upon the assumptions considered most likely ; for 1985, projections vary from 859 million to 1298 million, with some models showing China crossing the billion mark by 1975. Government population policy has varied from exaltation in the productive power of the masses—and thus the desirability of a large population—to the need for control with an emphasis on quality, i.e. education. The former was stated in 1952 and was current during the Great Leap Forward.

Efforts at control were relatively ineffective during the period 1954-1958, natural forces took over in the food shortages of 1959-1961, and, more recently, efforts to encourage later marriages, spacing of children, even sterilization are too new to be fully evaluated. But in all considerations of the Chinese economy, this dearth of population data must be remembered.

Finally, in considering the early achievements of the People's Republic, one must remember the important role of Soviet economic aid ; in taking into account the performance of the economy in comparison to that under the Nationalist government one must also remember that the Communist victory ended their destructive role and permitted the growth which any government would naturally seek.

Rehabilitation, 1949-1952. In many ways the period 1949-52, although less interesting to development economists than the subsequent years, was crucial to the whole economic history of the People's Republic. From a theoretical point of view only very rapid initial growth, i.e. recovery, could create that temporary surplus which would permit real investment in industry. This, together with Soviet aid, would prove the base for economic development. From the political point of view these years would show whether the Communist Party which had already some considerable administrative experience in the Upper Yellow River areas, could achieve control of the economy. With the apparent burden of a Korean War, would the Party be able to mobilize both people and other resources to reconstruct what twelve years of war had torn down ? The success of the new government in achieving its goals confirmed its reputation for success and made its direction of the first five-year plan psychologically less demanding.

By 1952 Communist estimates of national income were 69 million *yüan*, or with an index (1949= 100), 170, probably an underestimate. Ta-Chung Liu has compared his estimate of 60 million 1952 *yüan*, for 1933 with his revised estimate of 71 million *yüan* for 1952 and has concluded that, relative to this "normal" pre-war year of 1933, 1952 showed 20% gain (or 6% *per capita*), and that reconstruction had been completed. How was this achieved ?

Perhaps the most watched development was the successful check on the inflation during 1950 by a combination of techniques not dissimilar from those of the Nationalists but wholly different in their consequences because of the changed environment and enforcement of significant ancillary measures. Thus the new government instituted a savings campaign including bank accounts and government bonds denominated in a unit of account linked in value to the price of a bundle of consumer goods, i.e. a unit with a guarantee of fixed value not in terms of gold or some other metal but in terms of everyday commodities. The government coupled this with an intensive sales campaign directed at the well-to-do persons anxious to prove their loyalty to the regime. While the Nationalists had specifically rejected the commodity link, they had during the war attempted to sell foreign exchange and gold bonds—although they were forced to change their redemption plans. But the Nationalists knew the dangers of such commodity-related currencies unless the real situation could be changed. This the Communists did with the re-establishment of communications, the co-operation of business under the Common Programme, and the improved administration of the countryside with trained and honest cadre. The Nationalists too had tried coercion in their economic measures, but this had simply led to more corruption or to open defiance. The Communists, with the Korean War to rouse anti-foreign and unifying feelings, and with the usual advantages of a new government, were successful.

The checking of the inflation was only part of Communist monetary reform. Although interest rates were brought down as the inflation subsided, the monthly rate did not go below 2%, reasonable in a time of capital stringency. Nationalist low interest rates—they assumed interest to be a cost of production and thus a cause of inflation—was in fact a subsidy to those assigned official loans. At best the policy had led to a mis-allocation of resources, at worst it fed the inflation. At the same time the new regime centralized the banking system and initiated a plan whereby payments between government units and nationalized industries were made only by book-keeping transfers and not through cash payments. This permitted control of each transaction, and although this control was only as effective as the real plan on which the control decisions were made, it subjected the monetary sector to the state planners. Cash payments outside the socialized sectors were also tightly controlled ; later when they were excessive, that is, created an unwanted increase in aggregate demand, savings and bond campaigns could be initiated. But as S. C. Tsiang has pointed out, these were at least semi-fiscal in nature. Monetary policy played a subordinate and an accommodating role ; the monetary sector, which had played so spectacular a role in the Chinese economy since 1937, had been tamed.

Perhaps an even vaster task was achieving control over the commanding heights of the economy. This did not mean complete socialization. Chairman Mao Tse-tung had long enunciated two principles ; first, that the revolution must proceed through all its stages, that is, one could not proceed directly from feudalism to socialism without the bourgeois-democratic revolution—even if this was to be subject to the leadership of the Party, and, secondly, that all but a very small percentage of the Chinese people—all except such imperialist lackeys as compradores, the militarists, and the bureaucratic capitalists—were salvageable and could be taught to serve the revolution. Thus the so-called national bourgeoisie were expected to participate as partners in the reconstruction plans —indeed, the government of the People's Republic was, theoretically, not a dictatorship of the proletariat at all but simply under proletarian leadership and included representatives of other parties, e.g., the progressive elements in the Kuomintang. The Communists did not, therefore, seek to destroy those national bourgeoisie who could alone manage the modern sector of the economy, but, even then, by simply confiscating the property of bureaucratic capitalists and taking over government enterprises, the new regime had control of the commanding heights of the modern sector. Foreign property, other than American, was not confiscated, but high taxes and forced wage agreements soon led to the retirement, except in a few token offices, from active business and, in many cases, of foreigners to sale of their property for taxes.

At the same time in the countryside the Communists began their promised land reform, involving in the process the death of at least two million landlords. "Revolution is violence", wrote Chairman Mao. The redistribution of land took place after "struggles" which created revolutionary situations and permitted the people to pass through the appropriate historical stage. Thus the land redistribution apparently represented not simply the consequence of government decrees—for Chairman Mao felt this would be too easy to reverse—but rather the result of the actions of the people themselves properly led, of course, by that class-conscious element of the proletariat, the Communist Party. The basis had been set for the collectivization which was to follow.

If these tasks seemed proof enough that the Communists had been granted "the mandate of heaven", it must be remembered that they were achieved while China was fighting a significant, though limited, war against the United Nations in Korea. But this, startling as it may at first appear, is easiest to explain. China had a large, trained, and experienced army already in the field ; she had weapons and supplies captured from the Japanese and the Nationalists as well as new military aid from the Soviet Union. Although her casualties were large, they were small in relation to population, and, of course, United Nations forces refrained from damaging China's exposed industrial base.

Basis for the five-year plan, 1953-1957. Although China's modern sector was limited compared to that of the Soviet Union at the beginning of the latter's first plan period, China at the end of 1952 was better prepared than ever before to undertake rapid modernization of her economy. For the first time since the end of the Ch'ing, the country was really politically united and, perhaps for the first time in her history (would the Ch'in be an exception)? was under central government control in an administrative sense. Banditry had been suppressed, local and clan power structures had been broken— even though the new regime would not be completely free of provincial power developments. In the economic sector there was fiscal and monetary stability, improved economic administration, and a beginning made on essential services from dyke repair to health and education. And finally, there was the promise of Soviet aid for the projected first three five-year plans (1953-1967).

Soviet aid. Since Soviet assistance continued to 1960 when advisors were withdrawn—Chinese training in the Soviet Union itself continued on a decreasing scale through 1966—and since it was planned originally to extend over three five-year periods, i.e. from 1953 to 1967, its scope and impact may perhaps best be considered at this point. On a material basis Soviet aid was to consist of 300 industrial plants worth an estimated U.S. $3 billion, including steel mills, electric power, machine-tool, aircraft, chemical, electronic, and agricultural machinery plants. They were so designed and scheduled that they were to fit into the five-year plans as needed, and the plans themselves were to be drawn up on Soviet principles with the advice of Soviet economists. Technical assistance was a vital part of the Soviet aid package ; indeed, as Arthur G. Ashbrook, Jr. has observed,

> ..the Chinese communists were in the enviable position of skipping the costs and delays involved in (*a*) research and development, (*b*) design and blueprints, and (*c*) testing and evaluation. History gives no parallel example of a nation being offered a complete industrial system on a platter.

When the Soviet advisors left China in July 1960, their blue-prints with them, about 150 of the scheduled plants were in operation, but the Chinese were not prepared to take over responsibility for them nor had they the spare parts or the know-how to keep them in operation. By 1964 China's debts to the Soviet Union, for aid and other transactions, had been completely repaid, and China was, unnecessarily but inevitably, on her own. Although China paid for her aid in commodities needed by the Soviet Union, it is apparent that she was the net beneficiary from the relationship. But the political price was apparently too high.

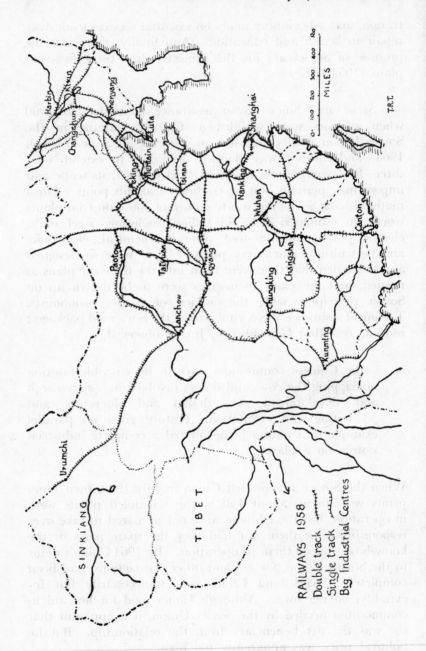

RAILWAYS 1958
Double track
Single track
Big Industrial Centres

Growth, 1953-1957. Estimates of growth during the first five-year plan vary from 5.6% average annual rate (Yuan-li Wu) to 8.8% (reconstructed Communist estimate), but the estimates of Ta-Chung Liu and K.C. Yeh giving 6% for net domestic product (NDP) have such a weight of research and professional skill behind them that we have, for the purposes of this history, accepted their validity. This gives a per capita annual average increase, assuming 2.3% population growth, of 3.6%. Lower still was the growth of household consumption, which Liu and Yeh estimate at 1.98%, a figure sufficiently low to bring into question whether there was any significant increase at all, and certainly the per capita level had not, by 1957, reached that of 1933.

TABLE 11. MAINLAND CHINA : GROSS DOMESTIC PRODUCT

	Total (billions of 1952 yüan)	per capita (1952 yüan)
1933	59·5	119
1952	71·4	126
1957	95·3	150
1958	108	166
1959	104	158
1960	96	143
1961	92	135
1965	108	150

Source : U.S. Congress, *An Economic Profile of Mainland China,* 1933-1957 estimates of T. C. Liu and K. C. Yeh: 1958-1965 exploratory estimates of T. C. Liu.

It would be wrong, of course, to judge the Chinese performance of growth by household consumption, because the plan was following the Soviet model. This calls for allocation of all surplus, after a minimum for consumption and an agreed level for the military, to investment, with heavy industry having highest priority, agriculture lowest. Gross capital forma-

tion was some 24% of GDP with an incremental capital-output
ratio of 3.9 (gross, total). Alexander Eckstein has estimated
that the percentage of investment in heavy industry increased
from 30 in 1952 to 44 in 1957, while that in farming decreased
from 14 to 9. His figures differ from Liu and Yeh, but all agree
in showing household consumption as a decreasing share of
the NDP and fixed capital formation as an increasing share;
defense was constant at 10%. In consequence of this investment allocation, we find, as expected, that the share of agriculture in the NDP declined, that of manufacturing, mining, construction, transport, etc. increased ; Liu and Yeh's figures
indeed show the former falling from 48% to 39% and the latter
rising from 20% to 30% of NDP. (In 1933 agriculture's share
was about 60%.)

These figures suggest that the Chinese government was
succeeding in carrying out a Soviet model development plan,
not as well as their own figures indicated, but certainly with a
degree of success comparing favourably with other undeveloped countries. One figure particularly, however, failed to
match the others—employment only rose 1.5% annually on
the average, and this would cause problems which contributed
to China's decision to abandon Soviet-type planning. There
were others. The stagnation in agriculture—and per capita
availability of foodstuffs during 1953-1957 period has been
estimated by Eckstein to have grown at 1.5% a year with the
possibility that even this growth is due solely to statistical
bias—the ending of Soviet credits, and the fast growing
population in the cities were problems which, when viewed
in the perspective of the developmental tasks remaining, must
have tended to frustrate the leadership. Their own figures
showed over 8% annual growth, but what is 8% compared
to the tasks ahead? Are the Chinese people to be limited and
bound by the faulty vision of Soviet planners, are they to be
tied to an alien model ? Was there nothing Chinese and
spectacular about the period 1953-1957 that could give the
Party inspiration for the development of a Chinese model ?
To the revolutionary the progress since 1952 seemed but the
plodding of a new bureaucracy, of a new class of experts; the
revolutionary took comfort in the socialist transformation of

the countryside and sought the solution for the future from this success. We must, therefore, consider the structural changes in the Chinese economy during the first plan period.

Structural changes. Despite their wide administrative experience before coming to power in China, the Communists could not immediately take over and themselves operate every facet of government and economy. In towns, for example, they might wait a year or more, studying, learning, before suddenly arresting reactionaries and moving, as it were, from the bourgeois-nationalist to the proletarian revolution. Thus the differing accounts of foreigners who left China in these early days of the regime can be partly accounted for by considering the stage the Communists had reached in their particular location. And so it was in the modern sector of the economy. The Communist government first focussed on certain foreign-run utilities, keeping the foreigners available until they were prepared to take over completely. In the Chinese-owned private sector, national bourgeoisie were permitted to continue in ownership, labour demands were toned down on Party instructions, and control was maintained by the banking procedures already touched upon. It was thought—perhaps even by the Party itself in the very first day—that this situation would continue for a considerable time, probably for fifteen years, but this is the age of compressed schedules and socialist transformation was completed in five.

The general line of the Chinese Communist Party called for the socialist transformation of agriculture, handicrafts, and capitalist industry and commerce. In 1950 regulations were promulgated requiring private industry to work only on approved plans and projects, but the atmosphere was still one of national co-operation. A change of tone came suddenly in the 1952 *wu-fan* or five-anti's campaign—anti-bribery of government workers, tax evasion, theft of state property, cheating on government contracts, and stealing economic information. This campaign was carried out in the now familiar method of mass denunciations and abject confessions. In an investigation of 450,000 private undertakings, some 340,000 were said to have committed "various illegal trans-

actions", and we are not suggesting that, given the broad
definitional base of the offenses, this figure is too high. But
the resulting fines and the "forced" savings reduced the liqui-
dity of the private sector and placed it even more firmly under
government control, while businessmen themselves were
afforded a more realistic view of their role in a socialist economy. Chu-Yuan Cheng has shown that the socialist transformation began with the Communist take-over in 1949 when
some 63% of industry (by gross value of output) was in private
ownership, 2% was state-capitalist joint ownership, and 35%
wholly state-owned. In the natural sequence of business
events this had changed by 1951 to 50%, 4% and 46% respectively, although a high percentage of private industry
was in the vulnerable position of executing orders and processing goods for the state. The role of private industry was
further weakened in 1952-1953 and the final transformation
took place from 1954 to 1956, by the end of which year 68% of
industry was state-owned, 32% were joint state-private enterprises. A similar pattern is apparent for the commercial sector.

The socialization can also be described in terms of the payment of private capitalists. (This has a rough parallel in the
agricultural sector.) First, private firms dealing with state
industries were guaranteed a "fair return", which was severely
restricted in 1953. In the second stage, the private businesses
were subjected to joint state-private operation, in which the
return to the capitalist depended still on the profits of the
business and on his ownership rights but was shared with the
state. Finally, in the third stage the business was taken over
by the state and the former owner recompensed by a guarantee
of 5% interest on the value of his property, which interest was
to be paid for seven years—later extended to ten.

In the countryside embryonic socialism in the form of
mutual-aid teams and elementary co-operatives was encouraged
as early as 1961, but the pace of socialization accelerated and
by 1957 was virtually complete. This process has often been
considered a cynical betrayal of the peasant who had been
promised his own land under the land reform programme,
but the fact is that the economic forces which originally diffe-

rentiated the income status of the rural population continued under Communism; land reform in the sense of land to the tiller and the inevitable small-holdings which this creates can be both undesirable and impossible. The evidence suggests that even in 1952 a reconcentration of holdings was apparent, the size of land holdings was uneconomical, the elimination of landlord had also eliminated the source of rural credit, and the fragmentary holdings increased in number by allotment of land to soldiers and other beneficiaries of the regime would preclude any rational, centrally-inspired development programme.

If the position in the countryside is not held by socialism, capitalism will assuredly occupy it.

Mutual-aid teams are an essential element of rural life and not necessarily connected with socialization; in China, however, they were the first step in a logical process forced by the economic realities of the agricultural sector and by the policy of the Communist Party. Such teams, of course, although they overcame some of the problems of small holdings by peasants, furthered the position of the better-off peasants by insuring them additional income from the use of stock and equipment. This "contradiction", i.e. growing personal wealth in a socialist society, led to a policy of encouraging formation of "elementary co-operatives", in which payment to the members was based not only on work performed but also on property and equipment brought into the co-operative. By the autumn harvest of 1965, 16,900,000 peasant households or 14% of the total, were members, despite widespread peasant opposition. This opposition provoked an intra-Party debate in which Chairman Mao Tse-tung insisted that the pace be not only maintained but increased to enable the agricultural sector to serve the requirements of the five-year plan and to prevent a resurgence of capitalism. A year later, in 1956, a programme of organizing advanced co-operatives similar to the Soviet *kolkhoz* was instituted. By the end of the year 96% of rural households had joined co-operatives, by the end of 1957 the task was completed with 120 million households in some 752,000 units, of which 668,000 were advanced-type co-operatives. At this stage individual ownership rights were lost to the co-operative and payment was for labour alone, although a key policy question remained unresolved, *viz.* the right of the peasant to auxiliary income from private plot or livestock. This problem remains a basic issue to this day, materially affecting total output of the agricultural sector.

Although the co-operative movement arose from the needs of the economy, it too had its contradictions, for now the issue arose as to incentives, management, and subsidiary activities, all part of the natural balance of rural life which had been tampered with. The question the government had to face was whether to solve these by economic means or by non-economic means; the former solution would be more in keeping

TABLE 12. CHINA AND SELECTED COUNTRIES :
INDICES OF INDUSTRIAL PRODUCTION

	Mainland China	Taiwan	India	Japan
Prewar[a]	37·1	n.a.	58	64·6
1949	27·2	39	67	32·5
1952	56·1	65	76	57·7
1957	109·4	113	104	116·3
1958	143·8	122	107	114·7
1959	181·6	138	117	137·5
1960	188·5	157	130	171·2
1962	109·6	195	150	221·1
1965	147·6	312[b]	184	298·1

a. 1933 for China, 1937 for India and Japan.

b. Or 336 if the *IFS* index excluding sugar is used.

Sources : *IFS* and R. M. Field in U. S. Congress, *An Economic Profile of Mainland China.*

Note : These figures show average annual growth rates from year of recovery of pre-war peak (India, 1951 ; China, 1955 ; Japan, 1955) to 1965 of 6·7%, 6·4% and 13·8% respectively.

with Soviet planning, the latter with what became the Great
Leap Forward, with "continuous revolution". In 1957 the
Party inclined towards an economic solution including a rational plan of management, concessions to well-to-do peasants
which enabled them to maintain some private property, and
general concessions in permitting members to raise domestic
animals, draught animals and poultry on their own account.
But by April 1958 the first commune had been established and
these policies temporarily reversed.

Eight great years ! What then did the Chinese economy
look like after eight years of the People's Republic and five
years of planned development ?

First, there was much the Chinese government could take
pride in, even though their statistics dangerously exaggerated
the progress. We have already considered the various rates of
growth, but we should stress again that the Chinese measure of
success was based upon growth in industry, especially heavy
industry, and these had responded to development policies.
Output of crude steel, for example, had risen from 1.35 million
metric tons in 1952 to 5.35 million in 1957; there had been an
increase in petroleum from 0.44 million metric tons to 1.46
million; electric power from 7.3 to 19.3 million kwh; cement
from 2.9 to 6.9 million metric tons. High rates of growth were
shown for non-ferrous and ferrous metals, chemicals, machines,
building, and paper manufacture. And the socialist transformation had been completed. But for all this, the regime had
to face dissatisfaction in the countryside and stagnation in agriculture, which, if permitted to continue, could undermine
development in the industrial sector where growing unemployment and underutilization of plant were threatening.

We may conclude that the progress of these first years was
flawed, not disastrously, but sufficiently to force the regime
to reassess its programmes. Yet there was nothing in the
record to 1957 to suggest that this reassessment could not have
taken place within the context of the three five-year plans
which were basic to Soviet economic co-operation.

THE GREAT LEAP FORWARD

Into the Great Leap Forward the Chinese threw all their frustrations, their dreams, their anti-foreign proclivities, their revolutionary zeal, and their hopes for progress. The cost : ten years of economic growth lost—perhaps more, for the temptation to try the impossible again is ever present and the favourable circumstances of 1952—successful reconstruction and Soviet aid—may not be duplicated. The whole tone of Chinese economic policy changes in 1958 and we must, in a sense, make a break with the former period as firmly as we did with the 1949 disappearance of the nationalist government. But, while we must consider this new tone and the economic philosophy behind it, we must also recall that the circumstances of 1957 were not wholly satisfactory and that some re-evaluation was called for. There was economic reason behind the Great Leap. And to understand how apparent initial success of the new policy could so quickly degenerate into chaos, we must remember in what follows that a one or even two-year extraordinary growth in GDP is extremely easy to achieve. Thus the greater than average growth of GDP in 1958 should not be surprising—anyone can work longer hours or keep a machine running longer if only he doesn't try to keep it up too long or care what the extra work produces. Now let us examine the post-1957 record.

National income statistics. During the first year of the Big Leap Forward, 1958, official Communist figures show a 30% growth of NDP for an economy which, up to that year and under the Soviet planning model, had been increasing—again by official figures—at some 9% on the average. Statistical analysis of this and the following years with the same level of intensity as during the first five-year plan is impossible due to the changed function of the statistical services and subsequent refusal to publish any significant or consistent series, but Ta-Chung Liu's "exploratory estimate" suggests that the actual growth was closer to 14%. Were such a figure part of a consistent trend, it would be impressive; as an isolated event it is a sign of poor planning. Indeed, in 1959 Liu's estimates show a decline in NDP, while official figures insist on continued growth. We may assume, however, that the People's Republic reached a peak NDP in 1958 with a total 108 billions of 1952 *yüan* (71 billion *yüan* in 1952), that a low was reached in 1961 with NDP at 92 billions of 1952 *yüan*, and that the 1958 level was not again reached until 1965.   Per capita figures are, of course, more depressing, for 1961's level brought the economy back to the 1955 figure of 135 (1952) *yüan*, and it has not yet (1966) recovered the 1958 peak of 166 *yüan*.

United States Department of Agriculture estimates for food crops show a similar pattern; a significant increase from 185 million metric tons in 1957 to 194 million in 1958 followed by a decline and a low for 1960 of 160 million.   In 1965 food crop production had about returned to the 1957 level.   Cotton on the other hand has not so recovered, with a peak of 1.9 million bales in 1958 compared to 1.6 million in 1957 and 0.9 million for each 1961 and 1962, with only 1.3 million for 1965. Official estimates for the 1958 food crop were originally 375 million tons, that is twice the 1957 level.   It is absolutely essential to accept the fact that the Chinese themselves believed these figures (as did some non-Chinese—but that is another story).   Subsequently the Chinese admitted error and revised their estimates down to 250 million, i.e. still about 55 million too high.   Reports of food shortages were assumed to be the result of transportation bottlenecks, presumably as the railway system struggled with the bumper harvests. Indeed so complete was the government's acceptance of reports from the field that they announced a new "three-three" system, in which one-third of the land would be put to forest and one-third left fallow to prevent overproduction of food.

In the industrial sector recovery has been faster with 1959-1960 peaks recovered by 1963 and continued progress in selected industries.

"Pantsless Communism".   Obviously the Great Leap Forward failed, and equally obviously the Chinese were slow to discover the facts, slower still to admit failure.   But "failure" implies that something was being tried, and that this "something" was sufficiently important to form the basis of a funda-

mental struggle not only within the Chinese Communist Party
but also between this party and the Communist Party of the
Soviet Union. The disagreement has been characterized by
the leading participants, both extremely literate in their
particular mediums, as "pantsless" versus "goulash" communism.

We know too that a "leap" in communist jargon suggests
a qualitative as well as quantitative change, and thus the
importance of 1958-1959 rests not only with the figures but
also with the methods. Underlying it all lies the relevance
of Chairman Mao's theory of continuous revolution ; in a
sense the uniqueness of the Chinese revolution was being
tested. To admit the revolution failed is impossible for a
Party member : he is thus faced with one of two choices,
either the Leap need not have failed had it been carried out
with proper revolutionary fervor or the Leap philosophy
is not an essential element of the Chinese revolution, which
can, therefore, consistently follow Soviet models at the present
stage. If we are permitted the right to grossly simplify
these political complexities—and surely an economist may
be permitted to do so—and if we were to personify, we should
have something approximating an explanation for the intra-
party struggle between Chairman Mao Tse-tung and Chief
of State Liu Shao-ch'i which appears to play so significant
a part in the Cultural Revolution as seen in early 1967.

Chairman Mao had written of the great power of the
Chinese people if only their productive potential were
liberated. While economists considering the law of diminishing returns and possible additions to both land and
capital might suppose that China was burdened by too great
a population. Mao saw the people as China's strength. Or
as Liu Shao-ch'i then put it : "Man should be viewed as a
producer rather than a consumer", thus reversing the Sun
Yat-sen approach. But to be practical, the question should
first be put this way: Are there techniques, labour-intensive
in nature and as yet untried, which could make a significant contribution to the output of the agricultural sector ?
And again, if these techniques require longer hours or harder
work can the peasant be induced to undertake them without

increased material reward ?   And finally—this is a somewhat different problem—are the peasants underemployed so they can be used on a wide variety of Labour-intensive projects not directly connected perhaps with production on their own co-operative (or, later, commune) ? The Party under the leadership of Chairman Mao thought "yes" on all counts, and the task of implementation was set the government.

The Mass Line and downgrading the expert. The affirmative answers of Chairman Mao depended first on the validity of the new techniques—deep ploughing and close planting, for example—proposed ; secondly on the willingness of the peasant to have his productive capacity liberated, that is, accept cultural or political rewards rather than material benefit ; and thirdly, on the organizational skill in identifying an underemployed peasant and getting him to subsidiary work and then, very important, back again to his land in time for his next task.

We might suppose that the "expert" would remain skeptical. He would object that the new techniques were not proved, that people work best under material incentive, and that the tasks to be set the underemployed had not been fully thought out. Chairman Mao would counter by saying that the expert did not know the people and that the peasant, if properly led, could not only perform the tasks, but would actually decide their nature at a local level, without national direction, in the manner of the wartime guerilla administration. Thus the "expert" was in the way of what some saw as a major breakthrough, and the "expert" was downgraded; the Mass Line was approved. S.C. Tsiang quotes a Chinese economist, Teng T'o as advising in 1966 that,

> prior to the announcement of new economic policies and measures, more consultation should be held with economists, for in this way many mistakes can be avoided. . academic economists should be extensively engaged to take charge of economic operations.

This was unacceptable in Peking in 1966 ; it was more so in 1958.

There is certainly validity in each of Mao's propositions. This made the Great Leap Forward plausible. There is a certain necessity in the policy implied ; this made the Leap acceptable. But certainly a major political drive was essential; this made the Leap appealing to revolutionaries, it also made the Leap's actual course hard to determine and delayed the essential reaction when it failed. With China's balance of trade turned to an export surplus, with the need to develop agricultural output both for export and to feed domestic industry or risk under-utilization of capacity, China had to "walk on two legs", that is, develop industry and agriculture simultaneously. If the rate of growth of industry was only barely acceptable to the leadership, the development of agriculture could not be allowed to take place at the price of an industrial slowdown ; both had to grow together. Additional resources had to be found in the agricultural sector. They were to spring from the peasant, as we have outlined, from new techniques and from new undertakings. And, just as the peasant was to be liberated, so the productive capacity of the city worker would result in a growth in output in the modern sector beyond all precedent. This too was part of the Great Leap Forward.

1958 policy and structural change. Thus beginning in 1957 and mounting in intensity during 1958 a series of new policies were announced, initiated, expanded, and implemented. First, into an already disrupted countryside, went the call for the people's commune, defined officially as the

> basic unit of social structure of our country, combining industry, agriculture, trade, education, and the military ; at the same time, it is the basic organization of social power.

The communes differed from advanced-type cooperatives in their size and their scope. As first conceived, they were the heralds of communism, for, since they combined economic and governmental functions, the state had withered away to subsist in the commune. At this stage the individual member of the commune was allowed no private means of production, family life itself was challenged through communal eating facilities, communal nurseries, and the former cooperative unit became the production brigade, the basis of labour organization. The payment of wages by ticket to communal mess halls on the basis of work done, attitudes, skills, and strength was intended as a final step in the divorcing of the peasant from the land, that is, the proletarianization of the peasant. This task of social reorganization was all but complete by September 1958. Suffice it to note here that by 1961 the process had been *de facto* reversed, and that, although the commune remained in existence, it performed its functions in so decentralized a manner that it resembled several individual cooperative units. Then, too, the peasant was allowed his private plot and his livestock activities. Quite obviously the attempt to induce extra work and to mobilize the underemployed, especially the women, by communal living and political motivation failed in China.

With the communes organized in the countryside, the government set down new targets for the workers to fulfil, but these targets were set not on the basis of carefully blended plans but rather on the basis of political slogans calling, e. g. for the surpassing of Britain in fifteen years. These targets were, however, a minimum. The lower unit of government was expected to send back its own target revised upward; this *revised* target was also to be forwarded to the next lower political unit as a *mandatory* goal ; this unit in turn upped the target and sent the higher figure down to the next level. Final targets were fantastically high and preliminary reports in 1958 indicated that they were being reached ; the goals for the next twelve years were about to be obtained in one. We know now that this did not happen, but we should begin to understand the atmosphere which made it seem possible.

Consequences—agriculture. The faith of the Communist Party in the doctrines expounded during the Great Leap is exemplified by the determination of the Party to take significant risks in the vital agricultural sector. With 80% of the people directly dependent upon the land, with the industrial development programme keyed into agricultural growth, the Party nevertheless undertook the further reorganization of the countryside, devising a completely new series of techniques embodied in Chairman Mao's Eight-Point Charter ; deep ploughing, fertilization, irrigation, close planting, pest control, field management, the use of improved seed, and the use of improved implements—all highly technical innovations which should have been preceded by thorough and scientific experimentation and planning. While there may indeed be no hope of progress without some mistakes, the delicate balance between population and resources in China cannot be subjected successfully to such strains. China is the second largest agricultural producer in the world (after the United States), but she must feed nearly one-fourth of the world's population with only 7.8% of the world's cultivated land !

The disruption which reorganization of the countryside and agricultural innovation must have caused was, when combined with the attempt to meet unreasonable targets, sufficient reason for the failure of the Leap in the agricultural sector. However, the poor harvests in 1959 and 1960 were accentuated by bad weather conditions and the demoralization of the peasantry helped bring another poor harvest in 1961. Since then there has been retrenchment and recovery, but the recovery in production has been mainly in the private rather than the socialist sector.

The new policies also required the peasant to contribute to labour-intensive work projects during the "off-season", and some 40% were reported mobilized. Despite the regimentation of the communes, the proletarianization of the peasantry, and the liberating of women's productive capacity, labour shortages developed both in industry and on the farm. This requires further explanation.

As intended, the "underemployed" peasant was set the additional task—the building of dykes, the digging of irrigation ditches, and the establishing of local small-scale industries, the most notorious of which were the "back-yard" steel furnaces. These projects in themselves created problems, for the planning of irrigation works is a technical task requiring some expertise if land is not to become waterlogged or salinity impair fertility ; or, small-scale industries may not produce what is needed, they probably will not produce it where it is needed, and they certainly will not produce it at acceptable quality. (We should note, of course, that these criticisms would not necessarily be valid if sufficient time were taken for planning and training ; this was not done in China and the omission proved fatal—fatal not only for the material worth of the projects but also for the political theory of the mass line, which depended for its validity on the ability of the untrained to make just this sort of decision without time and without training.) While all this would have resulted in misallocation of resources and some damage to the land, it does not in itself explain the shortage of labour which developed during the Great Leap. This can only be done by stating that as a matter of fact workers were not brought back from these projects in time to undertake their essential agricultural tasks. Furthermore, some even migrated to the cities where labour was also short under Great Leap production pressures ; there they remained even as unemployment grew in 1961, although some at least went home during urgent campaigns which reached their peak in 1962. Imported food, using scarce foreign exchange resources, was required to feed them ; as production fell on the land, the government could not obtain sufficient for its over-populated cities.

We should perhaps recall that the concept of "underemployed" is an extremely tricky one. That there are times in a primitive agricultural regime during which it is possible to remove a peasant for some other task without loss of agricultural output must be accepted. It is the basis of forced labour projects common to most pre-modern societies. It has also, with less than universal acceptance, formed the theoretical basis of a development theory advanced by Arthur Lewis and others. The problem in China apparently must be that these "underemployed" are, without the knowledge of the "experts", performing ancillary tasks about the farm or cooperative which are essential to total output, including traditional handicrafts. Furthermore, *per capita* availability of foodstuffs in China was less than in 1933, or about the period Tawney observed the peasants "roughing" through the winter. There is certainly the possibility that the peasants were not physically capable of performing the tasks required of them. Disrupting the rural routine as a practical task and without disturbing production is never simple or obvious ; it has proved especially difficult in China.

Consequences—industry. The impact of the Great Leap Forward on the modern industrial sector came from three separate causes ; first, from the acts of those within the sector ; secondly, from the disruption of the agricultural sector ; and thirdly, from the withdrawal of the Soviet advisors. To deal with this last, we have already briefly noted that their departure left some projects uncompleted, others with Chinese still not prepared to take over or to supply parts and other services. As for acts by those within the sector, the demand for higher production was a direct consequence of the abandonment of sound planning and the initiation of the two-level target system described above for agriculture.

Workers did indeed increase output ; the statistics, even as reviewed, support this (See Table 12 above). But the increase came at the cost of quality and adequate maintenance. Furthermore, production was undertaken for its own sake, that is, without regard to demand ; factories diversified their production without regard for competing facilities. And the Communist financial system was not organised to check such wasteful uses of resources ; there proved to be no effective monetary control, for such control had been geared to a plan, and the plan was now nothing more than a series of impossible targets. The attempted organization of urban communes and the extra burden on labour certainly affected morale adversely ; there is now evidence that the Chinese proletariat like their peasant compatriots work better under a system of material incentives.

The consequences of the industrial practices followed during the Great Leap Forward were long lasting, in the physical damage to equipment, in the stocks of sub-quality components, and in labour morale. Recovery was, however, faster than in the agricultural sector despite the fact, noted above, that the industrial sector was affected by the crisis in agriculture. Resources for investment had to be diverted for the import of foodgrain ; cotton and other raw materials

for Chinese industry were in short supply. There was depression in China during 1961-1962, an unusual phenomenon
in a Communist-ruled country.

The agricultural and industrial consequences of the
Great Leap are reflected in China's international trade
account. From a peak of US $4.3 billion in 1959—it
was US $1.9 billion in 1952—Mainland China's total trade
dropped to US $2.7 billion in 1962 and had not fully re-
covered by 1965. Even more significant have been the changes
in the composition and direction of trade, reflecting both the
economic and the political reorientation which the Big Leap
and Soviet reaction have caused. During the period of
growth, China typically imported industrial materials,
machinery and equipment (83% of total imports in 1959)
from Communist countries (66% of total 1959 imports)
and China exported agricultural products, principally food,
industrial materials, and textiles. In contrast, and reflecting
the shortcomings of the agricultural sector as well as the new
priority assigned it, China's imports of agricultural products
and chemical fertilizers were 47% of China's total imports
in 1965 compared to only 4% in 1959. Imports of machinery
remained below the 1959 level despite the general recovery of
trade. Perhaps more significant has been the shift in the
direction of trade with over 70% of imports now originating
in the non-communist countries. For a time exports to the
Soviet Union remained high to repay Soviet credits, and
continuing efforts have been made to decrease China's de-
pendence on the Soviet Union and other communist countries.

China's balance of trade account turned from deficit to
surplus in 1956, although it was in balance for 1960 if non-
monetary gold exports are included. The balance of payments
statement, for which see Table 15 at the end of this chapter,
presents problems in interpretation because special items, e.g.
the transfer of Soviet assets to the Chinese, distort the trends.
But, generally, after the period of growth, the surplus on
merchandize account was modified by freight, interest, and
other current payments to leave a small credit balance on
current account—except in 1960. Some 70% of Chinese
overseas remittances from the period 1950-1964 occurred

during the years through 1957, reflecting the impact of the Great Leap on the Overseas Chinese as well as the limitations imposed upon relatives in China attempting to use the remitted funds. On capital account a partially offsetting shift is apparent, although the size of errors and omissions prevents nice analysis. In the period to 1957 China's capital account showed a credit balance due principally to Soviet credits ; thereafter, with the exception of 1961, the account was in deficit as a result both of drawings on credits China had extended and to the rapid repayment of Soviet credits.

The international accounts confirm the seriousness of the economic setback resulting from Great Leap policies. China's relations with the Soviet Union so deteriorated that she was unable to continue the import surplus which is so useful to the developing country. The failure of the agricultural sector forced a distortion in China's trade policy and the use of limited foreign exchange resources on the import of consumption items. Since 1963 China has contracted for complete plants to be constructed and set up by non-communist sources, and arrivals of these were not fully reflected in the trade statistics of 1965. If recovery on the Mainland continues, we may expect a relative growth of industrial imports, but there is no indication that the favourable circumstances of the first five-year plan period will ever be repeated.

Despite the impact of the Great Leap Forward, China has continued a modest foreign aid programme, having made commitments to some 21 countries between 1956 and 1965, including Ceylon (US $41 million) and Pakistan (US $60 million). The total commitments reached US $845.5 million, but actual *expenditures*, i.e. the value of goods actually delivered to the recipient countries, was but US $200 million, compared to US $2 billion by the Soviet Union. In addition to goods, China has provided technical assistance, especially for labour-intensive type projects, with Mali, Nepal, Guinea, and Yemen the principal recipients. China's scholarship programme has been severely limited.

The aid programme is, of course, best explained in political terms and with reference to Soviet-Chinese rivalry for influence in the undeveloped world. But the poor performance as measured by expenditures in relation to commitments is best explained in terms of the strains on the Chinese economy since the Great Leap.

Validity of Leap principles. The issues, both economic and political, which created the Great Leap Forward are not dead ; indeed, they play a significant role in the present (1967) Cultural Revolution. Nor is this simply the consequence of an old revolutionary who doesn't know when to quit. As we have already suggested, there is considerable validity to the propositions that an "expert" can learn from the people, that labour intensive projects make economic sense in a country with large labour resources, and that modern techniques need to be adapted to the factor supply situation in each particular situation, and even that persons can be persuaded to work without relation to material reward—as witness the United States Peace Corps.

Indeed, one can take the position that unless the principles expressed in these propositions are incorporated into a country's development plan, the plan is likely to have considerably less impact on the level of living, even on the growth of national product, than would otherwise be the case. We can go further : unless some "missionary" zeal can be instilled in the people, the transfer of resources from the agricultural sector will be difficult to administer and the communication between bureaucrat and peasant will be no more intimate than that between a colonial district officer and the village headman. But when the government appeals to idealistic rather than materialistic values, the people expect that it will not waste the additional work performed. Here is where the government of the People's Republic failed. One long-run consequence of the Great Leap Forward is that the aura of inevitable success no longer characterizes the actions of the Chinese Communist Party, and its dealing with the peasantry has outrun the initial store of goodwill earned during the early period of land reform.

Recovery and readjustment. The failure of the Great Leap Forward forced the government to adopt new policies for a period of recovery and readjustment, say from 1961 to 1965, when the new third five-year plan (1966-1970) was presumably inaugurated. (Concerning this plan too little is known or rather rumoured to enable it to have a place in a work of economic history). We turn briefly to the new policies of 1961 to conclude our story.

The Party enunciated the ambiguous new policy line of "agriculture as the foundation and industry as the leading factor", but it was in practice something more than a return to the pre-Leap policy in that, for the first time, the key significance of agricultural development *per se* was recognized. For a Party that was supposed to understand the needs of the countryside—as the old Kuomintang was supposed not—this twelve-year lag may seem strange. The answer is, of course, that both parties understood the needs of the countryside, but the Kuomintang could not and the Communist Party did not wish to devote the resources to grant those needs, except to the extent politically and economically necessary. This necessity was forced on the Party in 1961.

The new line is also recognizable as a policy of "balanced growth", or, as Eckstein has put it, recognition of the interdependence of agricultural and industrial development and of consumption and investment. But such a balanced growth will probably not maximize the theoretical—and apparently unobtainable—rate of growth, and, therefore, we find China dropping those slogans calling for the surpassing of Britain in the immediate future and substituting "the building of an independent, comprehensive, and modern economic system within a not too long historical period." Recent events indicate that these changes have not been universally accepted in China.

The new line implied a relaxation of pressures on the peasants, especially in the organization of the commune. As we have seen, the commune by 1961 had become *de facto* a political aggregate of advanced co-operatives, hence the commune as a unique economic phenomenon proved of such a temporary nature, perhaps of one or two years' duration, that it no longer warrants detailed study in a brief economic history.   The new line also involved a change in attitude to population, and measures were instituted to check the rate of growth.   While the new line stressed restoration of food consumption and gave increased priority to consumer industry, it also encouraged the expansion of industry on a "narrow front", e.g. those which had created bottlenecks during the Leap, which were related to the needs of agriculture, or which would tend to cut imports.   Eckstein lists the production of special steels, synthetic fibres, and petroleum as examples in each category.   Fertilizer production and utilization, on the other hand, had been growing steadily and has continued to do so throughout the Leap and the recovery period.   While the peculiar organizational features of the Leap were abandoned, so also were the new technical practices including deep ploughing and close planting—"learning from old farmers" was the new slogan.   This abandonment of "miracle techniques of cultivation" was accompanied by partial restoration of private plots and incentive payment schemes.   Backyard steel furnaces and other industrial aberrations had already been abandoned.

Conclusion.   With planning on a pragmatic year-to-year basis, the recovery of the Chinese economy began slowly but surely from its 1961 crisis.   We have already examined the figures briefly, and we should recall that they indicate the potential of continued growth at comparatively favourable rates for the foreseeable future.   We have also noted that the current Cultural Revolution may be threatening this new growth, but that the lesson of the Great Leap Forward seems to have been sufficiently well learnt that attempts to launch another leap have so far been successfully defeated.

The first years of the People's Republic, that is, through 1957, had a lasting impact on the economy and effected a real structural change which continues of fundamental significance despite the interlude of Great Leap.   But the growth of the 1950's which appears so favourable when divided by five, seems less so when divided by ten or fifteen, and the economist's criticism of the regime must be that the sacrifices, that is, the use of resources, were unnecessarily large for the results achieved.   This fundamental criticism in no way affects the nation's real achievements or its hopes for some future development. Nevertheless, the experiences and the scars of the Great Leap Forward may have sufficiently affected the relations of government and people as to have some impact on the ability of government to implement programmes of the same range and nature as before. The government may be forced to modify the Soviet model for development, while the passage of years with the growth of population has narrowed the agricultural base. There is now less flexibility than in 1952, less room for manoeuvre or for error.

As in the Ch'ing, the Chinese still seek a Chinese solution to their economic problems. The Middle Kingdom cannot be tied to a Soviet model any easier than it could to the plans of those missionaries of steam power who hammered on the doors of Ch'ing officials with proposals for factories, mints, railroads, and financial schemes of comprehensive nature and dubious origin. And the Chinese are correct in seeking such a solution, but since 1949 this search and the resulting experimentation has been costly. Allowing for the inherent difficulty in ruling so vast a nation as China, for the technical problems involved in "solving" the agricultural problem and achieving balanced growth in the unique Chinese context, we may repeat our judgement that the present government has proved unable fully to follow up the initial advantages its success in 1949 and its reconstruction programme 1949-1952 provided.

This quotation from Walter Galenson appears particularly appropriate for a text directed in the first place at an Indian audience :

A good deal of impatience with the seemingly slow pace of Indian economic development is often expressed in the United States. But, in fact, have the Indians performed any less well than the Chinese in the years that have elapsed since the two countries embarked on central planning ? It may turn out on closer examination that without the fanfare of breakneck industrialization, Great Leaps, Red Guards, and the like, the Indians have done at least as well as the Chinese, at a smaller cost to the people.

This is not an assertion, but a question. If it turns out to be true, our current view on appropriate economic relations with India might well be altered.

Would someone please answer the professor's question ?

TAIWAN : DEVELOPMENT IN ONE PROVINCE

Background. With a 1965 per capita GNP of NT $8800 (=US $220), Taiwan has enjoyed continued growth despite her large (12.4 million) population, its high rate of growth (3%), and the province's small area (13,886 sq. miles). Over the past five years, the increase in GNP has averaged some 8% per annum, including a 4% increase in agriculture. Savings in 1964 were 24% of GNP and, in the following year, the U.S. aid programme, which had financed some 35% of Taiwan's investment over a ten-year period, ceased. Prospects for the future continue bright; Taiwan has become the case of a successful aid recipient.

And why, indeed, some have asked, should this not be so? Taiwan has received aid to an amount some three times the average to underdeveloped countries, it inherited an industrial base from the Japanese, and a skilled and literate peasantry and labour force with managerial talents readily available. It is very easy to dismiss Taiwan as a special case and pass over the significant development lessons which it provides. For the record of this province since 1952, the year in which the refugee mainlanders may be said to have settled into the economy, has been achieved not with aid alone, but with a combination of foreign aid and sound economic policies. Those overly concerned with the politics of the National Government of the Republic of China would be well advised to look beyond the cliches.

Taiwan has always been something of a special case. As a semi-tropical island off the China coast, it attracted the attention of European powers looking for areas of exploitation in the Far East close to the eldorado of the elusive China market. The American merchant Augustine Heard, Jr., urged Hainan for the Americans; he urged Taiwan (Formosa) on the Belgians through the Duke of Brabant, then heir to the Belgian throne. The Belgians considered the economic potentials, but rejected a Taiwan venture in favour of the African Congo. The French failed to capture the island in 1874, and the Japanese long had their ambitions set. But it was, at least in part, this separateness which enabled Taiwan to be a special case, even under the Ch'ing. Part of Fukien Province until 1887, Taiwan first had its own administration in 1885 when Liu Ming-ch'uan was appointed governor. Even before this, development of the island's coal industry had been urged and the first telegraph, from Kaohsiung to Tainan was completed in 1877.

Governor Liu had a reputation in Peking and the support of Li Hung-chang. With the latter's promise of an inter-provincial subsidy of 440,000 *taels* for five years—a typical *ad hoc* Ch'ing fiscal arrangement—and with additional sums for mining ventures, he began development of the Keelung coal mines, construction of the Keelung-Taipei railway, shipping communication with the mainland, telegraph lines the length of the island and to Amoy, and modernization of Taipei, including, in 1888, electric lighting. Typically his enthusiasm outran his economic discretion. The electric lighting was too expensive, and his modern school—to which he sent his own son—ran into similar problems and was closed down. Samuel C. Chu's article on these activities lists other financial difficulties and notes how Ch'ing administrators were left to piece together a patch-work of financial "deals" which might fall apart at any moment. Typical too were the problems Liu had with foreign advisors and with conservative co-administrators. When Liu was replaced by Shao Yu-lien, modernization continued although on a rationalized basis. Certainly by the time of the cession of Taiwan to the Japanese under terms of the Treaty of Shimonoseki, the province was in some sense "model"—it was certainly different.

The Japanese contribution to the island's economy is undoubted. While it has been suggested that they exploited Korea, they built up Taiwan, seeing it both as a source of sugar and rice for Japan itself and as an industrial base in the Japanese co-prosperity sphere they hoped to create. But their most important single contribution was probably the creation of a relatively large literate population.   Thus the Chinese, mostly immigrants from Fukien but with some Hakka and Cantonese, had received a basic education, were used to following technical instructions, experimenting with new techniques and commercial crops, and had had some industrial training at the foreman level.   Nevertheless, the development of sugar and heavy industry made complete sense only if Taiwan were part of a larger economic union—as the Japanese planned and as the Chinese National Government expected in 1954.   The unqualified contribution to the modern sector was the overhead, the railways, roads, and power system; perhaps least significant at first were those industries, e.g. aluminium, which depended on imported raw materials.

Growth immediately following Chinese political recovery was slow, partly because of damage to the economy, the necessary reorientation of trade, and lack of materials, and partly because of the chaotic condition of the mainland economy. The island was spared the worst rigours of the post-war inflation through remittance control and a separate currency. Nevertheless, there was serious inflation, and a new currency— the *New Taiwan* dollar (NT $)—was successfully instituted soon after the Government of the Republic of China left the Mainland and established its capital at Taipei.   (The provincial capital is at Taichung.) There is, unfortunately, insufficient space to detail the economic history of Taiwan in the 1950's.   What follows is an outline of the economy's development, intended to arouse questions as to cause.

Statistics. If we compare Taiwan with the Mainland in 1952, we find that agriculture (with forestry and fishing) accounted for 35% of Taiwan's gross domestic product at factor cost; the Liu-Yeh estimate for the Mainland is 48% of GDP.   By 1959 Taiwan's structure had changed to show the "manufacturing plus" sector (including mining, transport, and construction) at 32% compared to agriculture at 30% ; on the Mainland, as we have seen, manufacturing grew relative to agriculture but, by 1957, had not surpassed it in importance.   Certainly, the industrial base on Taiwan was significantly more important.

TABLE 13. TAIWAN : ECONOMIC INDICATORS

	1950	1952	1956	1960	1965
Money Supply (billions of NT $)	0·58	1·29	3·23	6·11	14·84
Wages : Daily earnings (1958 = 100)	20	41	86	126	186
Cost of Living (1958 = 100)	34	58	88	131	147
Industrial production (1958=100)	35	53	82	129	265
Agricultural production (1958 = 100)	n.a.	71	85	103	n.a.
Private investment (billions of NT $)	n.a.	2·51	4·21	10·76	17·1b
Private consumption (billions of NT $)	n.a.	10·95	23·03	40·69	65·70b
Gross national product (billions of NT $)	n.a.	15·75	32·30	59·63	110·00
Total available product (GNP & import surplus)	n.a.	16·63	33·97	64·32	n.a.
Population (millions)a	7·6	8·0	9·2	10·6	12·4
Aid imports as % of total	n.a.	43	42	36	n.a.

a. International Financial Statistics. This figure excludes certain groups, e.g. military. At end of 1960, for example, figure should be 11·4 million, and estimates in the text are so based.

b. 1964.

Source : *International Financial Statistics.*

Even from this base, the rate of growth of Taiwan's GNP was not spectacular—it averaged 6.8% in the six years from 1954 to the end of the second four-year plan in 1960. Total available product, however, increased at a faster rate, from NT $16.5 billion in 1952 to NT $20.5 billion in 1954 and NT $32.0 billion in 1960 (TAP=GNP + net factor income paid to abroad + net imports of goods and services, cited here in constant 1952 prices). If we consider the pre-war situation during the Japanese period, the implications of the role of foreign trade will all the more be obvious, for then an export surplus reduced TAP below GNP. Thus pre-war per capita real TAP was surpassed in 1952, GNP not until 1955. The import surplus was made possible, of course, through U.S. aid.

During the first two four-year plan periods, agricultural output increased at an average annual rate of 5%, which is exceptionally high. Manufacturing output increased at 12%. Government expenditure, i.e. the consolidated budgets of the national, provincial and local governments, remained between 10% and 12% of national income.

The agricultural record deserves some further consideration. Without any net addition to the area of cultivation, crop production increased 4% per annum due to irrigation, multi-cropping practices, improved seed, and increased use of fertilizer. With the exception of sugar, pre-war production peaks were quickly surpassed, although rice production could not maintain its export level and also meet the requirements of a growing population. Even then, sugar production was sufficient to meet domestic requirements and quota levels authorized by the International Sugar Agreement and the United States. Statistically more dramatic was the 10% per annum increase in fishery production, through development of pond, coastal, and deep-sea fishing. Timber production grew at 7% per annum, although this was partly at the price of erosion and sound replanting policies. Livestock production lagged at 3% per annum.

In industry there had been a break from the bureaucratic traditions of the Mainland. Although the government inherited the Japanese industrial complex, in the period 1952-60 government's share of industrial production declined from 55% to 40% of gross output. In good Dr. Sun tradition, it remained in control of public utilities—and also such key industries as fertilizer, petroleum refining, aluminium, sugar (centrifugal), and forestry. Electric power production increased from 1.4 billion kwh in 1952 to 3.6 billion in 1960, thus achieving a per capita production second only to that of Japan in the ECAFE area. There was a fully integrated system of 27 hydro and 10 thermal power stations with installed capacity of 709,000 kw, and the 1960 peak load of 633,000 kw was 3.5 times that of the pre-war peak. While the economic indicators in Table 13 tell the general story, specific note should be taken of the development of the plastics and polyvinyl chloride production; cement, too, showed exceptional growth; and the figures for tinned pineapple (490,000 cases in 1952 and 2,219,000 in 1960) indicate one consequence of a dynamic agricultural policy. Steel production rose from 18,000 to 200,000 metric tons.

The rising importance of Taiwan's industry is also illustrated in the province's export figures. In 1952, 78% of the total exports of US $120 million were composed of rice and sugar, 14% "other agricultural", and 8% "other exports". This pattern changed significantly in 1959 and 1960, due partly, it is true, to a decline in the quantity and value of sugar and rice exports in 1959. In 1960, sugar export volume increased, but the total value of rice and sugar declined further. Nevertheless, there was also a striking increase in "other exports" from the US $18 million of 1957 to the US $64 million of 1960, an increase which changed the proportions for that year to 46% of total exports in rice and sugar, 38% in "other exports". At the same time, the composition of imports changed significantly from 1952 to 1960; consumer goods declined from 50% of imports to 30%. There was a corresponding increase in the import of raw materials and capital goods, and, for the latter, figures indicate a change from 31% to 42% of total imports between 1957 and 1960.

Typically, Taiwan had a deficit in the goods and services balance ranging from US $81 million on 1953 to US $132 million in 1960. This deficit was modified by a net credit balance on various donations and capital inflows, including overseas Chinese capital. But the most important offset was U.S. aid, which was sufficiently large to permit Taiwan to finance her deficits and build up foreign exchange reserves. In 1960, for example, U.S. aid imports were 36% of total imports of US $252 million.

The government utilized some 28% of the gross national product during the second four-year period, 1957-1960; revenues were 22% (15% of GNP equivalent in tax receipts). The result was budget deficits, which reached a high of NT $2 billion in the fiscal year 1960-61 (cash basis), financed principally from U.S. aid counterpart funds, but also by borrowing from the banks. The inflationary impact of the former method of financing depends, of course, on the net changes in the counterpart accounts, and these have grown in every year except 1953. Defence expenditures accounted for approximately 50% of government expenditures, although there are naturally problems involved in considering the hidden subsidies and payments in kind to the military.

As the economic indicators (Table 13) show, these developments have occurred during a period of rapidly expanding money supply and rising prices. Since in 1950 prices rose four times and the money supply doubled, the general trend during the first two planning periods may seem relatively mild: from 1954 to 1958 money supply increased an annual 25% per annum, wholesale prices 9%. There then occurred a break in the trend, with the increase in money supply only 9% but with wholesale prices up 12% per annum. Bad harvests in 1960 aggravated the situation, with a 21% rise in the food index (18% in the general cost of living index).

Basic to development of the Taiwan economy has been the U.S. aid programme, which, excluding military hardware, totalled over US $1 billion between the national government's evacuation of the Mainland and the end of the second four-year plan in 1960. (Of the US $4.5 billion in U.S. aid to China between World War II and 1960, approximately US $3 billion has been military, of which nearly US $2 billion has been supplied since 1949). The programme was implemented on the following general principles as the result of annual negotiations; a total dollar allocation was approved based on the size of the Republic of China's defense burden, the capacity of the economy to absorb aid, and the demand of other countries relative to U.S. aid appropriations. The bulk of the aid was in the form of non-project commodity imports, i.e. programme aid, while some 25% has been project aid, and a small proportion specifically designated for "technical co-operation", principally in the fields of education and agriculture. All this was supplemented by the sale, for local currency, of U.S. surplus agricultural products under Public Law 480 (title one) and loans from the Development Loan Fund (after 1959). Of the US $86 million *expended* in fiscal 1960, for example US $17 million was for project (including DLF), US $54 million for non-project commodity imports, US $2.4 million for technical cooperation, and US $13 million under PL 480.

In theory the distinction between project and non-project or programme aid may be difficult to justify. One can argue that, if the aid-donor does not have control over all resources of the aid-recipient, his project aid may only result in diversion of other resources to low priority activities; if the aid-donor does have such control, the distinction is irrelevant. In practice, the aid-donor concerned with results must determine that the overall allocation of resources is reasonably sound; then non-project aid may be designed to release needed local resources for development projects, project aid may be directed towards high priority projects which require close scrutiny and technical assistance from the aid-donor. This is, of course, aid with strings, but the alternative, say in the style of the Reorganization Loan of 1913, is useless. The "strings" need not be foreign direction of development programme; rather this implies a recognized role for the aid-donor in the formulation and, sometimes, the execution of development policy. Such a role was sought by the Soviet Union on the China Mainland and was finally denied. Despite the inevitable and natural frictions which must arise, the Republic of China did permit the United States such a role in the development of Taiwan.

The effectiveness of the U.S. aid programme on Taiwan is not, then, to be measured solely by its dollar value—no more than the Soviet aid to the People's Republic. First, there is the donor's contributory policy role. Secondly, through technical assistance—which extends beyond the item so labelled in government statistics—the United States increased the effectiveness of its dollar aid; thirdly, through the Investment Guarantee and Investment Development programmes, the U.S. encouraged development through American private investment. Special local currency funds were available for this purpose. Of course, all this is subject to the very legitimate query, "But what if the aid-donor advises incorrectly?" Fortunately, as an economic historian we are able to reply that both the Soviet Union and the United States did, as a matter of fact, advise with reasonably good sense. But it is just as reasonable for a potential aid-recipient to reject aid based on what it considers an ill-advised programme. And, just as the People's Republic has done, such a country must take the consequences.

Planning. The increase in Taiwan's GNP has been stated, but it has not been explained. Nor have we attempted, except in the introductory comments, to consider the post-1960 period. Our first task is to account for the 6-7% annual increase in real income and to see that this formed the base for the continued and more rapid increase since the end of the second four-year plan. While we shall make comparisons with events on the Mainland, we do not wish anyone to suppose that policies and methods which could be implemented in one province—and a province with a special history and different resources—are directly relevant to the economy of a great empire, or continent, if that better describes Mainland China. Nevertheless, there are points at which comparisons are, at least, interesting.

From a negative point of view, we can show that development occurred despite continued inflation, high government expenditure, and budget deficits. The most obvious comparison is with the National Government's post-war Mainland policy through 1949. In Taiwan, the hyper-inflation of 1950 was checked. True, prices rose faster than the money supply after 1958, but quasi-money rose even more rapidly, suggesting that there was a transfer from current to time and savings accounts and more efficient utilization of money balances. The relatively faster real growth of total available product (TAP) would be relevant here, but equally so would be the psychological impact of the consumer goods made available through the U.S. aid programme. Government rice and other "payment-in-kind" programmes would also contribute to the stability of a monetary sector in which the income recipients were heavily weighted with those eligible for such payments. There was an emergency atmosphere, a sense of austerity, and a minimum of conspicuous consumption. And throughout real output was increasing; the inflation was demand-pull, consequent to the failure of voluntary savings to meet the requirements of both government deficit spending and real investment by the private sector, despite American aid. Yet this was a matter of timing; production did increase in sufficient time to prevent a flight from the currency.

From the fiscal point of view, there was little change in the percentage of gross national product taken in the form of tax revenue, but, in contrast with Mainland administrations, tax revenue did at least keep up both as a percentage of GNP and as a percentage of total government expenditures. The government claim on GNP, say 28%, was high, but not excessive if reasonably financed, which phrase may be defined in terms of the consequences. These, growth with inflation, were not totally unsatisfactory. Within reasonably flexible limits, it is not the size of government expenditures which is so significant as the method of their financing in a particular economy; this is related both to the import surplus which is aid-financed and the economy's rate of savings. Of course, the purpose of the expenditure is also significant; in Taiwan development outlays totalled about 4% of the budget, and there is no evidence that the government competed with the private sector for key resources or were in other ways disruptive.

Obviously the Taiwan Provincial Administration, backed by the National Government in Taipei, had a firmer control politically than had the previous governments on the Mainland. With no civil war to disrupt production—and this was more important than the defense expenditures themselves—or to hinder administrative reforms, especially in the field of taxation, the government could take the severe measures necessary to secure resources and could execute the policies necessary to encourage production in both government and private sectors.

With this in mind, we turn to the government's overall planning policy. From 1949 to 1953 emphasis was placed wholly on agricultural reform, with the Sino-American Joint Commission for Rural Reconstruction leading a vigorous and comprehensive programme, technically competent and highly effective, to increase agricultural production. Here the Japanese tradition served the people well. Those familiar with the problem of teaching new methods to peasants must imagine undertaking such a job when, first, many peasants can read (and have electric lights at home for night study if need be!), secondly, are already organized in farmers' associations which have a tradition of extension work, and thirdly, the extension work is being undertaken by persons who are both competent *and* willing to go into the field. (Perhaps it is more accurate to say there are no peasants in Taiwan, only farmers.) Some economists have warned that universal primary education might not be justified. The young men so educated leave the farms for the towns long before the towns can absorb them ; better to leave them alone for the time being. But education cannot be turned on and off, and the proposition is absurd for many reasons ; it is only cited here because it has been advanced by some with development experience. Judged in the Taiwan context, the proposal to cut down on primary education fails because such education is needed by the farmers if agricultural productivity is to be increased.

There are two further requirements : first, there must be competent advice and complete follow-through ; secondly, the peasant must have sufficient incentive. The first point refers to several problems under a single heading. The development of improved seeds and techniques in a central experimental station, e.g. Los Banos in the Philippines, is relatively simple. But despite the fact that all concerned pay constant lip service to the difficulty of applying the lessons learned from these centralized experiments to the field, such application is often made too hastily and without local testing. Secondly, unless agricultural advice is offered on a continuing and sustained basis, the peasant will find himself subject to the whims or well-meaning inspirations of district officers or amateur enthusiasts. Finally, the government must stand behind its advice. That is, if a new crop is urged, it must stand ready to buy it at a minimum price. Since the nation's entire development programme is bound to depend eventually on the success of the agricultural sector, the peasant cannot be expected to shoulder the basic risks of experimentation. In any case, he won't do it.

There is no evidence—in China or Southeast Asia, at least —that the peasant will not respond to sound advice or economic motivation ; there is evidence that he will not respond to the enthusiasms of laymen or professors of agriculture. The JCRR programme on Taiwan, backed by government marketing decisions and in co-operation with the local government and the farmers' associations, did have just that combination of requirements which we have suggested are essential for success. And this includes in the complete service from seed to sack, adequate rural finance—at reasonable rates of interest, always higher, that is, than city-bred, LSE trained politicians are likely to consider reasonable.

The JCRR programme has been concerned with the application of fertilizer, with the techniques of inter-cropping, with the optimum utilization of new water regimes—especially the problems created by double-cropping from ground-water supplies and deep wells—with new commercial crops— including finding overseas markets and coordinating with processors—with opening new areas where special problems had prevented previous exploitation, and with extension work in general. This has covered not only crops, but also forestry and fisheries, indeed, almost every aspect of rural life.

We also stated that the peasant must have sufficient incentive. This introduces the history of land reform, so successful in Taiwan. Briefly, the programme began in 1949 with reduction of rent to 37.5% of the value of the main crop combined with measures to ensure security of tenure to the tenant. Undoubtedly, this measure was not fully effective, but it permitted the second step, that is, "land-to-the-tiller". With the landlord limited in the amount of land he might hold, he was forced by a 1953 law to sell the rest to the government at a price equal to 250% of the value of the principal crop, a figure which makes sense in the context of the rent restriction which had limited the value of the land to a landlord. The government paid the landlord 30% in the shares of government enterprises—those taken over from the Japanese—and 70% on 10-year government bonds, which were amortized in 20 semi-annual instalments fixed in real terms. The intention here was both to give the landlord an interest in the industrial sector and to reassure him on the value of his compensation. The farmer was permitted to buy the land thus released over a similar time-period at a burden equal to 40% of the value of the principal crop. This provision, i.e. specifying "principal" crop, was to be important in view of the considerable development of other crops, i.e. vegetables and wheat on rice land in between the two rice crop periods. The government also sold land in its possession.

There has been a very slight decrease in the area of farms, although probably not in consequence of land reform *per se*. The question nevertheless arises as to how such a division could be expected to promote agricultural production.

While there may be a limit to the increase in production that increased application of labour to a small land area can create—and certainly a point at which diminishing marginal returns are reached, it is apparent that this point had not been reached in Taiwan. This, however, is partly because of a poor definition of "land" as an area rather than as a "time-area" concept. By this we simply mean that the land had not been fully utilized throughout the year and thus to say that labour was applied more intensively to the same small farm is not as accurate as saying that labour was applied to the land during a period in which the land had been idle. The improved techniques available to the Taiwan farmer were all at first of a labour-intensive nature and often involved using more capital (fertilizer) or more land (existing land during idle periods). The coming of the Japanese-type all-purpose farm tractor at a time when labour shortages have been felt in Taiwan industry may have an impact on size of farm, but that was not the problem of the 1950's.

The incentive needs of the farmer must, however, be reconciled with the investment requirements of the development plan ; resources must be made available for the growth of the industrial sector, and a large proportion of these will probably have to come from agriculture. Despite U.S. aid, Taiwan faced this problem. It was solved in a maze of complex food requisition and compulsory purchase schemes, distribution of fertilizer at prices which in effect included an excise tax, and a series of arbitrary land-tax classifications. None of this can be justified theoretically. All that can be said is that the impact of these measures was never sufficient to undermine the positive contributions of the JCRR programmes. Since, too, the resources so obtained had to be obtained, we have here a question of administrative technique, which, though obviously open to abuse and relatively inefficient, was evidently not too abused and was sufficiently efficient. The results indicate that on balance the handling of the agricultural sector and of the farmer was sound, sufficiently so to give the Republic of China political recognition by those emerging nations which required her agricultural experience.

In this pre-plan period, industry was being rehabilitated. The first four-year plan, 1953-1956, had as its declared purpose the maintenance of a high rate of growth, improvement of the government's fiscal position, and decreasing of U.S. aid. The first only was achieved, although the fiscal position was improved in the sense that reform enabled the government to maintain its economic position without deterioration. The plan was, moreover, little more than a collection of priority projects and an assignment of government investment funds on the basis of previous use—30% went to agriculture and 70% to industry. Nevertheless, this in itself reflected a decision to push agricultural production as fast as technological improvements would allow, short of heavy investment in costly irrigation schemes, while devoting the balance of available funds to industry.

In the second plan, industry, including transportation and public works, was again stressed with assignment of 76% of available funds. Since production targets were changed annually, comparison of final results with the original goal is not too meaningful in a brief survey. The third four-year plan, 1960-1964, was the most ambitious, with investment some one-third higher than in the previous plan period and with a rate of growth of 8% per annum, which seemed unreasonably high at the time, but which has since been achieved. Perhaps most significant of all has been the continued high rate of agricultural growth. Indeed, in 1960, Taiwan was on the eve of a breakthrough, and from the perspective of 1967, this is indeed how we can interpret the various changes, revealed by the statistics quoted, especially for the period 1958-1960.

The similarity with Mainland planning is, at a very superficial level, apparent. Both stressed industrial development and the transfer of resources from agriculture ; both relied on foreign aid for that surplus which is reflected in the difference between TAP and GNP. In both economies the contribution of industry changed relative to agriculture over the period 1953-1960. Both governments put through an effective land reform—effective in the administrative sense of actually getting land to the tillers. But the differences are even more interesting.

First, consider the overall plan concept. Although Taiwan stressed industry, the government pushed agricultural improvement as rapidly as technologically possible—with the exception of major irrigation schemes. Thus the "success" of Taiwan's land reform from a production point of view is really the success of an integrated programme in which the reform was, in fact, but one facet. Indeed, one can conceive of growth in Taiwan's agricultural output without land reform—although undoubtedly political and social justice would have suffered and the task would have been more difficult—but growth without the adequate allocation of investment funds and the work of JCRR is not conceivable. Thus the Mainland reform was economically unsuccessful, partly because neither the peasant nor the government were prepared for the responsibilities resulting. While it may be argued that the Chinese Communist Party never intended to leave the land under individual ownership, it can also be shown that the beginnings of a reconcentration of land had begun in China shortly after the reform, which had, therefore, failed in its own context.　To the extent that growth in agriculture depends upon peasant motivation, the Taiwan record is more consistent, despite the necessary activities of the Taiwan Food Bureau ; year after year, the Taiwan farmer became more assured that government policy had awarded him a share in the national income, not as a temporary expedient, but as of right.　And the growth of per capita GNP served as an assurance that the government would not be forced to modify this policy.　On the Mainland the alternation between "economism" and "continuous revolution" tactics, which are reflected, for example, in the policy regarding private plots and peasant livestock activities, reflects a *de facto* opportunism which is unlikely to inspire peasant confidence or full co-operation.

　　As for industry, in Taiwan growth occurred at the relative expense of the government's share in manufacturing enterprise, that is, the private sector built on the economic services, the overheads, provided by the government.　Consistency of policy, the simplification of the maze of regulations surrounding economic activity, and the encouragement of investment by overseas Chinese and others—and this includes the establishment of industrial estates, the improvement of power facilities, the financial resources of the China Development Corporation —all these have permitted the private sector to play a major role.　Here again, there is no single factor responsible for the significant growth in industry after 1958, but rather a complex of factors, including the soundness of the agricultural base. Thus, when in 1960 economic stability, the need for a higher level of exports, and the prospective ending of grant-type aid forced a readjustment in the province's industrial sector, the economy was able to sustain its rate of growth despite some failures and the operation of old-line industries at less than full capacity.　The type of reaction, the type of activity which characterizes the private sector was, of course, not present in Mainland China.

Any comparison between Taiwan and Mainland China must stress the different resources bases, especially manpower. To develop one province may be easier than developing the whole of China; the essential difference between the Mainland record and Taiwan's may then simply be a reflection of the problems of ruling so large an area as China. There is certainly evidence to support this, including the economic development theory which posits the need for a certain critical level of investment if a breakthrough is to occur. With trained manpower and a heavy concentration of foreign aid directed to a relatively small area, development is possible; dissipated over a vast land mass, general development is unlikely. Related to this point of view would be the importance of the timing element, the essential coordination of economic policies which some have described as the "balanced growth" approach to development. Yet another explanation is to suggest that comparison of the two areas after 1957 is irrelevant, since, on the Mainland, politics was in command. And thus it may be that the consistency of the government's role in the Taiwan economy is at least as important as any specific policy; if so, here we have certainly discovered a fundamental difference between the Mainland and Taiwan.

TABLE 14 : CHINA : PRODUCTION OF SELECTED COMMODITIES, 1911-1957

	Cotton yarn 1000 spindles	Pig Iron 1000 MT	Steel 1000 MT	Coal 1 million MT	Cement 1000 MT	Electricity billion kwh
1911	736	83	39	9	—	—
1918	1,134	329	57	18	—	—
1928	3,610	477	30	25	608	—
1933	4,731a	609	30	28	764	1.6
1936	5,103a	810	414	40	1,306	2.5
1937	844b	5,900	5,300	124	6,900	19.3
1957c	third	seventh	ninth	fifth	eighth	twelfth
1957d	807b	1,900	1,700	44	5,700	13.7
1957e	517b	7,100	12,600	52	15,200	81.3

a. excluding Manchuria.
b. million meters.
c. China's world rank.
d. India's production.
e. Japan's production.

Sources : Yearbooks and Alexander Eckstein.

TABLE 15 : CHINA : BALANCE OF INTERNATIONAL PAYMENTS 1903—1960
(Million of dollars)

	Chinese $		US$	Ch$	US$					
	1903	1930	1935b	1936c	1937	1946	1947	1948	1950-57	1960
Imports	− 492	− 1965	− 1119	− 1146	− 468	− 775	− 653	− 282	− 9615	− 1980
Exports	+ 374	+ 1476	+ 562	+ 812	+ 265	+ 179	+ 276	+ 237	+ 9030	+ 1980
Balance of trade	− 118	− 489	− 457	− 334	− 203	− 596	− 377	− 45	− 585	0
Current expend.	+ 74	+ 205	+ 95	+ 238	+ 41	+ 35	+ 3	+ 4	− 360	− 80
Overseas Chin. remit.	+ 114	+ 316	+ 260	+ 320	+ 132	+ 76	+ 74	+ 90	+ 855	+ 50
Service of foreign loans	− 69	− 111	− 108	− 128	− 34	− 25	− 36	− 46	+ 490	− 180
Other remittances	− 35	− 227	+ 55	− 70	− 29	− 25	− 50	− 46	− 80e	− 8
Capital import	+ 42	+ 202	+ 140	− 366d	+ 7	+ 80	+ 90	+ 77	+ 1405f	0
Balance	+ 8	− 104	− 125	− 340	− 86	− 455	− 302	0	− 20	− 290
Specie (net)a	− 8	− 53	+ 357	+ 335	+ 86	+ 355	+ 190	0	+ 230g	− 50
Errors and Omissions		+ 157	+ 232	+ 5		+ 100	+ 112		+ 250	+ 340

a. After 1936=foreign reserves and monetary specie. Non-monetary specie is included in the trade statistics.
b. Conversion rate : Ch$1 = US$ 0·362625,
c. Conversion rate : Ch$1 = US$ 0·294375.
d. Includes all capital movements (net) other than debt amortization.
e. Includes "transfer of Soviet assets", $330 m. and "drawings on Chinese grants and credits" $ 475 m.
f. Drawings on credits received.
g. Includes "expropriation of convertible currencies", +$250 m.; changes in holdings of monetary gold, −$35 m.; and "changes in clearing account balances with the Free World", +$15 m.

Note: This table is derived from several sources, including H. B. Morse, *Chinese Yearbook*, C.I.A., and Kia-ngau Chang. For the post-1949 period, the headings are inappropriate, but the C.I.A. figures have been forced into this mold for ease in comparison. Again with the exception of the post-1949 period, this table is to be taken in a very general sense. Many and devious are the adjustments which have been made, and it is doubtful if the resulting figures really mean much unless the reader has gone through each such adjustment himself. In a short, introductory text, it is impossible to supply sufficient information for this. Hence this table is supplied more as illustration of the problems involved in statistical analysis with Chinese data than with providing a final balance-of-payments statement.

READING LISTS

The brief economic history of modern China which we have just concluded obviously cannot cover the vast range of economic topics throughout the hundred-year-period. The following reading lists, arranged topically, should be useful for following up on problems or controversies which appear to have economic interest for you. Material in Chinese is not included and the lists are not all-inclusive. But many of the works contain lengthy compilations of references, while certain bibliographies have also been cited. The material on the People's Republic, including the latest publications, has been assigned its own section.

If one wished to go beyond books into more specialized articles and English-language research material, here are brief suggestions. The *Journal of Asian Studies* (of the American Association of Asia Studies) and its annual bibliography should be consulted regularly; for contemporary China, add the *China Quarterly* (London). A selection of articles from this latter journal has been published by Roderick MacFarquhar (ed.), *China under Mao: Politics Takes Command* (London, 1966). Quantitative research on specific topics in Chinese economic history between 1840-1949 is beginning to be published, reaching a scholarly standard comparable that in the best European studies, but these articles may be found in any journal of economics or economic history. For the Ch'ing, the newspapers may be read, and for these, King and Clarke's *Research Guide* is useful. You should also consult the reports of the Imperial Maritime Customs, usually listed as "China, Inspectorate General of Customs", and especially the *Decennial Reports*. From 1912 on there are at least three series of annual handbooks, published in Tientsin, Shanghai and London, variously titled, *China Handbook, The Chinese*

Year Book, The China Year Book, all with detailed articles on practically every topic. They are well supplied, too, with statistics of varying quality.

In France, Mouton & Co. are publishing a series of texts and documents in the field of modern Chinese history ; one at least has been on economic history—Marie-Claire Bergere's on the 1910 banking crisis in Shanghai. Harvard, Columbia, and Washington University presses have series on China which include economic works. The University of Michigan has an important monograph series, and American universities with Asian studies or research centres sometimes have reprints of articles by members of their faculty available.

For work on the period since 1949, you will wish to consult Nai-Ruenn Chen's bibliography of English-language works on the Mainland China economy (Berkeley, 1963). But high on the priority list would be the various translation services of the U.S. government, especially the translations of the daily press and of periodicals issued by the Consulate-General of the U.S. in Hong Kong. Publications from mainland China itself are available, published by the Foreign Languages Press, and are very enthusiastic. *China Reconstructs*, for example, is a periodical picturing in colour developments in the economy. There are also pamphlets on laws, regulations, visits to factories and communes, and explanations of current government priorities and campaigns— to the extent these are known to the writers themselves. For the economist, they suffer from the faults of the Great Leap Forward. *The Peking Review* you would read in any case. *China's Foreign Trade* is another periodical of relative significance. As for the history of Chinese Communist Party policies, this can be most easily learned from the collections of selected documents cited in list *H* below, although you should also consult more specifically political collections and surveys, e.g. Stuart Schram's *Political Thought of Mao Tse-tung* (London, 1963), since economics and politics are so intimately involved. There is a four volume selection of the works of Chairman Mao available from Peking ; the little red book of *Quotations from Chairman Mao Tse-tung* (Peking,

1966) is important in its own right, but contains surprisingly little of concern to the professional economist, except, perhaps, by indirection. Even reading the plays ("Comrade, You've Taken the Wrong Path") and novels (*Railway Guerrillas*) will give you an appreciation of the intellectual atmosphere in Mainland China, and this, as much as or more than knowledge of development theory, will help explain the Great Leap and current economic events there. And for no reason at all read Lu Hsün's, "The True Story of Ah Q ".

Many branches of the U.S. government, including the C. I. A., Agriculture, and the Census, issue material on the Mainland economy in pamphlet or article form. Much of the government's past research has been gathered together in the *Economic Profile* published by the Joint Economic Committee of the Congress and cited below. In Japan, the work of the Institute of Asian Economic Affairs should be noticed. The Committee on the Economy of China, under the chairmanship of Professor Walter Galenson of the University of California, Berkeley, is sponsoring a series of monographic studies, which are available first in mimeograph form ; the Rand Corporation in Santa Monica, California, also sponsors defense-oriented research.

For a publication close to the Mainland scene but excellent in coverage and judgement, you should read the Hong Kong published *Far Eastern Economic Review* and its *Yearbook*.

Study of Taiwan (Formosa) is more difficult, since little of a comprehensive nature has been written. The study of the U.S. aid programme there by Neil H. Jacoby, supplements and brings up to date the material in this book. The Government of the Republic of China, the banks, the universities, and the U.S. aid mission have, from time to time, issued bulletins and studies on specific topics. ECAFE publications also contain material on Taiwan, and the *International Financial Statistics* (IFS) and *Balance of Payments Yearbook* of the International Monetary Fund should be consulted. The government-sponsored periodical *Industry of Free China* is an important current source.

There is no economic history of the British Crown Colony of Hong Kong, although several works have material relevant to its study, e.g. George B. Endacott's history and my own *Money in British East Asia*. Bibliographical information is provided by the excellent lists published in the Colony's annual report, a book-length effort available in both Hong Kong and London. Economists are naturally fascinated by the industrial revolution which has transformed Hong Kong since 1952, and the initial stages have been described by Edward Szczepanik, but such efforts are hampered by the lack of national income accounts. The recent progress is still to be found only in departmental reports, surveys, and articles. Readers will have noted, of course, that we have considered Hong Kong generally without the scope of this present history.

A closely related study is the economic history of the Overseas Chinese, or their role in the economic history of Southeast Asia. There is an extensive bibliography in this field, but it is at this point, perhaps, that we must draw the line—at least as far as this book is concerned !

But what if you could only read one or two titles from each of the sections below ? Excluding the general section, this is still a difficult—perhaps personal—question, but . . . .

From *B*, Fairbank on *Trade and Diplomacy :* from *C*, I frankly suggest my own ; from *D*, certainly Hou's work on foreign investment—it is unique in having been written by an economist—and Feuerwerker on Sheng Hsüan-huai ; from *E*, Fei's study of *Earthbound China* is sociology, but should be read, so should Buck's work on *Land Utilization ;* from *F*, Carl Crow's books is irreverent and enjoyable, but for more sober economics Tawney's study is a classic ; from *G*, Kia-Ngau Chang's book is authoritative and less highly specialized ; from *H*, the U.S. Congress' *Profile* or Eckstein's 1966 study.

With all this material in the English language, is there any need for the student to know Chinese ? An economic historian or development economist wishing either to know something

significant about Chinese economic history or to study a particular problem for comparative purposes, probably can satisfy
his immediate needs without reading anything in Chinese, but
he can never be quite sure.   The student who plans to contribute to the field of economic history of China must read
Chinese.   The proof of this assertion may be found in the
footnotes and bibliography of almost any of the recent works
cited.

A. General and Background

Clubb, O. Edmund, *20th Century China*, New York, 1964.

Cowan, C.D. (ed.), *The Economic Development of China and Japan*, London, 1964: including, Mark Mancall, "The Kiakhta Trade"; Kwang-Ching Liu, "British-Chinese Steamship Rivalry in China, 1873-85" ; Albert Feuerwerker, "China's Nineteenth-century Industrialization: the Case of the Han-yehping Coal and Iron Company, Ltd."; Jean Chesneaux, "The Chinese Labour Force in the First Part of the Twentieth Century"; K. R. Walker, "A Chinese Discussion in Planning and Balanced Growth. A Summary of the Views of Ma Yin-ch'u and his Critics".

Cressey, George B., *Asia's Lands and Peoples*, New York, 1965.

Fairbank, John K., E.O. Reischauer, and A. Craig, *East Asia : the Modern Transformation*, Boston, 1965.

Feuerwerker, Albert, "Materials for the Study of the Economic History of Modern China", *Journal of Economic History*, 21: 41-60 (1961).

— (ed.), *Modern China*, Englewood Cliffs, N.J., 1965 : including J. Lossing Buck, "Chinese Agriculture"; F. Schurmann, "Peking's Recognition of Crisis"; A. Feuerwerker, "Economic Conditions in the late Ch'ing Period ; Douglas S. Paauw, "The Kuomintang and Economic Stagnation, 1928-1937"; Peter Schran, "Some Reflections on Chinese Communist Economic Policy".

—and S. Cheng, *Chinese Communist Studies of Modern Chinese History*, Harvard, 1961.

Ho, Ping-ti, *Studies in the Population of China, 1368-1953*, Harvard, 1959.

Hu, Chang-tu and others, *China, its People, its Society, its Culture*, New Haven, 1960.

Hucker, Charles O., *China: a Critical Bibliography*, University of Arizona Press, 1962.

King, Frank H.H. and Prescott Clarke, *A Research Guide to China-coast Newspapers, 1822-1911*, Harvard, 1965.

Koh, Sung Jae, *Stages of Industrial Development in Asia*, Philadelphia, 1966.

Liu, Kwang-Ching, *Americans and Chinese, A Historical Essay and a Bibliography*, Harvard, 1963.

Reischauer, E.O. and John K. Fairbank, *East Asia : the Great Tradition*, Boston, 1961.

Shen, T.H., *Agricultural Resources of China*, Ithica, N.Y., 1951.

Teng, Ssu-yu and John K. Fairbank, *China's Response to the West, a Documentary Survey, 1839-1923*, Harvard, 1954 2 vols.

Tregear, Thomas R., *Geography of China*, London, 1965.

B. Foreign Trade

Cheng, Yu-kwei, *Foreign Trade and the Industrial Development of China*, Washington, 1956.

Collis, M., *Wayfong: A History of the Hongkong and Shanghai Banking Corporation*, London, 1965.

Fairbank, John K., *Trade and Diplomacy on the China Coast, 1842-1854*, Harvard, 1953. 2 vols.

Greenberg, Michael, *British Trade and the Opening of China, 1800-42*, Cambridge, 1951.

Jardine, Matheson and Company, an Historical Sketch, Hong Kong, n.d. (This is a well-done "house history", not for sale, but of considerable interest to economic historians.)

Mackenzie, Sir Compton, *Realm of Silver : One Hundred Years of Banking in the East*, London, 1954.

Remer, Charles F., *The Foreign Trade of China*, Shanghai, 1926.

Wright, Stanley F., *Hart and the Chinese Customs*, Belfast, 1950.

C. Ch'ing Economic Policy and Organization

Beal, Edwin, G., Jr. *The Origin of Likin, 1853-1864*, Harvard, 1957.

Ch'u, T'ung-tsu, *Local Government in China under the Ch'ing*, Harvard, 1962.

Hinton, Harold C., *The Grain Tribute System of China, 1845-1911*, Harvard, 1956.

King, Frank H. H., *Money and Monetary Policy in China, 1845-1895*, Harvard, 1965.

Stanley, C. John, *Late Ch'ing Finance : Hu Kuang-yung as an Innovator*, Harvard, 1961.

Sun, E-tu Zen, (trans. and ed.), *Ch'ing Administrative Terms*, Harvard, 1956.

Wright, Mary C., *The Last Stand of Chinese Conservatism: the T'ung-Chih Restoration, 1862-1874*, Stanford, 1957.

D. Ch'ing Industrialization and Modernization

Allen, G. C. and Audrey G. Donnithorne, *Western Enterprise in Far Eastern Economic Development*, London, 1954.

Carlson, Ellsworth C., *The Kaiping Mines, 1877-1912*, Harvard, 1957.

Ch'en, Gideon (Ch'i-t'ien), *Tso Tsung-t'ang, Pioneer Promoter of the Modern Dockyard and the Woollen Mill in China*, Peiping, 1938. This and other studies by Ch'en have been recently reissued in Taipei, Taiwan.

Chu, Samuel C., *Chang Chien : Reformer in Modern China*, New York, 1965.

Feuerwerker, A., *China's Early Industrialization : Sheng Hsüan-huai (1844-1916) and Mandarin Enterprise*, Harvard, 1958.

Hou, Chi-ming, *Foreign Investment and Economic Development in China, 1840-1937*, Harvard, 1965.

Liu, Kwang-Ching, *Anglo-American Steamship Rivalry in China, 1862-1874*, Harvard, 1962.

Sun, E-tu Zen, *Chinese Railways and British Interests, 1898-1911*, New York, 1954.

E. The Rural Economy

Buck, John Lossing, *Chinese Farm Economy*, Chicago, 1939.

—*Land Utilization in China*, Shanghai, 1937.

Chang, Chung-li, *The Income of the Chinese Gentry*, Seattle, 1962.

Fei, Hsiao-tung and Chang Chih-i, *Earthbound China*, Chicago, 1945 ; London, 1948.

Yang, Martin (Mou-ch'un), *A Chinese Village, Taitou, Shantung Province*, New York, 1945.

F. 1911-1936

Arnold, Julian et al., *Commercial Handbook of China*, Washington, 1919-1920.   2 vols.

Chesneaux, Jean, *Le Mouvement Ouvrier Chinois de 1919 à 1927*, Paris, 1962.

—*Les Syndicats Chinois, 1919-1927*, Paris, 1965.

Crow, Carl, *Four Hundred Million Customers*, London, 1937.

Kann, Edward, *The Currencies of China*, Shanghai, 1927.

Liu, Ta-Chung, *China's National Income, 1931-1936*, Washington, 1946.

Lowe, Chuan-hua, *Facing Labor Issues in China*, London, 1934.

Ou, Pao-san, *National Income of China, 1933, 1936, and 1946*, Nanking, 1947.

Sun Yat-sen, *The International Development of China*, New York, 1922.

—*San Min Chu I* (trans. Frank W. Price) Shanghai, 1928.

Tamagana, Frank M., *Banking and Finance in China*, New York, 1942.

Tawney, R.H., *Land and Labour in China*, London, 1932.

G. War-time Inflation, 1937-1949

Barnett, A. Doak, *China on the Eve of the Communist Take-over*, Praeger, New York, 1963.

Chang, Kia-Ngau, *The Inflationary Spiral : the Experience in China, 1939-1950*, New York, 1958.

Chou, Shun-hsin, *The Chinese Inflation, 1937-1949*, Columbia, 1963.

Young, Arthur N., *China and the Helping Hand, 1937-1945*. Harvard, 1963.

—*China's Wartime Finance and Inflation, 1937-1945*, Harvard, 1965.

H. The People's Republic

Aird, John S., *The Size, Composition and Growth of the Population in Mainland China* (International Population Statistics Reports, Bureau of the Census), Washington, D.C., 1961.

Barnett, A. Doak, *Communist China and Asia, Challenge to American Policy*, New York, 1960.

Bowie, Robert R. and John K. Fairbank (eds.), *Communist China, 1955-1959: Policy Documents with Analysis*, Harvard, 1962.

Buck, John L., Owen L. Dawson and Yuan-li Wu, *Food and Agriculture in Communist China*, New York, 1966.

Chao, Kang, *The Rate and Pattern of Industrial Growth in China*, Ann Arbor, 1965.

Chao, Kuo-chun, *Agrarian Policies of Mainland China : a Documentary Study, 1949-1957*, Harvard, 1959 and 1960. 2 vols.

—*Economic Planning and Organizations in China: a Documentary Study, 1949-1958*, Harvard, 1959 and 1960.   2 vols.

—*Agrarian Policy of the Chinese Communist Party: 1921-1959*. Bombay, 1960.

Chen, Nai-Ruenn, *Chinese Economic Statistics: A Handbook for Mainland China*, Chicago, 1967.

Cheng, Chu-yuan, *Communist China's Economy, 1949-1962*, Seton Hall University Press, 1963.

—*Economic Relations Between Peking and Moscow : 1949-1963*, New York, 1964.

China, Government of the People's Republic of, *First Five-Year Plan for Development of the National Economy of the People's Republic of China in 1953-1957*, Peking, 1956.

China, State Statistical Bureau, *Ten Great Years*, Peking, 1960.

Ecklund, George N., *Financing the Chinese Government Budget*, Chicago, 1966.

Eckstein, Alexander, *Communist China's National Income*, New York, 1958.

—*Communist China's Economic Growth and Foreign Trade*, New York, 1966.

Emerson, John Philip, *Nonagricultural Employment in Mainland China: 1949-58*, U.S. Bureau of the Census, Washington, D.C., 1965.

Galenson, Walter, Alexander Eckstein, and Ta-Chung Liu (eds.), *Economic Trends in Communist China*, Aldine Press, 1967.

Hudson, Geoffrey (ed.), *The Chinese Communes*, London, 1960.

Hughes, T. J. and D.E.T. Luard, *The Economic Development of Communist China, 1949-1960*, 2nd ed., London, 1961.

Ishikawa, Shigeru, *National Income and Capital Formation in Mainland China: an Examination of Official Statistics*, Tokyo, 1965.

Jones, Philip P., and Thomas J. Poleman, *Communes and the Agricultural Crisis in Communist China* (Food Research Institute Studies, III, I), Stanford, 1962.

Li, Choh-ming, *Economic Development in Communist China: and Appraisal of the First Five Years of Industrialization*, Berkeley, 1959.

—*The Statistical System of Communist China*, Berkeley, 1962.

Liu, Ta-Chung and Kung-Chia Yeh, *The Economy of the Chinese Mainland: National Income and Economic Development, 1933-1959*, Princeton, 1965.

Mah, Feng-hwa, *The Foreign Trade of Communist China*, (forthcoming).

Orleans, Leo, *Professional Manpower and Education in Communist China*, Government Printing Office, Washington, D.C. 1961.

Perkins, Dwight H., *Market Control and Planning in Communist China*, Harvard, 1966.

—*The Steel Industry in Communist China*, New York, 1965.

Remer, C.F. (ed.), *International Economics of Communist China*, Ann Arbor, 1959.

Treadgold, Donald W., (ed.), *Soviet and Chinese Communism, Similarities and Differences*, Seattle, 1967.

United States, Central Intelligence Agency, *Communist China's Balance of Payments, 1950-1965*, Washington, D.C., 1966.

United States, 90th Congress, Joint Economic Committee, *An Economic Profile of Mainland China*, Washington, D.C., 1967.   2 vols.

Walker, Kenneth R., *Planning in Chinese Agriculture: Socialization and the Private Sector, 1956-1962*, London, 1965.

Wu, Yuan-li, *Economic Development and the Use of Energy Resources in Communist China*, New York, 1963.

I. Taiwan and Hong Kong

Barkley, George W., *Colonial Development and Population in Taiwan*, Princeton, N.J., 1954.

Chen, Cheng, *Land Reform in Taiwan*, Taipei, 1961.

Chu, Samuel C., "Liu Ming-ch'uan and the Modernization of Taiwan", *Journal of Asian Studies*, 23 : 37-53 (November 1963).

Endacott, George B., *A History of Hong Kong*, London, 1964.

—(ed.), *An Eastern Entrepot*, Department of Technical Co-operation, Overseas Research Publication No. 4, London. 1954.

Gallin, Bernard, *Hsin Hsing, Taiwan: A Chinese Village in Change*, Berkeley and Loss Angeles, 1966.

Jacoby, Neil H., *U.S. Aid to Taiwan, A Study of Foreign Aid, Self-Help, and Development*, New York, 1966.

King, Frank H.H., *Money in British East Asia*, HMSO, London, 1957.

Ma, Ronald, A. and Edward F. Szczepanik, *The National Income of Hong Kong, 1947-1950*, Hong Kong, 1955.

Shen, T.H., *Agricultural Development on Taiwan since World War II*, Ithica, N.Y., 1964.

Spaeth, David H., *Economic Development of Agriculture in Taiwan*, U.S. Department of Agriculture, Washington, D.C. 1965.

Szczepanik, Edward F., *The Economic Growth of Hong Kong*, London, 1958.

J. Other works cited

Bresciani-Tourroni, C., *The Economics of Inflation*, London, 1937 (p. 334).

Brunnert, H.S. and V. V. Hagelstrom, *Present Day Political Organization of China*, Peking 1910 (in Russian). A reprint of the A. Beltchenko and E. E. Moran translation has recently been published in Taipei.

Lewis, William Arthur, *The Theory of Economic Growth*, London, 1963.

Marshall, Alfred, *Money Credit, and Commerce*, London, 1923 (pp. 38-50).

Mayers, William F., *The Chinese Government (3rd edition)*, Shanghai, 1897.

Morse, Hosea B., *The Trade and Administration of China*, London, 1921.

Smith, Adam, *An Inquiry into the Nature and Causes of the Wealth of Nations* (Modern Library ed.), New York, 1937 (p. 311).

Yen, Chung-p'ing, *Selected Statistical Data for China's Modern Economic History* (in Chinese), Peking, 1955.

And for Arthur G. Ashbrook, Jr., Ta-Chung Liu, Yuan-li Wu, Marion R. Larsen, S. C. Tsiang, and John S. Aird see list *H* above under United States, 90th Congress.

INDEX

A CONCISE ECONOMIC HISTORY OF MODERN CHINA